SCOTLAND

HOME OF GOLF

2002-2003

pastime publications ltd

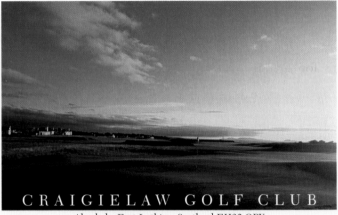

CRAIGIELAW GOLF CLUB

Aberlady, East Lothian, Scotland EH32 OPY
Tel: 01875870800 • Fax: 01875 870620 • www.craigielawgolfclub.com
Email: info@craigielawgolfclub.com

The byword for classic crestable performance golf and leisurewear

At the HEART of the GAME of GOLF

GOLF & LEISUREWEAR

www.glenmuir.co.uk

Preferred Supplier to the
34th Ryder Cup Matches

GOLF
FOUNDATION
Official clothing supplier

Scotland

PGA
PARTNER

Contents

This edition published by Pastime Publications Ltd,
5/9 Rennie's Isle, Edinburgh EH6 6QA
Tel/Fax: 0131 553 4444
E-mail: pastime@btconnect.com
Website: scotland-for-golf.com

2002 © Pastime Publications Ltd

First published by the Scottish Tourist Board 1970

Printed and bound in Scotland

UK and Worldwide distribution

PUBLISHED IN
Scotland

CRAGGAN GOLF COURSE

Craggan is now an **18 hole course** of 2,406 medal yards, designed by Bill Mitchell of the PGA. The first nine holes were opened in 1995 and the extension in 2000. This parkland course situated bedside the River Spey in the Highland region of Scotland boasts magnificent views of the Cairngorm mountains to the south and the Cromdale Hills to the east and is easily accessible from the A95 Speyside road one mile south of **Grantown-on-Spey**. There is also an 18 hole putting green which is free if you have paid for the golf course and adjacent to the course there is **trout fishing**.

For more information, telephone: **01479 873283**

North Inch Golf Course

Hay Street, Perth, Tel: 01738 636481

Medal 5442 yards, SSSI 66

Situated near the City Centre, this course is extremely accessible by foot or car. A mixture of links and parkland, the course lies adjacent to the picturesque River Tay. Parties and larger groups are welcome, just contact the club for teeing availability and up-to-date prices.

PERTH &
KINROSS
COUNCIL

GOLFING VACATIONS IN SCOTLAND

THISTLE GOLF

Thistle Golf is a company run by golf enthusiasts for those of similar mind throughout the World who wish to experience and savour the special delights of playing in Scotland . . . the Home of Golf

Thistle Golf (Scotland) Limited, Suite 423, The Pentagon Centre, 36 Washington Street, Glasgow G3 8AZ, Scotland
E-mail: info@thistlegolf.co.uk   Tel/Fax: +44 (0) 141-248 4554

Travel Trust
Association
No. R4554

Our company is affiliated to the Travel Trust Association Limited through which your vacation is guaranteed by means of a Trust Fund.

Craigie Hill

Craigie Hill is a Club steeped in history and was founded in 1911. Set in beautiful Perthshire, the course is located on the western edge of the historic City of Perth. The 18 hole golf course was designed around the natural contours of the land, and includes some of the most breathtaking scenery of any course in the area. The vista includes the magnificent meandering of the River Tay, spectacular Kinnoull Hill, splendour of Perth City and the snow covered Grampian Mountains, as well as the Crieff Hills.

For further details telephone the Secreatary on 01738 620829

Introduction

For many the name Billy Casper conjures up thoughts of that golden era in the 60's and 70's when Gary Player, Arnold Palmer and Jack Nicklaus (to name but a few) became golfing icons. Billy, on the other hand, was less visible, being a Mormon, a teetotaller and dedicated family man who did not seek out the cameras. But consider his record:

He won his first U.S. Open in 1959 at Winged Foot and another in 1966 in an extraordinary contest with Arnold Palmer who was seven shots ahead with eight holes to play in the fourth round. This culminated in an 18-hole play-off in which Palmer collapsed completely over the last nine holes.

In 1968 he won a then-record $205,168 in prize money making him only the second golfer to win over $1,000,000 on the U.S. Tour. He followed this up with a win at the U.S. Masters in 1970 and represented his country no less than eight times in the Ryder Cup making a ninth appearance as non-playing Captain and so it goes on.

I am telling you this because we are proud to be associated with the Billy Casper Organisation through his son, Byron (named after Byron Nelson, his godfather). As a result of this Partnership, we are able to offer our readers a UNIQUE number of benefits, not the least of which is the opportunity to purchase original, signed golfing memorabilia (*see* pages 24/25) as well as exclusive membership to Billy Casper's Golf Collection offering incredible discounts to stay and play at some of Scotland's most celebrated venues such as Dornoch, Skibo, Nairn, St Andrews and many others. Also, we are planning a Tournament with Byron that

will allow participants to meet his father and get some lessons as well as enjoy his company afterwards at dinner.

There will be a number of other special offers and we will feature them on our web site at www.scotland-for-golf.com as and when they evolve.

Notwithstanding all this, we continue to work on our Guide to bring you the most up-to-date information on Scotland's courses. Our 'featured courses' section introduces you to another 68 clubs and hidden gems. We are determined to show you that there is so much more to enjoy than you ever believed. It may take a little more planning to get to these locations but our Guide will make that part of it so much easier *and even enjoyable.*

The Gazetteer is becoming more informative as more and more of the courses listed take up our offer to write about their features and facilities, and this year we have highlighted those who have indicated to us that they are particularly happy to receive visitors.

As ever, we are keen to bring to you a guide that is indispensable when it comes to planning a golfing tour to Scotland and to this end we are anxious that you, the reader, contacts us to tell us how we can improve the content. You can do this by contacting us through our web site or emailing us at pastime@btconnect.com. We hope you enjoy browsing through *Scotland Home of Golf 2002/2003* and look forward to welcoming you to our legendary courses as soon as possible.

Thank you.
Graham Wilson, Publisher

Donald Ford

Not the greatest of starts to a new millennium

On reflection, one of Scotland's coldest – and most protracted – winters for years was a portent. Almost overnight, we went from winter to summer, but not until May, by which time greenkeepers' plans for the new season were in tatters and at least four weeks in arrears. Early season conditions across Scotland, particularly on inland courses with a heavy arboreal presence, left a lot to be desired and there were numerous moans and groans over the state of greens at many venues. As ever, though, quality prevailed and by the time a very ordinary June and wet July had come and gone, Scottish courses were once again an absolute delight to visit. Scotland's leading sportsmen, however, were far from delighted.

The first year of the new millennium was, whichever way you look at it, a pretty bad one for Scottish sport. On the international scene, our professional football and rugby teams did not fare well, while at club level performances were again mediocre, to say the least. (Soccer in Scotland has reached a new low when Glasgow Rangers can start a European campaign with eleven foreign players on the field.) In spite of a rating as top seed and a self-declared best-ever preparation, our national cricket team failed to qualify for the 2003 World Cup. Our hockey team was equally disappointing – on its home territory – in the qualifying stages for the next Commonwealth Games.

At individual level, there was little to excite the thousands of Scottish sporting followers who long for the opportunity to celebrate a new world champion. With the notable exception of snooker, we seem unable to produce the right material or quality of support that creates the atmosphere for an emergent Scottish champion. Granted, there was a point at Lytham when we thought Monty really was on the way but as he confessed afterwards and some of us had guessed, his confidence over the putter had failed him.

David Coulthard again threatened the Ferraris but an inferior machine and some bad luck ended his chance once more. Colin MacRae performed miracles in the World Rallies but just missed out – and so it went on. Even our best – our only – star of squash deserted to England as Peter Nicol left none of us in any doubt that he could not remain at the top unless he transferred his 'home' to England. Scottish athletics was shown to be in a real mess too, with the legendary Alan Wells offering –

even from his own distant home in England – to help out.

There were a few, a very few, glimmers of hope and it was golf which provided most of them. Scotland's lady professionals, Catriona Matthew, Kathryn Marshall and Janice Moodie, had outstanding performances across the world and in the U.S.A. in particular. We have never had riches such as these at the top of women's golf. Apart from the obvious hope that more championships come their way, as a nation we surely must be optimistic that their performances will rub off on the increasing numbers of young girls around the Scottish clubs who have taken up the sport and hope that they show the same dedication and desire for success as their peers.

Yet, even as good reports came back from foreign fields of the girls' exploits, a row was brewing over the new National Golf Centre at Drumoig. A deficit of many thousands of pounds having been incurred in getting Scotland's amateur golf showpiece off the ground, the S.G.U. incurred the wrath of club treasurers and members around the country by announcing that they, the clubs, would foot the bill for the deficiency, through a levy on subscriptions.

Not surprisingly, the natives became restless and this saga may have a lot further to run before a satisfactory solution is found. It would be nice, nevertheless, if someone in authority was humble enough to confess that mistakes had been made and a few hands were held up in admission. I, for one, would feel much more respect for an honest statement and a request for frank discussion rather than a blunt demand for cash to right a massive – and unexplained – overspend. (Come to think of it, this sounds all too familiar. For 'Drumoig' read 'New Scottish Parliament Building' – the second paragraph of this introduction was spot on – it was a stinker of a year!)

Then there was the matter of the Ryder Cup; not just the encounter scheduled for the Belfry which was, mercifully, postponed after the indescribable events in the United States but the one which Scotland failed to win the right to stage in 2009. It is hard, if not impossible, to accept that the criteria on which the committee made its choice had anything to do with the quality of golf courses on the short list. Had it been so, Scotland surely must have won.

More fools we Scots for thinking that's what would swing it. In effect, squalid materialism – filthy lucre – was too much of a temptation to the committee and a course which isn't even constructed to the required standards got the vote.

There is consolation in the 2014 event coming to Gleneagles, but why on earth could it not have been the other way round? The end of 2001 could not come quickly enough.

On a less distressing note, I discovered some more of Scotland's golfing riches through the lens, but also got the chance of a game on courses I had not previously visited. The New at St.Andrews, for example, is quite superb. Overshadowed for obvious reasons by the Old Course, it is in some respects an even harder challenge and it was a change to be able to see where you were going from the tee! The Eden, too, was put to the test; shorter but no less enjoyable with a few cracking holes which make you think regularly about the next shot.

I also experienced the Green Hotel courses at Kinross, early in the season, granted, and just too soon to catch the greens at their best. These are, however, very popular tracks for outings and interest never wanes. I had my first trip around Muckhart, whose twenty seven holes allow you to choose 'two nines from three' as a variation from the norm. Three contrasting challenges they are, too, with the nine original holes (our back nine on this occasion) probably the most fun and in spanking condition.

Then there was Mortonhall, Edinburgh's most under-rated course, without a doubt. A kind member read my cry from the heart at never having played it and duly invited me along to put things to rights. The course is enormous – not so much in its length although it is no pushover from the medal tees – but in the wide open spaces on the majority of fairways. There's a 'Gleneagles' feel about it, in a way, as fellow golfers are hidden from sight through many of the holes being ring-fenced with trees or hummocks. Great sport (with a long putt on the eighteenth bringing yours truly a one-hole victory. How selfish can you get?)

Dunfermline Golf Club (Pitfirrane) was kind enough to ask me along to their Cel-Am in August. A first time around again proved to be a most enjoyable one.

Then there was Muirfield. A few years ago I wrote to the Secretary for the Club's permission to include the course in my Millennium golf publication 'The Great Scottish Courses', which featured my own photographs and editorial on sixty four of the country's finest venues. The blunt reply indicated that the members abhorred the use of the course for commercial purposes and permission was refused. The temptation was to engage in a protracted diatribe with the Secretary but, in spite of the blatant hypocrisy involved, I felt that I was unlikely to cause a change of mind and therefore did nothing more.

Regular readers of Home of Golf will be aware that we now annually choose one of the Championship courses – generally where the next Open will be held – and with the aid of the local professional, do a complete examination, hole by hole, of how the world's top players take on the challenge. For 2002, therefore, Muirfield was the obvious choice. Bearing in mind the treatment my request had been given, it seemed prudent that my publisher make the approach this time around; alas, the outcome was the same, the reply being equally blunt. (It was with considerable dismay that I spotted a shot of Muirfield in a 2002 calendar; a law for the rich and another for the poor?)

In some forty years' golf around Scotland, during which time I have photographed some three hundred courses and played almost one hundred and fifty of them, I have had nothing but help from club secretaries (admittedly, on occasion, after a bit of pushing and shoving!) and the welcome by members and greenstaff on the course has been superb.

The Muirfield attitude, however, flies totally in the face of the immense hospitality which is offered all around Scotland and while it must be admitted that there are odd committees who are not enthralled at publicity directed towards their course, they realise the final objective is to put Scotland's golfing riches – as well as its legendary warmth of welcome – before the growing numbers of potential tourists across the world.

Do not, dear Reader, therefore allow our Muirfield experiences to colour your judgement of Scottish golfing hospitality. The various editorials which follow hopefully convey the true warmth and openness of the welcome which awaits visiting golfers across the wide spectrum of Scottish clubs, from the best and biggest to the most modest. As always, we hope you will put Scotland at the top of your 2002 holiday planning, in the guarantee that the Home of Golf will fulfil the predictions of such articles as follow hereafter.

Finally, however, it would be remiss of me – on behalf also of my publisher – not to send our own words of sympathy and comfort to all of our readers and enthusiasts of the Scottish game in the U.S.A. It goes without saying that the terrible horrors inflicted on you last September effortlessly crossed the Atlantic into the Scottish clubhouses where thousands of you have made friends and acquaintances over the years.

We in Scotland shared every second of the tragic events with you and while we found it all heart-breaking, it compared not a jot to the agonies and grief you must all have suffered. In spite of the doubts and anxieties which many of you may now justifiably have about travelling, we just want to let you know that you will always be welcome here – whenever you feel the time is right. Haste ye back – and don't forget to bring your clubs.

The right way to tackle Cruden Bay

Cruden Bay professional Robbie Stewart guides Donald Ford around one of Scotland's most visited links and explains in detail how to take on the Aberdeenshire venue voted number six in the UK's list of holiday courses.

Robbie Stewart hails from Lossiemouth, a famed breeding ground of great golfers. Indeed, he was but nine years of age when his father, himself off a highly respected three handicap, first introduced him to the demands of the Moray links. Like so many others, Robbie was instantly hooked. Dad's coaching was essentially on the grip and the basics of the swing – he did not go over the top with advice or criticism. It seemed to work; Robbie was Moray Under-12 champion three years running.

He considered himself, even at nine years of age, a late developer, although by the age of fifteen he was playing off one. Paradoxically, that had gone up to three at the point when he turned professional four years later, turning his back on a potential career in banking to take his first post of assistant to Keith Campbell at Gleddoch, Langbank, where he was to spend three very happy and productive years.

In 1982, he obtained his PGA qualification, marked by one major success – that of the Scottish PGA award as 'Trainee of the Year' – but also by one glorious failure as he lost the final of the Scottish Assistants' Championship. In the same year, he applied for the post of professional at Nairn (a fairly ambitious move for a twenty-two year old, as he now realises) but lost out to Robin Fyfe, who retains that post to this day. Robin left Largs to take the Nairn job, and in stepped Robbie to replace him at the Ayrshire club. It's amazing how things turn out!

He spent almost ten years in Largs, then in 1991 successfully won the race for the vacant Cruden Bay post. The upheaval of a long move – especially with his wife Heather and three children to think about – was a serious consideration, but the success which Robbie has made of the job, and the contentment of the whole family within their new surroundings, fully reflects the wisdom and bravery of the decision.

Now respected as one of the North of Scotland's best coaches, with firm views on exactly how much technical stuff ought to be passed on to youngsters with a good grip and basically sound swing, his tournament experience has been minimal. He is overly modest, however, about his very first PGA victory, which came in 2000 at the great new links of Kingsbarns, in its own inaugural professional tournament.

A keen supporter of Aberdeen F.C. (I won't hold that against him as I myself loved playing there!) he willingly undertook the task of escorting your editor around this great links and letting him in on a few of the secrets of an outstanding and heavily played venue. (He probably gave me the insight into all of them but at my age it's not easy to remember everything!) I now happily pass these on to the reader. Should the opportunity to come here present itself, I would advise anyone not to turn it down. It is likely to be a golfing experience which you will remember for a very long time.

THE COURSE:

It was probably the legendary Eric Brown (best known at club level for his long association with Buchanan Castle, but for two years the professional here) who put Cruden Bay firmly on the golfing map. Harry Bannerman, himself one of our best known club professionals, followed in his footsteps and in the early 1990's a series of architects began to take notice of the quality reports which the course was getting. The upshot of it all was that, in 1993 and 1994 Cruden Bay was included in the list of the top 100 in the world. The most recent rankings have it at number 52.

Steadily the popularity of the venue grew. Golf architect Pete Dye averred that it was one of his 'three favourite courses'. Donald Steel also attached his considerable ability and reputation to the club by becoming a consultant. The club spirit and pride at the lofty status being enjoyed rubbed off on all concerned, and it really has been no surprise to anyone connected with Cruden Bay that it has made such an impression on the world stage.

Credit for the original course design belongs to Tom Simpson. Robbie offered a new insight into his planning of the layout by claiming that Simpson thought his entire way around, finding the ideal route

for every hole. He then worked out the best way to play the course from start to finish - and promptly hid the secret from all eyes! In particular, he had a target area for the drive at every par four and par five in the round, while his piece de resistance was to walk the course backwards to confirm his thoughts on each.

Like all great links, the need for the golfer to constantly think ahead is paramount at Cruden Bay. Wind direction, of course, is crucial. A northerly with any degree of force makes the course a monster, firstly, with three difficult holes from a cold start into the teeth of the wind, but critically when you turn away from the twelfth green. No quarter is asked or given as you face the narrow targets of thirteen to fifteen (the latter one of very few dog-leg par threes in the world – how it rates stroke index of 12 is baffling!) and then contemplate potential nightmares at the three closing holes, once again into the cold north wind.

Turn the wind around one hundred and eighty degrees and it's a totally new challenge. The great string of holes in the lee of the big sand hills takes on a new perspective, particularly 'Bluidy Burn', one of the two tremendous par fives on the course. This time, as you climb aboard the thirteenth tee, it's an entirely new ball game. If you have the making of a score, negotiate the

aforesaid skimpy fairways at thirteen and fourteen and strike a quality teeshot – wind assisted this time – on fifteen, thoughts of collecting the sweep money focus the mind.

There is scarce a hole without a character of its own. The fourth is one of the great par threes, requiring correct club choice, sweet strike and then total carry of the 193 yards to the elevated green. It is literally "green or bust". The two par fives are quite superb, while the aforesaid short fifteenth is without peer in UK golf. Strangely, as Robbie was quick to point out with a twinkle in his eye, 'it's the hole that visitors always remember but which the members usually wish to forget!'

He is one of those who adhere to the principle that a truly great golf course should have six hard holes, six easy ones and six full of fun. 'That's the trademark of a good golf architect', he reckons, then concludes, with more than average respect and pride in his voice, " and that's exactly what we offer at Cruden Bay".

THE ROUND:

High pressure had dictated that Scotland's weather was settled and generally fine for several days. A front approaching from the North Sea, however, had spawned a thick layer of grey cloud with spells of wetting drizzle; Cruden Bay was thus uncharacteristically gloomy when we reached the first tee. Of much more significance was the conspicuous disappearance of the wind. Robbie estimated that no more than thirty days a year were not subjected either to the prevailing strong southerlies or a biting wind coming down from the Arctic, both of which would cause a major re-assessment of the game plan.

The course itself was softish after a fair amount of rain earlier in the month, with little or no warmth thereafter to dry it out. In effect, that completely negated the normality of customary late summer pace across the links. The transformation thus required on approach shots, in particular, was of major significance, as I was to discover at more than half the holes. In one sense, it was disappointing that I would not be enjoying my first round on the course in the same conditions in which I had often photographed it; paradoxically – and selfishly – it also greatly assisted my own performance and no doubt avoided a fair deal of potential embarrassment!

Robbie had warmed up with ten minutes on the putting green and a few practice swings; not, I know, his normal build-up to a round, but he later admitted to some early stiffness after a gym session the previous evening. This was not the accepted warm-up routine the modern professional golfer accepts as essential but as I was to discover, his performance got steadily better as the round wore on and he finished off in a veritable blaze of glory!

We played off the boxes, reducing the task by some 370 yards. This was of little significance at the par threes or the shorter par fours, but it was easy to appreciate the increased level of difficulty from the back tees at the sixth, seventh and ninth in particular and especially at each of the closing five holes. While the 6022 yards is not at all taxing, the challenges posed by this great course at every single hole more than compensate for any criticism of length – especially in the customary breeze. Not since my Turnberry adventure in the company of Guy Redford (last year's featured 'stroke-by-stroke' choice) had I looked forward so much to a round.

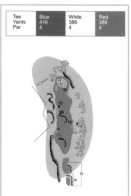

Tee Yards Par	Blue 416 4	White 386 4	Red 386 4

1ST. HOLE

SLAINS

386 YARDS, STROKE INDEX 7 The first tee points north; the drive should be lined up on the tower above the horizon. As with many of the par fours, there's an ideal landing area on a flat plateau about 220 yards out, but beware; out of bounds threatens on the left and with the sloping fairway everything falls left to right. If all goes well, there is a mid-iron approach of around 170 yards left. The bunkers to right and left of the green are not tight to the putting surface and are avoidable if the shot is struck well.

Robbie's first teeshot – with a two iron – was not struck as he would have wished; a 3 wood from rough was then pulled left but a lovely 30-yard pitch over the bunker was followed by a single putt from 10 feet for his par four. (R.S. - 4; D.F. - 5)

2ND. HOLE
CROCHDANE
319 YARDS,
STROKE INDEX 13

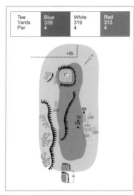

Tee Yards Par	Blue 339 4	White 319 4	Red 313 4

Northwards again
with the drive crucial
to easing the
difficulty of approach
to a high green.
(A new tee will add
some twenty yards
and bring the first of
the bunkers down the
right into play.) However, the driving line should be
left to gain slightly higher ground and assist the
problem of judging an approach to a raised target. Do
not be short with that; take one more club to ensure
you make it – it's a lot easier to chip back from the rear
of the green than to re-attempt a blind pitch from the
foot of the steep slope at the front!

Robbie again took the 2 iron off the tee to find the
perfect line in on the left. His 9 iron was also spot on;
two putts secured his par. (R.S. - 4; D.F. - 4)

3RD. HOLE
CLAYPITS
270 YARDS,
STROKE INDEX 17

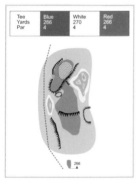

Tee Yards Par	Blue 286 4	White 270 4	Red 266 4

Tom Simpson's
design of this lovely
little hole has been
widely copied. It
features a "wall of
death" some forty
yards long, hidden
from the tee by a
cross-fairway ridge but running everything that's struck
left round towards a fascinating green. Out of bounds
lines the entire left-hand side, there's a sizeable hillock
to the right and the teeshot should dissect the gap
between them – aim for the 'hump'. The big hitter will
look to drive the green, but out of bounds lies
immediately to the rear if he overdoes it. The sensible
approach is to land around the end of the aforesaid
"wall of death" and look for birdie with an up and
down from thirty yards out. There's a killer of a fold in
the green, mind you, a crucial feature if the flag is to
the left rear.

Robbie's 2 iron ("I'll only use the driver if the wind's
in the north") again was superb and his pitch with an
8 iron left him a 6 foot putt; down it went! (R.S. - 3;
D.F. - 3)

4TH. HOLE
PORT ERROLL
183 YARDS,
STROKE INDEX 11

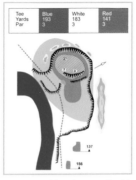

Tee Yards Par	Blue 193 3	White 183 3	Red 141 3

One of Scotland's
great par threes, this
is the only hole on
the course which runs
west to east. It
requires, without
exception, a total
carry from tee to
green, requiring the use of a driver from the back tee if
the wind is in your face. It goes without saying that
you need to be up, so take at least one more club.
Finishing below the green leaves a blind pitch almost
impossible to judge properly, while the continuation of
the up-slope behind the green will prevent major
problems if you should overcook the teeshot. The ideal
target on a difficult green is pin-high right.

Robbie used a 7 iron and landed pin-high; his birdie
putt ran out of steam an agonising couple of inches
from the cup. (R.S. - 3; D.F. - 3)

5TH. HOLE
THE BUCK
444 YARDS,
STROKE INDEX 3

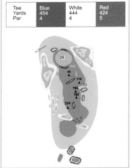

Tee Yards Par	Blue 454 4	White 444 4	Red 424 5

The first of three
terrific holes amidst
the big Cruden Bay
sand dunes will find
the vast majority
reaching for their
driver as you turn
southwards for the
first time. A wide fairway awaits and a quality teeshot is
essential to set up a reasonable chance of making the
green in two. It will, in addition, almost certainly take
out of play the first of three bunkers some fifty yards
short of the green. A second trap, further up and to the
right of the green, catches anything pushed, while the
bunker in the face of the dune to the immediate front

left of the green will snaffle anything pulled or underhit. This latter hazard caught both of us, causing Robbie his only major trauma of the round. Unseen, until you step over the little ridge on the apron of the green, is a wicked fall-off to the left from the middle of the putting surface. Be content with a bogey at a tough par four.

Robbie's driver took him past the bell (264 yards). Normally using his 2 iron to take out the risk of sand, he went down to a four, did not get the desired contact and finished in the front left trap. Two to get out and two putts was a disappointing end after the perfect drive, (R.S. - 6; D.F. - 6)

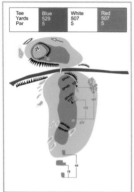

Tee Yards Par	Blue 529 5	White 507 5	Red 507 5

6TH. HOLE
BLUIDY BURN
507 YARDS, STROKE INDEX 5

This is the first three-shotter of the round - a quite superb par five. The drive from the tee amidst the dunes should be lined up on the left-hand door of the greenkeeper's sheds. That should allow happy landings in the wider spaces to the right of the fairway. Too far right, however, is fraught as a bunker and the seventh green on the wee course are waiting out of sight. Thereafter, the second should be laid up short of the burn and though the dunes are intimidatingly close, ideally left-side to avoid bunkers. Control and confidence are then required for a wedge shot of around 90 yards to Tom Morris' original green, higher and almost at right angles to your line of approach. Another fold in the putting surface causes headaches too.

Robbie demolished the difficulties here with a superb teeshot, four iron into position 'A' short of the burn, then a wedge from 80 yards to ten feet. Left with a wicked putt, a mere inch deprived him of a deserved birdie. (R.S. - 5; D.F. - 6.)

7TH. HOLE WHAUPSHANK
355 YARDS, STROKE INDEX 9

This is a deceptively difficult hole where the dog-leg

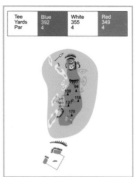

Tee Yards Par	Blue 392 4	White 355 4	Red 349 4

demands that you line up the drive 'on the hump', in Robbie's words. A two iron or three wood may be enough, but ideally you look to find the generous landing area to the right hand side. That allows a clear sight of the flag some 150 yards distant. Should you try to bite too much off the corner, however, disaster awaits in the shape of three horrid little pot bunkers and thick rough. The long, narrow green slopes up from front to back and if the approach heads for the right hand segment, it will kick away. Again, an extra club is advisable and once there, take extra time over the first putt.

Robbie did exactly what he advised against, his two iron from the tee just failing to reach safety across the corner of the dogleg. A wicked lie in tough grass had him reaching for a 'U' wedge; that came up short and a chip and two putts could not rescue the damage. (Just as Guy Redford said to me at Turnberry last year –'make one mistake on links and you'll struggle to prevent one or two more.') Robbie was not happy, but it perfectly illustrated how deceptive the hole is. (R.S. - 5; D.F. - 5)

8TH. HOLE ARDENDRAUGHT
225 YARDS, STROKE INDEX 15

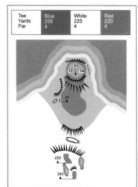

Tee Yards Par	Blue 258 4	White 225 4	Red 220 4

It sounds like a German beer and few golfers fail to lick their lips as they step on to the tee. Accuracy, however, is paramount in order to avoid horrific rough on the hillside to the right and create any chance of judging the pitch which will set up the birdie. The valley in front of the green prevents many from using the driver; it is much better practice to pitch in from the left –

albeit thirty yards further – on the same level as the putting surface, which by the way is the smallest of the round. Should you pass the flag, be wary of the first putt as the downhill roll is fast, especially in summer.

Robbie's 2 iron to his chosen landing area was perfection, as was his pitch to some 8 feet. The putt duly obliged for his birdie. (R.S. - 3; D.F. - 5 - no comment!)

Tee Yards Par	Blue 462 4	White 430 4	Red 393 5

9TH. HOLE
HAWKLAW
430 YARDS,
STROKE INDEX 6

Normally into a south-westerly, this is a testing par four for even the lower handicaps. It is not laden with problems and the degree of difficulty probably rests on the absence of features which render distance estimation difficult. The driving line is simple – split the fairway between the bunkers to the right and left of you as you look up the rise (out of bounds runs down the right from tee to green). Ideally, you must get up and over with the drive to open up the view to the green, some 200 yards away. Downhill, it looks less than it is, so again take an extra club - or two - and the target is not a big one. One greenside bunker to the right threatens a push.

This is the one hole at Cruden Bay which is perhaps out of character with the rest, but is yet a stiff conclusion to the outward nine.

Robbie creamed a magnificent teeshot miles over the hill, struck a "canny" 9 iron and was appalled to see it at the back of the green! A beautifully weighted first putt made a formality of his par. (R.S. - 4; out in 37; D.F. - 4; out in 41)

10TH. HOLE **SCAURS**
366 YARDS, STROKE INDEX 6

Undoubtedly the 'Craw's Nest' of Cruden Bay, with spectacular views from the tee. Perched on the edge of the steep, grassy hilltop, the hole stretches out perhaps a hundred feet below you. The ideal drive is to the left-hand side of the fairway and short of the burn. (The big hitters regularly try - and fail - to carry it!) Too far

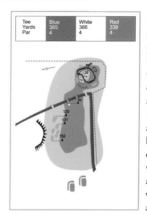

Tee Yards Par	Blue 385 4	White 366 4	Red 339 4

right – you ought not to be – will find you out of bounds; too far left and you will certainly catch one of five bunkers around the 11th.green. The approach makes or breaks the hole. It's a difficult green with a vicious ridge right across the middle, while three bunkers and grassy hollows offer protection around it. If the pin is at the back, be up. Try, in any event, to finish on the same level to avoid the real risk of three putts.

Robbie once more smacked his two iron into pole position. An 8 iron, however, was a club short (after all he had said!) and he was left with a banana-shaped forty-footer from the lower level. You've guessed – he knocked it in! (R.S. - 3; D.F. - 4)

11TH. HOLE **MISHANTER**
139 YARDS, STROKE INDEX 16

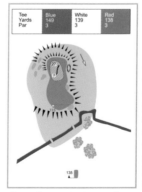

Tee Yards Par	Blue 149 3	White 139 3	Red 138 3

As you descended to 'ground level' after your drive on the tenth, it was worth a look over to the eleventh green to confirm the pin placement. It's a long, narrow green with yet another tricky shelf virtually down the middle. That apart, it is heavily trapped to the left hand side, also at front right, but at all costs avoid a teeshot in this latter area. There's a steep drop, with thick rough, making recovery for par if you miss the green a near impossibility. As usual, club choice is crucial to success.

Robbie's choice from the box was a 9 iron; it finished well short (the pin was at the back) but another superb long putt overcame that misjudgement to present him with par. (R.S. - 3; D.F. - 3)

(One interesting footnote – Robbie decided to name

his house in Ellon after this hole. I'm not sure of the wisdom of that choice – it's the Doric for 'mistake'. Take your own conclusion!)

12TH. HOLE **FINNYFAL**
305 YARDS, STROKE INDEX 14

The last southbound par four is shortish, the key being the run-up and entrance to a small green which falls away fairly steeply to both the front and back. The drive requires to be struck well enough to allow you to

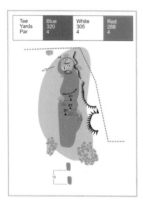

Tee Yards Par	Blue 320 4	White 305 4	Red 288 4

pitch and run onto the very tricky surface. Fine placement is needed from the tee, however, to miss a threatening bunker on the right deviously positioned in exactly the place from which you would ideally wish to attack the pin! Keeping the teeshot leftish is thus the best advice. A high approach with a wedge, particularly in summer, is not a real option and success or failure will depend on the accuracy of the crucial second shot.

Robbie's 2 iron from the tee was just too far left of his target position on the fairway and finished in clingy rough. He struck a superb wedge (the option of the pitch and run now gone) 95 yards to the back of the green and rolled in an eight foot putt to secure his fourth 3 in five holes, three of them birdies. (R.S. - 3; D.F. - 4)

13TH. HOLE **BENTS**
540 YARDS, STROKE INDEX 8

Turning for home again on the thirteenth tee, we felt the first breeze of the day on our faces. Out came Robbie's driver for a rare appearance to counteract the effect of the wind at the second three-shotter of the round. The key is to ensure that your third shot is played from the least difficult angle of approach (the left side) to an angled, hidden green sitting at the foot of a steep, tall grassy hill. To get there, you first must ensure the drive pulls up short of the burn. With the normal wind behind, it is reachable, so a three wood or

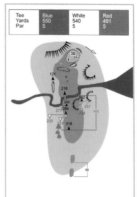

Tee Yards Par	Blue 550 5	White 540 5	Red 491 5

two iron may be in order. Bunkers, a kink of the burn and rough all put more emphasis on the line, which is better right than left. The second, normally a fairway wood or long iron, is straightforward enough, but the finishing spot is critical. You'll need anything from a four to an eight iron to find the green, which lies at an angle of 60 degrees to your line - and you can't see any of it!

Robbie pushed his drive into rough, but hit a perfect 3 wood to pole position on the left fairway. His 7 iron looked great, but when we reached the top of the crest before the green, he was well short - it is very hard to judge when you have nothing to look at! Another lovely approach putt, however, made par a formality. (R.S. - 5; D.F - 5)

14TH. HOLE **WHINS**
362 YARDS, STROKE INDEX 2

Rated the second hardest hole on the course, this is a great driving hole and certainly the tightest of the round. While left-sided bunkers await a drive struck too far left, the inclination is to head that way from the tee as heavy rough in the dunes above the beach on the right will ruin any chance of par if you finish up therein. The landing area, however, is again fairly generous so there's no excuse! The next problem is the accurate judgement of a

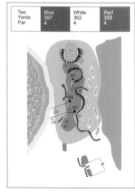

Tee Yards Par	Blue 397 4	White 362 4	Red 358 4

second shot up and over a ridge to yet another invisible target – this time sunk in a 'basin' perhaps 160 to 180 yards distant. Difficult though it is to judge, the steep slope downwards to the front of the green almost

guarantees that the underclubbed or short approach will make the putting surface, but with the pin to the rear (as it often is) it can leave an enormous first putt – read on! There is help on the tee; the greenkeeper shows the pin location on his board, so there really is no room for excuses.

Robbie normally hits a driver here, lined up inside the left-hand bunkers; this time he used his 2 iron again, which he struck beautifully and it finished perfectly. His wedge looked great, but with no run on the green, he was left sixty feet from the pin (mischievously placed only eight feet from the back edge!) For the first time in the round, his putter failed him and he took three to get down. (R.S. - 5; D.F. - 5 - stroke index 2 does not now look odd for an apparently straightforward hole!)

15TH. HOLE **BLIN DUNT**
225 YARDS, STROKE INDEX 12

Perfectly titled and a quite unique par three featuring a blind teeshot and a dogleg!

So nearly a par four, you wonder if the printer has juxtaposed the stroke indexes of this hole and the one before it. The line from the tee is the marker pole some fifty feet up the hillside in front of you and slightly left; it is crucial that you take at least one more club. There's nothing to see on the right apart from dunes, marram grass, the beach and Slains Castle on the horizon!

Going that way leaves a fraught pitch downhill to the sunken green – not clever at the best of times but impossible in summer

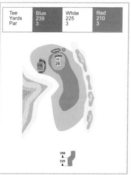

– while too far left is preferable but not if you catch the long grass beneath the sixteenth tee, as a certain professional did!

Robbie struck his two iron well, but pulled it too far and finished in wicked shape on the aforesaid bank below the next tee. He superbly repaired the damage with a brilliant pitch but his saving putt lipped the hole. (R.S. - 4; D.F. - 5 - no comment!)

16TH. HOLE **COFFINS**
175 YARDS, STROKE INDEX 18

By simple mathematics, one hole on the course has to have a stroke index of 18 but I would not have made it this testing little hole. For a start, you see no more than the top of the flag. It lies at the foot of a long downslope which begins only just beyond the halfway point from the tee. Since the green continues the

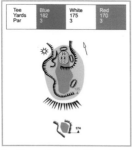

Tee Yards Par	Blue 182 3	White 175 3	Red 170 3

decline – only two coffin grass bunkers (hence the hole name) to the rear stop the overruns – it follows that stopping the ball from a height is a virtual impossibility. Club choice is very difficult but picking the landing point some 50 yards out and floating the tee shot onto it is even more so, particularly when dry weather has taken all the 'give' out of the slope. At the end of it all, if you have judged it well, you still have to putt out on a devilish green!

Robbie struck a 7 iron from the tee, the soft conditions for once allowing the 'high road' approach. A twelve foot putt finished agonisingly on the lip. (R.S. - 3; D.F. - 4)

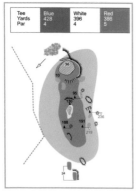

Tee Yards Par	Blue 428 4	White 396 4	Red 386 5

17TH. HOLE
BILIN' WALLIE
396 YARDS,
STROKE INDEX 4

'Choose one side of the hump or the other' advised my guide 'and have a real whack at it!' The 'hump' is a big mound which splits the broad fairway into two segments, the one to port normally offering the better line in for the second shot. Should you head to starboard, however, the essential requirement is to carry the slope about 225 yards out and avoid going further right into one of two sand traps. The green, although flattish, is guarded at the front by deep bunkers though with the wind generally behind you, getting aboard in two ought not to be the most difficult of tasks; anything from a five to an eight iron is the norm, depending on the result of your choice from the tee, but make sure you clear the sand and the slope.

Robbie got the driver out and the ball eventually decided to land about 290 yards later! That exquisite teeshot left him another 'canny' 9 iron, which dutifully pulled up eight feet from the hole. In went the putt for a matchless birdie. (R.S. - 3; D.F. - 4)

18TH. HOLE
HAME
395 YARDS,
STROKE INDEX 10

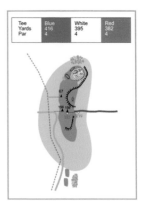

Tee Yards Par	Blue 416 4	White 395 4	Red 382 4

On reaching the eighteenth tee, the average player will almost certainly feel his knees knocking as he surveys the proximity of the out of bounds fence tight to the left-hand side. (This will get worse when the new tee, some twenty yards further back, comes into use!) While the burn does threaten on the right-hand edge of the fairway some two hundred and twenty yards out, it goes underground and thus a straight drive takes out all the aforementioned hazards; the white exit gate to the left of the green is the ideal line. Successfully over these potential nightmares, a medium iron struck well will cope suitably with the long, angled green – one of the longest on the course, in fact. Wrong club selection (there may be a choice of three or four depending on the flag position) or anything under-hit will leave a frightfully long first putt; if the greenkeeper was out of sorts when he laid out the day's pin positions, you will then do well to secure par across a tricky putting surface.

Robbie ended the round by reducing this hole to a sumptuous drive, a 9 iron to eight feet and another single putt - his sixth three on the inward half. (R.S. - 3; back in 32; round in 69 (one under par). D.F. - 4; back in 38; round in 79 (nine over par)

EPILOGUE

With regular interruptions by yours truly, either with questions or for advice (and a few stories were thrown in along the way too!) it took us four hours to make the trip. The time, at least from my point of view, had simply flown. Robbie's increasing looseness of muscle was evidenced by his five-stroke improvement on the inward nine, and by a blistering finale in particular, his last three holes being near-perfect. He was the first to admit, however, that we had enjoyed an exceptionally quiet day on the links. While a whisper of wind developed around the thirteenth tee as we turned for home, it caused nothing more than a modest change of mind on club selection. At no point did it upset swing or flight trajectory; the periodic drizzle, in fact, threatened more discomfort than anything that the slight ripple of wind created.

As we held our post-mortem over a bowl of cream of leek soup and toasties in the sumptuous lounge, the panorama below us almost disappeared in the Stygian gloom. The drizzle which had punctuated play became more persistent and the telescope for the benefit of members and visitors (is this the finest clubhouse perch in Scotland?) seemed quite superfluous. Not even the gathering greyness, however, could detract from the feeling of pure enjoyment of a simply wonderful golfing experience.

It is almost impossible to find negatives about Cruden Bay. From the design which has integrated nature's seaside terrain with golfing architectural skills at their best has evolved one of the world's outstanding links. There is, nevertheless, not a hint of complacency around the club. The Greens committee, of which Robbie is an important member, is constantly looking at course improvements. A new tee at the eighteenth to make life harder for the better player by bringing the burn into play is one. Replacement of an unsightly long path is another. A new toilet is being built in the dunes beside the eighth tee; to be environmentally friendly, the finish will exactly match that of the original – now ancient – wooden clubhouse. Olaf's well is to be re-landscaped; two more new tees are under construction.

Apart from the fantastic location and the magnificence of the course – let us not ignore completely the presence of the second course which itself beautifully complements the big one around it – there is no difficulty in recognising why Cruden Bay has taken its place among the elite of Scottish links golf clubs.

Sound guidance from all concerned ensures that it will retain its magnetism for members and visitors alike. As a role model in the running of a golf course and, nowadays, the essential facilities demanded around it, this club stands supreme.

Mike Aitken's Top 10 Hidden Gems

S cotland is blessed with so many fine golf courses, it's inevitable that some are less renowned than others. This has led to a spate of articles in recent years celebrating the country's hidden gems.

It's an attractive if flawed concept. In a country which likes to think of itself as the home of golf, just about every course in the land is accessible if you know where to look.

While many of the lay-outs in this article gleam like diamonds, it would be stretching a point to talk of buried treasure.

In truth, all of the ten courses I've selected, in no particular order, for this article are as easy to find as the Old Course itself.

I make no apology for what is a personal selection other than to explain the bias towards courses in the Lothians and Borders. Having lived most of my life in Edinburgh, this is simply the area I know best.

1 Ratho Park, near Edinburgh

Parkland
5900 yards
SSS68
Par 69

Tree-lined, sparkling green in spring and ablaze with golds and browns in autumn. Beautiful greens, generally soft and ideal for the lofted iron specialist. In the shadow of nearby Dalmahoy, Ratho is a star in its own right, one of those rare parkland courses which everyone who plays it seems to like. One of James Braid's ?00 or so Scottish designs, this unpretentious, attractive par 69 is beautifully maintained. It demands accuracy off the medal tees and a straight driver will be rewarded with a morale boosting score. Anyone who is wayward, however, will make the acquaintance of a splendid selection of trees which can soon induce a sense of claustrophobia.

I've been a member of this friendly club for most of my life and can think of nowhere I would rather play 18 holes of social golf. A major refurbishment of the changing rooms in 2001 means the clubhouse now matches the quality of the course. By way of an added bonus, the club sandwich is probably the finest in the country.

2 Lundin Links, Leven

Links
6394 yards
SSS71
Par 71

The second of the great Fife links as you head northwards along the coast. Leven 'joins on' behind Lundin's 4th.green to offer two terrific tests back-to-back.

I was introduced to this splendid links many moons ago on the annual outing organised by the Edinburgh

Press Club. In the days before the Forth Road Bridge linked Edinburgh with Fife, we travelled by bus and ferry from the capital, leaving the city before dawn and returning in the dead of night. It felt like a great adventure.

Today, Lundin Links is easily reached by car and the short journey is readily repaid by a game on one of the qualifying courses for the Open. Anyone with a tendency to hook the ball will stand on the first tee and glance towards the sea with trepidation. There's every chance you'll be looking for your ball on the beach! Graced by wonderfully quick greens – a colleague putted off the first the last time we played there – Lundin Links is flawed only by two holes of parkland on higher ground (the 12th and 13th) which seem to belong to another course. Otherwise, this is seaside golf at its best.

❸ The Roxburghe, near Kelso
Heath and parkland
6925 yards
SSS 74
Par 72
Built for championships and assuredly the hardest golfing test in the Borders. Not for the faint-hearted, needing much long iron use and with huge, difficult greens.

One of the best new courses in Britain, never mind the Borders, Dave Thomas' design hosted its first professional tournament, the Scottish Seniors Open, in 2001. Players of the calibre of Colin Montgomerie, Nick Faldo, Jesper Parnevik and course record holder Sergio Garcia have also played here and enthused about the experience. The signature hole, the 15th, which swoops down from an elevated tee to the River Teviot with a viaduct standing in the distance beyond the green, is one of the most visually stunning in the game. Very much the brainchild of the duke of Roxburghe, the course has worked wonders in focusing attention on the game in a hitherto overlooked part of the country.

❹ Elgin, Morayshire
Heath and parkland
6416 yards
SSS71
Par 69
Hugely entertaining inland course with fifteen of the eighteen played north/south or vice versa. Highly respected by the pros who never find it an easy touch.

I played Elgin for the first time a couple of years ago when I was staying in the town for the Walker Cup at

nearby Nairn. The course was a delightful surprise, both testing and charming. The views were breathtaking and the mixture of heath and parkland holes were most attractive. The tenth, a 436 yard par 4 to an elevated tee, particularly sticks in the mind, but the whole experience was most enjoyable.

❺ Montrose, Angus
Links
6485 yards
SSS 72
Par 71
Some say the golf course was here before the town! A highly respected Open Qualifying course; damage limitation required if the wind gets up, but great links.

While the conditioning of this ancient links might not be on a par with championship courses of the calibre of Carnoustie and Turnberry, Montrose offers a piece of the game's history at a bargain rate. Golf was first played here in 1562, which makes the links the fifth oldest in the world. Today's lay-out was designed by Willie Park Jnr around the turn of the century and shouldn't be missed by any golfer with more than a passing interest in the game's heritage.

❻ Whitekirk, Lothian
Heath
6526 yards
SSS 72
Par 72
Building a reputation as a high quality venue, with superb practice and off-course facilities. Not an easy ride, but stunning views in all directions ease the pain!

Jim Jefferies, the former Hearts and Bradford manager, now running Kilmarnock in the SPL, introduced me to this compelling test not long after the course was opened. Unlike some new courses, where money was no object, Whitekirk was built on a relatively tight budget. No one, though, should fall into the trap of regarding this hillside location as second rate. Testing enough to host one of the competitions on the Mastercard Tour, Whitekirk is well worth the short detour inland from those renowned courses at Gullane and North Berwick.

❼ Muckhart, Clackmannanshire
Heath
6086 or 6069 or 6485 yards
SSS 69 or 69 or 70
Par 71 or 70 or 71
Confused by the facts and figures? Play any two of the nine hole segments for the round. Most agree the

original 9 'Cowden' is still tops; it's a great 'outings' venue.

I would never have come across this charming club near Dollar but for the good offices of Alastair Wilson, the former Scottish Brewers executive, who once organised a sportswriters outing to his home course. With wonderful views of the Ochils, the course was a springtime treat. There are three nine hole tracks and you combine any two - another "first" for a hidden Scottish gem!

8 Queen's Course, Gleneagles
Heath/parkland
5965 yards
SSS 70
Par 68

The shortest, but many think the most enjoyable, of the three big Gleneagles courses. Wonderful early morning or evening; unimaginably glorious in autumn.

The Queen's always had to play second fiddle to the King's and now the PGA Centenary Course takes pride of place when it comes to hosting championships at the grand old resort in Perthshire. At just a touch under 6000 yards it's too short for today's long hitting professionals; for the rest of us, the Queen's is a treat. In my opinion, the most gorgeous of all the picturesque holes at Gleneagles are located on this little wonder.

9 The Kintyre, Turnberry
Links
6504 yards
SSS 72
Par 72

Created out of the former 'Arran' course and undoubtedly heading for greatness; may never upstage the 'Ailsa' but is equally demanding; the views are still great!

Donald Steel's reworking of what used to be known as the Arran opened to great acclaim in 2001. There are a number of holes that even surpass those on the Ailsa and could be part of a composite lay-out at future championships. For those who love links golf, perhaps the most appealing feature of the Kintyre is the stretch of land which carries the course to the sea for the first time.

10 Murcar, Aberdeen
Links
6287 yards
SSS 71
Par 71

Like Leven and Lundin in Fife, Murcar abutts Royal Aberdeen and offers the same challenge in the dunes. Shorter, perhaps, but very tight with planning essential.

Those of us who live in central Scotland don't get the chance to play in Grampian and the Highlands nearly as often as we would like. While there may be more famous courses around the Granite city, none are more challenging than Murcar. One of Britain's top 100 courses according to *Golf World* magazine, it would be hard to find a more daunting or dramatic test of golf anywhere.

Miracles at Muirfield

By Dougie Donnelly

You don't have to remind me – I know I have one of the best jobs in the world, one that allows me to be on first-name terms with some of the finest golfers in the world. It wasn't until I read *Golf World Magazine's* fascinating list of their top 100 courses in the British Isles, however, that I realised I have another reason to be grateful for being part of the BBC golf team for almost 15 years.

According to *Golf World Magazine*, the leading 12 golf courses are located north of the border, with Muirfield voted the very best in these islands by a panel of more than 80 experts.

I could not disagree with their choice, as subjective as it may have been, as the East Lothian links is truly magnificent. But as every golfer knows, part of the thrill of playing the great championship courses is in measuring your own humble skills against the great players who have teed it up on the same hallowed turf.

I will always have warm memories of Muirfield because it is where the most dramatic conclusion to any match I ever played took place. It is at this point, therefore, that I must introduce you to the Friday Club, a gathering of eight diverse personalities who are now in their 15th year of amiable – but intense – competition.

Formed one convivial evening in a Glasgow restaurant (where else?), our group meets eight times a year on a Friday, with each being responsible in turn for arranging the tee times and the festivities which inevitably follow. Five of the eight scores count towards the overall trophy, with a prize also on offer for the best fourball performance. You will understand, doubtless, that the golf is taken very seriously indeed!

Back to Muirfield, then, and a sunny August afternoon some years ago when Alan the Restaurateur and I found ourselves seven down after seven holes to Glen the Dentist and Davie the Motor Dealer. This, I would remind you, was Muirfield so, naturally, we were playing foursomes. The reader will appreciate that, at this point, sympathy for our plight was in scant supply. In fact, the gleeful predictions of a Friday Club record drubbing had become more than a little irritating.

"So what are the odds on you two hackers winning this one then? Five hundred to one?" chortled the man from the motor trade, giving the implications of his jocular comments no thought whatsoever. "I'll have a pound at these odds," replied my partner Alan quietly, to great hilarity from our over-confident opponents.

I will spare you the details of the following 10 holes. Suffice it to say that my newly motivated partner and I struck form with a vengeance. We subsequently, and to the utter disdain of our tormenters (now greatly subdued, of course), climbed triumphantly aboard the 18th tee one up.

I shall remember as long as I play this great game, the nine subsequent blows the four of us struck on Muirfield's renowned finishing hole.

In normal circumstances, Alan and I would not have been unhappy with the five we took to get down. I was upset that my three iron following my partner's arrow-straight drive had found the horrid greenside bunker, but the five at least forced our opponents into achieving par – no mean requirement here – to save the match, total embarrassment, and an unprecedented amount of cash.

It was not at all surprising that the Dentist and the Motor Dealer had long since ceased to communicate. After all, £500 was a much more impressive sum of money some 12 years ago than it is now. Quite apart from his profit from a good week disappearing into thin air, the Big Man was even more concerned about the hilarity and shame which would undoubtedly be heaped on him after defeat from such a dominant position.

It all served to concentrate his mind wonderfully. He chipped up bravely from light rough to about three feet. Then he closed his eyes – I was watching his every move – as the Dentist rolled in the putt to halve the match and save his skin.

I have played Muirfield several times since then. I have watched Nick Faldo win his Open Championship there. The drama of the Friday Club visit, however, remains my favourite memory of what I consider to be one of Britain's greatest courses.

For many years Dougie Donnelly has been BBC Scotland's anchorman of televised sport, from regular Saturday night Sportscene to live broadcasts of snooker, bowls, darts and, of course, golf. He is held in the highest regard by both his audiences and the vast number of professional sportsmen with whom he has rubbed shoulders and conducted interviews. Most recently he was part of BBC's team of commentators at the Sydney Olympics.

From the Ladies' Tee

Kathryn Marshall

Touring the globe, playing a game you love and earning a decent living. Doesn't it sound just absolutely fabulous? "Yes," agrees Kathryn Marshall before quickly adding: "But people sometimes forget that it's also a job. It's not all glamour; it's a very serious business.'

Marshall has been a seriously good golfer for most of her life, and has been on the professional circuit for ten years. Half smiling, she winces at the realisation that she is now one of the veterans of a lifestyle that includes playing on both the Evian Ladies' European Tour and the LPGA circuit in America.

As with anyone who chooses to play sport for money, the Scot's career has been speckled with highs and lows. The euphoria of victory contrasts sharply with the opportunities that have been missed as easily as a four foot putt.

"But I really do enjoy it," continued Marshall, warming to the theme, "The purses are increasing all the time and I love the competition. At times it can be very frustrating, especially if you're not playing well. But, overall, there aren't too many complaints."

Marshall, 34, is luckier than most in that she now shares the nomadic lifestyle with her husband, Scot. But, during their early years of married life, it wasn't quite so blissful.

Just two years after tying the knot in 1991 and just three seasons into her professional career, Kathryn bravely decided to head for America. She had spent her years in further education at the University of Arizona in Tucson, and had always harboured ambitions to play on the LPGA Tour.

She achieved her ambition by gaining her card for the 1993 season, but success on the golf course meant she spent too many heartbreaking months away from home, and evenings were usually taken up with long and tearful 'phone calls to Scot, who was working in Edinburgh as a civil engineer.

But as her career gathered pace and she started

"Europe is also growing, and I would love to come back more – and probably will – in the not too distant future."

plundering her fair share of dollars, the pair eventually decided that they could be as one on Tour and Scot, a handy low handicapper, took up a new career as his wife's caddie.

"We've now been travelling together for four years, and it's so much better," said Kathryn. "I used to miss Scot so much, but now we're together virtually all the time. To be able to travel the world with someone you love is perfect."

"Of course there are downsides. Airport delays are the biggest bugbear and, if you're missing cuts, it becomes very frustrating and can mean an awful lot of free time."

"Living in hotels can also become very tedious, but we spend around half the tournaments staying in hospitality; families that offer accommodation to the players. You go back to the same people every year and it breaks the monotony and we've made some really good friends."

Playing golf for a living is the absolute antithesis of a nine to five routine. Every day is different, but they are all very long. Rounds can stretch up to five demanding hours of concentration, while there is forever the call of the practice range, the putting green or the fitness trailer.

"You have early rises and late finishes," said Marshall as she tries to eradicate the myth that paying the mortgage by playing golf is an easy call. "As the money increases, the competition gets much stiffer."

"Everyone is working so much harder on every aspect of the game. The range is busy from dawn to dusk and all the players work out in the gym. A fitness trailer now travels to every tournament and you often have to queue up for a slot."

Not that it is all hard work. Scot and Kathryn spend many an evening at the movies and they also enjoy playing the role of tourists in the various cities around the globe. "But I don't have many late nights," rapidly dousing any notion that she might be a party animal. "I'm practically always in bed by 10pm."

At one time, they pondered with the notion of buying a house and moving permanently to America. But the pair then came across their dream home in Broughty Ferry, which is close to Monifieth Golf Club where

romance first blossomed during their days as junior members.

"I'm pleased we decided against living in the States," reflects Kathryn. "I now think we have the best of both worlds. We get to spend a lot of the year seeing the world, but it's always great to get back to Scotland. It will always be home."

"Mind you, when the season ends and we have a

continues page 26 >

EXCLUSIVE

Golf Memorabilia Offer

As a golfer, have you ever wondered what it might be like to own something truly unique – **a genuine piece of golfing history?**

Scotland Home of Golf, in Association with the **Billy Casper Group** are delighted to be able to offer you a service exclusive to the UK market.

Through our extensive contacts, we can obtain **unique articles**, unavailable to the general public, and get access to the giants of the game, past and present, to provide you with a memory **truly worth treasuring**.

Like what?
What about a personally signed, beautifully framed photo of **Billy Casper**, taken at his **1970 US Masters win?**
or perhaps you'd prefer **Gary Player's signature** on a photo of his **USPGA Championship** win?
or a great shot of the legendary Byron Nelson, with his signature elegantly engraved in copper?

These are just some of the standard items we can supply – but there's more.
What would you give for a genuine **Masters flag**,
signed by your favourite player?
Or an official **Ryder Cup**
jacket, signed by the
teams?

Whatever you want,
tell us! Whatever
item you'd ideally
love to own and
whose signature(s)
you want on it, we'll
get it for you as
soon as possible.

* But we can also supply items anywhere in the world, on request!

How can you get
these great items?
Simply fill out the order form on page 149
and post it back to us. We'll supply
standard items within 60 days, and provide a price for special request items
within 30 days. Each item comes with a certificate of authenticity, so you know
it's a genuine piece of golfing history.

Look out for our monthly auctions of special unique pieces on our website,
www.scotland-for-golf.com, starting later this year.

"I have a tremendous amount of respect and love for the game of golf and for the home of golf, Scotland. Through our **Scottish Golf Collection** I'd like to help golfers around the world realise their ambition of experiencing some of the world-class venues in Scotland."

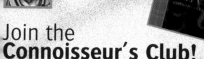

Join the
Connoisseur's Club!

Connoisseur's Club members will receive a copy of **Billy Casper's Golf Collection**, featuring 12 of

Scotland's most prestigious golfing venues and associated hotels, together with a suite of discount vouchers for use on green fees, accommodation and dining. The vouchers are activated and validated by a membership card which can be used for 12 months. After the vouchers have been used the club member can carry on receiving substantial discounts for the duration of their membership.

SAMPLE SAVINGS:

St Andrews: 50% off accommodation at the 5-star Old Course Hotel, plus 25% off green fees at the Duke's Course.

Carnoustie: 50% off accommodation at the 4-star Carnoustie Hotel, Golf Resort and Spa plus 25% off green fees at the Burnside's Course and 25% off the bill for 1-4 diners at the Dalhousie Restaurant.

Golf Event Service

Would you like to enhance your corporate golf event and make it truly special? **Scotland Home of Golf** and the **Billy Casper Group** have teamed up to offer a service to do just that.

Byron Casper, former professional golfer and son of the legendary 'Buffalo' Billy Casper, will host your day, play a round with you and help make the whole day a guaranteed success.

We can also offer further services for your day: send back the order form on page 150 for more information!

Billy Casper's
Golf Tips

STANCE AND BODY POSTURE

The stance should not be too narrow or too wide. The rule of thumb is the outside edges of your feet should not be wider than the outside edges of your shoulders.

The Posture: A wee flex of the knees and bend forward with the upper part of your body. The vision you must have when bending forward is like placing your seater on a tall bar or pub stool. Now with the bend from the waist and a wee flex of your knees let your arms drop down and place your hands together. This shows you how far from the ball you need to stand and how far your hands need to be away from your body at address.

THE DRIVER

You may not have looked at it this way before but for the more advanced player the drive consumes nearly 50% of the distance on most long holes. A drive in the fairway really sets you up with an excellent opportunity for a good score. The clubhead size, center of gravity, and loft along with the proper gram weight, flex, and length of the shaft are key factors in being able to use a driver effectively. The prime factor is the shaft or backbone of the club. The stiffness of the shaft is vital. There are many excellent shafts on the market today, it would do you well to spend some time testing a variety to really discover which shaft is best

suited for you.

Due to the length of the shaft the ball should be played forward towards your left toe if you are righthanded. Tee the ball high, a good ruleof thumb is at least half of the ball is above the top of the clubhead. With the ball placed forward in your stance you will contact the ball on the upswing. You see the longer the ball stays in the air the further it will travel unless you are playing into those strong breezes. And when you do play in those brisk winds, I recommend that you lower the tee and position the ball back at your left heel so the club will contact the ball closer to the middle of the ball which will cause the ball to fly lower and under more control.

THE SHORT PUTT
IS THE KEY TO GOOD SCORING

Assume a comfortable position over the ball, with the weight evenly distributed on both feet. The head and eyes must be directly over the ball and the hands are placed at the back of the ball. The stroke is slow and smooth. With the left hand moving the putter back away from the ball, the right hand helps to keep the putter square to the intended line. The putter must be kept low to the ground on the take-a-way or back stroke. The back of the left hand moves the putter back towards the ball with the right hand adding the power. Make sure that the back of the left hand carries the head of the putter through the position of the ball on the green. It is important that the golfer watches the putter strike the back of the ball.

LOOK OUT FOR A FULL COLLECTED EDITION OF BILLY CASPER'S GOLF TIPS COMING LATER THIS YEAR!

couple of months in the freezing cold of a Scottish winter it perhaps isn't quite so appealing."

While Europe and the US has become Kathryn's golfing 'home', most of her best -loved venues are perhaps, naturally, in her native land.

And she has little hesitation in naming three of her particular favourites, namely Carnoustie, Monifieth and the King's at Gleneagles.

"I absolutely adore Carnoustie," she says. "It's where I practise when I am at home during the winter and I think it is a great course and a great lay-out. I really enjoy links golf and I just wish we had the chance to play more links courses on Tour."

"I was so pleased when the Open returned to Carnoustie two years ago. It set a great test for the world's top men, and they certainly found it tough."

"Monifieth is where I started playing golf, and it's also got great memories because it is where I met my husband. We were both young members; real childhood sweethearts!"

"The King's at Gleneagles is another tremendous course. We played the WPGA Championship of Europe there for a few years and it was one of the best tournaments on either the European or LPGA Tours. There are lots of great courses in Scotland, but these three get my vote."

Asked to pick a career highlight, Kathryn easily plumps for two memorable weeks. The first was her win in the 1995 Jamie Farr Classic in Toledo – she was the first Scot to win on the LPGA Tour – and playing for Europe in the 1996 Solheim Cup.

This season, she has also had plenty memorable moments, crossing the six-figure mark in prize money, lying comfortably in the top 60 on the US money list. She also had packed away a good few pounds from the Evian circuit in Europe, with a good finish in the Weetabix British Open.

"I would love to win again," she said with a hint of desperation. "But competition is so strong these days that it is getting tougher all the time."

After ten years on Tour, she is delighted to see both the LPGA and Evian Ladies' European Tours thrive and prosper. "When I started in the States a prize fund of $500,000 was considered huge. Now we have 20 events at $1 million.

"Europe is also growing, and I would love to come back more – and probably will – in the not too distant future."

In the meantime, she is happy to pack away the air miles in regular trips chasing glory all around the world. "Scot and I are so lucky," she repeated. "As far as job satisfaction is concerned, it doesn't get much better." •

Jedburgh

HOLE	NAME	WHITE YARDS	YELLOW YARDS	PAR	STROKE INDEX
1	Gospel Hall	302	281	4	-
2	Pottsmuir	314	248	4	-
3	Dunion	381	301	4	-
4	Linthaughlee	197	179	3	-
5	Hundalee	184	171	3	-
6	Jethart	337	319	4	-
7	The Shed	417	403	4/5	-
8	Larkhall	320	292	4	-
9	Cheviot View	309	250	4	-
10	Gospel Hall	302	281	4	-
11	Pottsmuir	314	248	4	-
12	Dunion	381	301	4	-
13	Linthaughlee	197	179	3	-
14	Hundalee	184	171	3	-
15	Jethart	337	319	4	-
16	The Shed	417	403	4/5	-
17	Larkhall	320	292	4	-
18	Cheviot View	342	250	4	-

Jedburgh Golf Club

Dunion Road, Jedburgh,
Roxburghshire, TD8 6TA

Advance Bookings
T: 01835 863587

Holes: 9
Yardage: 5492 yds
SSS: 67

The first course you hit on the A68 route into Scotland is a favourite stop-off for English visitors in particular. Nine holes on rolling land west of the town provide a test of short irons and quality work around smallish greens, but Jedburgh is the perfect start to a Borders' golf tour – of which more and more now take advantage – with hospitality in the little clubhouse second to none.

Green Fees	Weekdays	Weekends	Are visitors
Round	£16	£16	welcome?
Daily	£16	£16	Yes

Nearest Airport: Edinburgh, 55.6 miles
Nearest Rail Station: Berwick-Upon-Tweed, 27 miles
Gazetteer Ref: p103   **Map Ref:** p157, F4

TO LOCATE THIS GOLF COURSE ON THE MAPS (p155-159) LOOK FOR THE FLAG WITH THIS PAGE NUMBER.

▼ Looking down to the clubhouse

Minto

Minto Golf Club

Denholm, Hawick
Roxburghshire TD9 8SH

Advance Bookings
T: 01450 870220

Holes: 18
Yardage: 5542 yds
SSS: 67

But a few miles up the road from Hawick, this lovely parkland layout sits amidst a wealth of arbor Geal splendour looking south over the Teviot valley. Perfect for parties and holiday golf, it's a busy course where excellent clubhouse fare complements the pleasures on the course. Interesting holes abound, most of whose challenge is, naturally, posed by the presence of flourishing timber – lots of it old and magnificent.

HOLE	NAME	WHITE YARDS	YELLOW YARDS	PAR	STROKE INDEX
1	Gibbie Glebe	396	-	4	2
2	Volunteers	309	-	4	16
3	Aintree	421	-	4	1
4	Stewart's View	165	-	3	10
5	Hoggie's Leap	480	-	5	15
6	Kirk Tower	188	-	3	8
7	Fat Lips	347	-	4	5
8	Benign Bishop	144	-	3	13
9	Kittock	335	-	4	9
10	Hangin' Stane	252	-	4	18
11	Dunion	369	-	4	12
12	Everest	267	-	4	6
13	Craigmount	311	-	4	14
14	Teviotdale	409	-	4	3
15	Ruberslaw	355	-	4	11
16	Road Hole	297	-	4	7
17	West Lodge	122	-	3	17
18	Shaw's Bush	375	-	4	4

Green Fees

	Weekdays	Weekends	Are visitors welcome?
Round	£22	£27.50	
Daily	£-	£-	Yes

Nearest Airport: Edinburgh, 54.4 miles
Nearest Rail Station: Berwick-Upon-Tweed, 35 miles
Gazetteer Ref: p103   **Map Ref:** p157, F4

TO LOCATE THIS GOLF COURSE ON THE MAPS (p155-159) LOOK FOR THE FLAG WITH THIS PAGE NUMBER.

Short 4th ▼

hidden gem

St Boswells (Melrose)

HOLE	NAME	WHITE YARDS	YELLOW YARDS	PAR	STROKE INDEX
1	Safely First	257		4	13
2	The Brae	349		4	4
3	The Milestone	168		3	17
4	Klondyke	343		4	5
5	Butts	272		4	11
6	High	367		4	7
7	Pandy	312		4	9
8	Marks	414		4	1
9	Ca'Canny	217		4	15
10	Ivanhoe	257		4	14
11	The Dyke	388		4	2
12	The Gully	168		3	18
13	Wester Ho	343		4	6
14	Wild Orchids	272		4	12
15	Tree Tops	367		4	8
16	Curling Pond	329		4	10
17	Black Hill	414		4	3
18	Home	271		4	16

St. Boswells Golf Club

Braehead, St. Boswells
Roxburghshire TD6 0DE

Advance Bookings
T: 01835 823527

Holes: 9
Yardage: 5250 yds
SSS: 65

You can look at this gorgeous little course and imagine, without difficulty, that it is cared for as the greens staff would their own gardens. Not content with lovely, lush fairways and high quality greens, course presentation resembles the best efforts of an Alan Titsmarch or Jim McColl rather than mere greenkeepers. The gurgling of the Tweed completes a perfect scene which can't be bettered for de-stressing golf.

Green Fees	Weekdays	Weekends	Are visitors
Round	£15	£15	welcome?
Daily	£-	£-	Yes

Nearest Airport: Edinburgh, 46.3 miles
Nearest Rail Station: Berwick-Upon-Tweed, 30 miles
Gazetteer Ref: p103   **Map Ref:** p157, F3

TO LOCATE THIS GOLF COURSE ON THE MAPS (p155-159) LOOK FOR THE FLAG WITH THIS PAGE NUMBER.

▼ River Tweed and St Boswells Golf Course

The Roxburghe

The Roxburghe Golf Course

Kelso, Roxburghshire TD5 8JZ

Advance Bookings
T: 01573 450331

Holes: 18
Yardage: 7111
SSS: 75

Championship quality, this one, needing no more than a few big tournaments to put it well and truly on the map. Dave Thomas has given bags of fairway space and big greens to hit, but threatens the wayward among us with huge sand traps. Even off the yellows, it will search out the best of your golf and it is not for the uninitiated; great scenery and sumptuous surroundings make this a very special venue and, surely, those big championships are just round the corner?

Green Fees	Weekdays	Weekends	Are visitors welcome?
Round	£50	£50	
Daily	£50	£50	Yes

Nearest Airport: Edinburgh, 58 miles
Nearest Rail Station: Berwick-Upon-Tweed, 25 miles
Gazetteer Ref: p103 **Map Ref:** p157, G3

HOLE	NAME	WHITE YARDS	YELLOW YARDS	PAR	STROKE INDEX
1	-	421	385	4	6
2	-	396	373	4	10
3	-	364	352	4	18
4	-	188	177	3	12
5	-	546	537	5	2
6	-	382	360	4	14
7	-	520	486	5	8
8	-	181	171	3	16
9	-	403	384	4	4
10	-	469	439	4	1
11	-	526	504	5	7
12	-	399	385	4	9
13	-	216	183	3	15
14	-	523	511	5	11
15	-	177	159	3	17
16	-	394	385	4	3
17	-	398	355	4	13
18	-	422	400	4	5

TO LOCATE THIS GOLF COURSE ON THE MAPS (p155-159) LOOK FOR THE FLAG WITH THIS PAGE NUMBER.

Short 4th ▼

Gatehouse

HOLE	NAME	WHITE YARDS	YELLOW YARDS	PAR	STROKE INDEX
1	-	211	206	3	9
2	-	354	338	4	5
3	-	320	288	4	3
4	-	322	316	4	7
5	-	131	120	3	17
6	-	549	532	5	1
7	-	280	272	4	13
8	-	189	186	3	11
9	-	165	160	3	15
10	-	211	206	3	10
11	-	354	338	4	6
12	-	320	288	4	4
13	-	322	316	4	8
14	-	131	120	3	8
15	-	549	532	5	2
16	-	280	272	4	14
17	-	189	186	3	12
18	-	165	160	3	16

Gatehouse Golf Club

Laurieston Road, Gatehouse of Fleet,
Castle Douglas
Kirkcudbrightshire DG7 2BE

Advance Bookings T: 01557 814766

Holes: 9
Yardage: 2521 yds
SSS: 66

Here's a fun course which will have you panting, scratching your head, wondering where on earth the green is and smiling in triumph – all in various degrees as you take on its nine testing holes. Put the drive in position A at the par fours, get your short irons into gear then gild the putter and you'll really enjoy lunch! The friendliest of clubs, beautifully set a mile out of the town, offers glorious views in all directions.

Green Fees	Weekdays	Weekends	Are visitors welcome?
Round	£10	£10	Yes, except Sundays
Daily	£15	£15	before 11.30am

Nearest Airport: Prestwick, 95.2 miles
Nearest Rail Station: Dumfries, 32.8 miles
Gazetteer Ref: p110   **Map Ref:** p157, D6

TO LOCATE THIS GOLF COURSE ON THE MAPS (p155-159) LOOK FOR THE FLAG WITH THIS PAGE NUMBER.

▼ 8th green

hidden **gem**

A warm Scottish welcome awaits you at our family run hotel, newly refurbished to the highest standard, consisting of 31 bedrooms all en suite, licensed bar (also serving home cooked food) and a la carte restaurant. The hotel is situated in the heart of Gretna surrounded by beautiful Dumfrieshire countryside. There are nine golf courses all within 35 miles. Fishing and shooting is also available nearby.

THE Gables HOTEL

1 Annan Road, Gretna, Dumfrieshire, DG16 5DQ · Tel: 01461 338300 · Fax: 01461 338626
www.gables-hotel-gretna.co.uk · info@gables-hotel-gretna.co.uk

The Baron's Craig offers luxurious accommodation with excellent facilities, and is ideally located for access to several golf courses including the superb 'Southerness' course. *Standing in extensive woodland and mature gardens, the imposing 19th century Baron's Craig Hotel is located in a region which is* steeped in history *and overlooks Solway and Rough Firth. Serving* tempting menus *and* fine wines, *the Baron's Craig can cater for the golfer, golfing parties and is the ideal venue for* corporate events. *The golfer and non-golfer can be assured of access to outdoor pursuits and a time to relax making their stay at the Baron's Craig Hotel* one to remember.

BARON'S CRAIG HOTEL

BARON'S CRAIG HOTEL, ROCKCLIFFE BY DALBEATTIE, KIRKUDBRIGHTSHIRE, DG5 4QF
TEL: 01556 630225 · FAX: 01556 630328
E-mail: info@baronscraighotel.co.uk · www.baronscraighotel.co.uk

---

Dumfries and Galloway Golf Club

2 Laurieston Avenue, Dumfries DG2 7NY · Tel. (01387 263848)

18 Holes, length 6325 yds. SSS 71

Charges: £26 round/day, £32 weekend.
For advance reservations
Tel: (01387) 256739

Practise area, caddy cars,
catering facilities available.

Visitors welcome weekdays
except Tuesdays

Secretary: Tom Ross
Tel: (01387) 263848,

Professional: Joe Fergusson
Tel: (01387) 256902.

The essential guide for fishing in Scotland

If you enjoy fishing, you'll love **Scotland for Fishing 2002/2003.** Edited by award-winning fisherman and journalist Mike Shepley, Scotland for Fishing contains all you need to know to get on the water at Scotland's best fishing sites.

If you order your copy direct from Pastime Publications, you can save £1 off the cover price. For just **£6.99** including post and packaging, we'll deliver the guide to your door anywhere in the UK.

Send your cheque, made payable to: Pastime Publications, Golf Reader Offer, 5 Dalgety Avenue, Edinburgh EH7 5UF, along with your address details. Then sit back and start planning your Scottish fishing holiday.

Allow 28 days for delivery.

Southerness

HOLE	NAME	WHITE YARDS	YELLOW YARDS	PAR	STROKE INDEX
1		393	372	4	7
2		450	405	4	3
3		408	383	4	9
4		169	132	3	17
5		496	479	5	11
6		405	367	4	5
7		215	215	3	15
8		371	342	4	13
9		435	404	4	1
10		168	141	3	16
11		390	371	4	12
12		421	387	4	6
13		467	436	4	2
14		458	418	4	8
15		217	195	3	14
16		433	414	4	4
17		175	164	3	18
18		495	480	5	10

Southerness Golf Club

Southerness, Dumfries
Dumfrieshire DG2 8AZ

Advance Bookings
T: 01387 880677

Holes: 18
Yardage: 6564 yds
SSS: 73

With its neighbour Powfoot across the Nith estuary, here we have the giants of links golf in southern Scotland. Southerness perhaps has the edge for degree of difficulty, especially as the vagaries of the wind have an amazing influence on your game, from the holes west of the clubhouse to those close to the Solway some half-a-mile to the south; the legendary twelfth is one of Scotland's great par fours.

Green Fees	Weekdays	Weekends	Are visitors
Round	£35	£45	welcome?
Weekly	£128		Yes

Nearest Airport: Prestwick, 126.5 miles
Nearest Rail Station: Dumfries, 16.3 miles
Gazetteer Ref: p109   **Map Ref:** p157, E6

TO LOCATE THIS GOLF COURSE ON THE MAPS (p155-159) LOOK FOR THE FLAG WITH THIS PAGE NUMBER.

▼ 12th green

Kirkudbright

Kirkudbright Golf Club

Stirling Crescent
Kirkcudbrightshire DG6 4EZ

Advance Bookings
T: 01557 330314

Holes: 18
Yardage: 5739 yds
SSS: 69

Dumfries & Galloway offers a host of perfect holiday golfing venues; this is yet another in the chain along the Solway which does repeat business with visitors year after year. Most of the eighteen holes are laid out, north to south, across the high ground to the east of the town; there's nothing taxing about them, mind you, and blame for lack of performance cannot be laid at the door of the course architect.

HOLE	NAME	WHITE YARDS	YELLOW YARDS	PAR	STROKE INDEX
1	Opperheimer	330	310	4	9
2	Knowes	367	355	4	5
3	Banks	273	261	4	13
4	Hastings	327	301	4	7
5	Whins	429	384	4	3
6	Valley	135	134	3	17
7	Avenue	380	378	4	1
8	Jessie Robertson	469	477	5	11
9	Pond	190	176	3	15
10	Boreland	344	330	4	8
11	Burn	326	279	4	12
12	Plantation	449	439	5/4	4
13	Spire View	167	161	3	16
14	Piggery	327	295	4	10
15	Clingans	228	213	3	14
16	Glebe	185	174	3	18
17	Glendroit	400	362	4	2
18	Galloway	391	383	4	6

Green Fees	Weekdays	Weekends	Are visitors
Round	£18	£18	welcome?
Daily	£23	£23	Yes

Nearest Airport: Prestwick, 101.9 miles
Nearest Rail Station: Dumfries, 28.2 miles
Gazetteer Ref: p110   **Map Ref:** p157, D6

14th green

Colvend

HOLE	NAME	WHITE YARDS	YELLOW YARDS	PAR	STROKE INDEX
1	Torrs Hill	259	251	4	10
2	Portling	115	111	3	18
3	Solway View	353	341	4	4
4	Whinny Bank	169	164	3	16
5	The Rowan	309	303	4	12
6	Teugh Brae	336	330	4	2
7	Douglas Hall	359	319	4	14
8	The Burn	190	178	3	6
9	Drumburn	297	286	4	8
10	New Barns	252	223	4	11
11	The Ruin	373	283	4	5
12	Devils Elbow	469	466	5	3
13	The Water Hole	181	122	3	13
14	Fairgirth	426	422	4	1
15	Barnhourie	516	507	5	7
16	Wee Dunt	155	139	3	17
17	Roon The Bend	222	218	4	15
18	The Oaks	269	266	4	9

Colvend Golf Club

Sandyhills, Colvend by Dalbeattie
Kirkcudbrightshire, DG5 4PY

Advance Bookings
T: 01556 630398

Holes: 18
Yardage: 5220 yds
SSS: 67

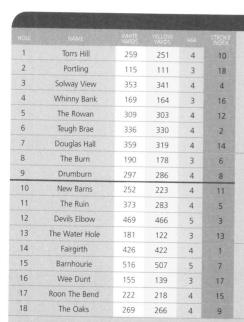

I make no apology for this most pleasurable of holiday courses appearing yet again in the D&G editorial. I find I simply cannot leave it out. Combining fun, the need for cunning, a few steep climbs, the chance of a flattering score and – once again – stunning Solway panoramas, Colvend has the lot. Throw in a clubhouse of ultimate friendliness and good fare and you have the whole picture. Come here – soon.

Green Fees	Weekdays	Weekends	Are visitors welcome?
Round	£20	£20	
Daily	£20	£20	Yes

Nearest Airport: Prestwick 120.8 miles
Nearest Rail Station: Dumfries 19.7 miles
Gazetteer Ref: p109   **Map Ref:** p157, E6

TO LOCATE THIS GOLF COURSE ON THE MAPS (p155-159) LOOK FOR THE FLAG WITH THIS PAGE NUMBER.

▼ 3rd green

hidden **gem**

Dumfries and Galloway

Dumfries and County Golf Club

Nunfield, Edinburgh Road
Dumfries, Dumfrieshire DG1 1JX

Advance Bookings
T: 01387 268918

Holes: 18
Yardage: 5928 yds
Par: 69

This lovely course at the south-west edge of Dumfries was a real surprise. I paid my first visit last year and instantly regretted not having done so ages before. It is in quite superb condition and in every aspect is a splendid challenge. The unique position of the clubhouse and the cleaving of the course by the road to Stranraer are idiosyncrasies which should not deter you from having a tilt at a layout every bit as challenging as its rival on the other side of town.

HOLE	NAME	WHITE YARDS	YELLOW YARDS	PAR	STROKE INDEX
1	Norwest	338	325	4	11
2	Summerhill	500	488	5	9
3	The Bell	442	422	4	5
4	Mabie On	146	139	3	18
5	Station	564	555	5	3
6	Burnside	323	323	4	13
7	Deil's Elbow	411	400	4	7
8	The Burn	205	195	3	15
9	Starryheugh	423	410	4	1
10	Fernie	410	395	4	4
11	Muckie Brae	448	362	4	2
12	Ridges	357	336	4	10
13	Pearmount	192	179	3	16
14	Plateau	324	316	4	6
15	The Gully	166	156	3	17
16	Cycle Track	365	360	4	8
17	The Dyke	353	344	4	12
18	Doonhame	342	334	4	14

Green Fees	Weekdays	Weekends	Are visitors welcome?
Round	£26	£26	Yes
Daily	£26	£26	

Nearest Airport: Prestwick 109 miles
Nearest Rail Station: Dumfries 1.6 miles
Gazetteer Ref: p109   **Map Ref:** p157, E5

hidden gem

18th green

Linlithgow

HOLE	NAME	WHITE YARDS	YELLOW YARDS	PAR	STROKE INDEX
1	Drambuie	312	296	4	15
2	Plantation	384	324	4	5
3	Hermit's Cave	279	268	4	13
4	Doon the Lum	376	372	4	3
5	Cocleroi	282	272	4	17
6	Glaur Aboot	250	237	4	11
7	Braehead Drop	168	168	3	9
8	Whinny Knowe	169	152	3	7
9	Deil's Dip	417	363	4	1
10	The Spinney	232	220	3	10
11	Donkey Lea	315	311	4	14
12	The Avenue	477	435	5	12
13	Lang Whang	490	475	5	4
14	Pulpit	273	267	4	16
15	Rest and be Thankful	278	246	4	8
16	Margaret's Bower	446	406	4	2
17	Wishing Well	169	154	3	18
18	Union Canal	412	399	4	6

Linlithgow Golf Club

Braehead, Linlithgow
West Lothian EH49 6QF

Advance Bookings
T: 01506 842585

Holes: 18
Yardage: 5729 yds
SSS: 68

Golfers either enjoy their sport here or go away in the huff – there appear to be no grey areas. The fact that it's a very tight driving course (at any one of twelve holes a miss-hit teeshot will almost certainly cost you dear) and that there are a couple of stiff climbs, seem to cause irritation. The course has never been in better nick, though, and if you get it going off the tee, you will be smiling all the way. Great views are just a bonus at a highly popular venue for outings.

Green Fees	Weekdays	Weekends	Are visitors
Round	£17	£10	welcome?
Daily	£10	£25	Yes

Nearest Airport: Edinburgh, 14 miles
Nearest Rail Station: Linlithgow, 3 miles
Gazetteer Ref: p127   **Map Ref:** p157, E2

TO LOCATE THIS GOLF COURSE ON THE MAPS (p155-159) LOOK FOR THE FLAG WITH THIS PAGE NUMBER.

▼ Par 4 at the 6th

Deer Park

Deer Park Golf & Country Club

Golf Course Road, Knightsridge West, Livingston, West Lothian EH54 8AB

Advance Bookings
T: 01506 446688

Holes: 18
Yardage: 6688 yds
SSS: 72

Livingston's testing eighteen holes – aimed originally at securing future tournament golf – is maturing year-by-year. It is a stiff course for the higher handicapped, without a doubt, and some of the longer par fours are a hard pull if the wind blows around Dechmont Hill. There is a great deal of satisfaction from a successful foray around a big course, however, and lots of variety ensures interest to the final putt.

HOLE	NAME	WHITE YARDS	YELLOW YARDS	PAR	STROKE INDEX
1	Royal Stag	332		4	17
2	Stables	513		5	2
3	Muir Trap	214		3	14
4	Long Park	450		4	1
5	Jim's Ain	367		4	9
6	Deer's Run	423		4	5
7	Fawns	189		3	16
8	Antlers	522		5	7
9	The Monastery	334		4	11
10	The Hind	165		3	18
11	Slaps and Stiles	430		4	8
12	Pines	481		5	4
13	Buck & Boe	350		4	15
14	The Law	505		5	2
15	Deer Hill	426		4	10
16	Ca Canny	222		3	12
17	The Rut	424		4	6
18	Knightsridge	341		4	13

Green Fees	Weekdays	Weekends	Are visitors welcome?
Round	£24	£36	
Daily	£24	£36	Yes

Nearest Airport: Edinburgh, 11.2 miles
Nearest Rail Station: Livingston North, 1.4 miles
Gazetteer Ref: p127 **Map Ref:** p157, E2

TO LOCATE THIS GOLF COURSE ON THE MAPS (p155-159) LOOK FOR THE FLAG WITH THIS PAGE NUMBER.

Across Deer Park ▼

Pumpherston

HOLE	NAME	WHITE YARDS	YELLOW YARDS	PAR	STROKE INDEX
1	Pentlands	410		4	7
2	Woodside	440		4	1
3	The Willows	184		3	11
4	Swans Nest	340		4	5
5	Magazine	185		3	13
6	The Cooler	251		4	9
7	The Whins	165		3	15
8	The Quarry	302		4	17
9	Clubhouse	440		4	3
10	Pentlands	410		4	8
11	Woodside	440		4	2
12	The Willows	184		3	12
13	Swans Nest	340		4	6
14	Magazine	185		3	14
15	The Cooler	251		4	10
16	The Whins	165		3	16
17	The Quarry	302		4	18
18	Clubhouse	440		4	4

Pumpherston Golf Club

Drumshoreland Road, Pumpherston,
Livingston, West Lothian EH53 0LF

Advance Bookings
T: 01506 432869

Holes: 18
Yardage: 6004 yds
SSS: 69

The notorious shale bings of West Lothian cradled the original nine holes of this now superb golf course. Extended only this year to a full eighteen, there is not a better presented test for golfers in the county and the new clubhouse is icing on the cake. For outsiders, it was rarely a revered venue but, mark my words, the development to a full eighteen will soon have Pumpherston a talking point in golf.

Green Fees	Weekdays	Weekends	Are visitors
Round	£18	£22	welcome?
Daily	£25	£33	Yes

Nearest Airport: Edinburgh, 8 miles
Nearest Rail Station: Uphall, 0.5 miles
Gazetteer Ref: p127   **Map Ref:** p157, E2

TO LOCATE THIS GOLF COURSE ON THE MAPS (p155-159) LOOK FOR THE FLAG WITH THIS PAGE NUMBER.

▼ 2nd green

Dundas Parks

Dundas Parks Golf Club

South Queensferry, Midlothian
EH30 9SS

Advance Bookings
T: 0131 319 1347

Holes: 9
Yardage: 6024 yds
SSS: 70

HOLE	NAME	WHITE YARDS	YELLOW YARDS	PAR	STROKE INDEX
1	Rhoddies	254	244	4	17
2	Pentland	496	487	5	5
3	Castle	418	408	4	1
4	Avenue	302	261	4	15
5	Pheasant Copse	392	382	4	9
6	Mons Hill	402	390	4	3
7	Beech	156	147	3	13
8	Roon' The Bend	393	385	4	7
9	Hawes	215	199	3	11
10	Rhoddies	254	244	4	18
11	Pentland	496	487	5	6
12	Castle	418	408	4	2
13	Avenue	302	261	4	16
14	Pheasant Copse	392	382	4	10
15	Mons Hill	402	390	4	4
16	Beech	156	147	3	14
17	Roon' The Bend	393	385	4	8
18	Hawes	215	199	3	12

This little nine-hole gem is one of West Lothian's best kept secrets. While the members would like to keep it that way, guests are always welcome; invariably they depart with nothing but praise for the appearance and condition of its lush fairways and receptive greens. After the rigours of last year's winter, there wasn't a better looking track anywhere in May than this one and when the rhododendrons are in their June splendour, a day's golf here is unforgettable.

Green Fees	Weekdays	Weekends	Are visitors welcome?
Round	£10	£-	Yes, except
Daily	£10	£-	weekends

Nearest Airport: Edinburgh, 8.2 miles
Nearest Rail Station: Dalmeny, 1.5 miles
Gazetteer Ref: p126 **Map Ref:** p157, E2

TO LOCATE THIS GOLF COURSE ON THE MAPS (p155-159) LOOK FOR THE FLAG WITH THIS PAGE NUMBER.

7th green ▼

hidden gem

Prestonfield

HOLE	NAME	WHITE YARDS	YELLOW YARDS	PAR	STROKE INDEX
1	Cragend	290		4	15
2	Hunter's Bog	151		3	14
3	Well's O'Wearie	551		5	6
4	Windy Gowl	451		4	2
5	The Dyke	179		3	12
6	Pentlands	377		4	7
7	Duddingston	510		5	9
8	Observatory	432		4	4
9	Peffermill	146		3	18
10	Forkenford	366		4	8
11	Spinney	440		4	1
12	Little France	436		4	3
13	Old Garden	145		3	17
14	Dog Leg	353		4	10
15	Paddock	370		4	11
16	Arthur's Seat	256		4	16
17	St. Leonard's	436		4	5
18	Home	325		4	13

TO LOCATE THIS GOLF COURSE ON THE MAPS (p155-159) LOOK FOR THE FLAG WITH THIS PAGE NUMBER.

▼ Short 2nd

Prestonfield Golf Club

6 Priestfield Road North, Edinburgh, Midlothian EH16 5HS

Advance Bookings
T: 0131 667 9665

Holes: 18
Yardage: 6214 yds
SSS: 70

Lying in the shadow of Arthur's Seat (and again but a five minute journey from the city centre) Prestonfield is yet another highly popular course with member and visitor alike. The start and finish to the round is at the top of the course where slopes and humps can be devilish; the flat section, where mature trees proliferate, never loses its interest in a succession of holes which in the majority of cases require more brainwork than brawn.

Green Fees	Weekdays	Weekends	Are visitors welcome?
Round	£20	£30	Yes
Daily	£30	£40	

Nearest Airport: Edinburgh, 10.4 miles
Nearest Rail Station: Edinburgh, 1.7 miles
Gazetteer Ref: p125   **Map Ref:** p157, F2

hidden gem

Duddingston

Duddingston Golf Club

137-139 Duddingston Road West
Edinburgh, Midlothian EH15 3QD

Advance Bookings
T: 0131 661 7688

Holes: 18
Yardage: 6420 yds
SSS: 72

HOLE	NAME	WHITE YARDS	YELLOW YARDS	PAR	STROKE INDEX
1	Deer Park	495		5	8
2	Westward Ho'	170		3	11
3	Abercorn	407		4	6
4	Death or Glory	488		5	2
5	Ditch	338		4	17
6	Burn	201		3	15
7	Mansion Head	381		4	4
8	Gates	524		5	10
9	Avenue	321		4	13
10	Capability	185		3	12
11	Woodlands	443		4	1
12	Village	377		4	7
13	Temple	426		4	3
14	High and Dry	150		3	18
15	Shade's	325		4	16
16	Arthur's Seat	386		4	5
17	Pond	500		5	9
18	R.D.B.M.	356		4	14

For classical parkland golf it is hard to imagine that there is anything as opulent as this superb course. The Shade family put it firmly on the map years ago and it has gone from strength to strength over the last few years. A magnificent test of golf with loads of variety in challenges posed from start to finish, every part of your game will be fully tested. Satisfaction aplenty derives from a good round, fully underlining just how high the standard is.

Green Fees	Weekdays	Weekends	Are visitors welcome?
Round	£35	£-	Yes, except
Daily	£45	£-	weekends

Nearest Airport: Edinburgh, 14.5 miles
Nearest Rail Station: Edinburgh, 3.6 miles
Gazetteer Ref: p125   **Map Ref:** p157, F2

TO LOCATE THIS GOLF COURSE ON THE MAPS (p155-159) LOOK FOR THE FLAG WITH THIS PAGE NUMBER.

13th ▼

Glencorse

HOLE	NAME	WHITE YARDS	YELLOW YARDS	PAR	STROKE INDEX
1	Whinny Bank	225		3	11
2	Lawrencelaw	355		4	4
3	Viaduct	208		3	16
4	Graham's Road	451		4	1
5	Forresters Rest	237		3	7
6	Auchendinny	273		4	13
7	Railway	308		4	9
8	The Precipice	164		4	18
9	Vale O'Logan	331		4	5
10	Whinny Haugh	335		4	6
11	Logan Bank	211		3	14
12	Milton Bank	211		3	15
13	Stey Brae	434		4	2
14	Scaldlaw	329		4	8
15	Whistle Bare	236		3	12
16	Greenlaw	375		3	3
17	The Hedges	215		3	17
18	Hill's O'Hame	319		4	10

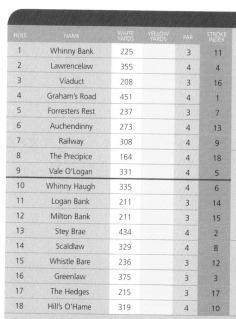

Glencorse Golf Club

Milton Bridge, Midlothian
EH26 0RD

Advance Bookings
T: 01968 677177

Holes: 18
Yardage: 5205 yds
SSS: 66

This popular Midlothian venue opened its doors to 150 new members last year. In no time at all the vacancies were filled and a highly popular course is now more heavily played than ever. Not long, but varied, with no little head scratching over choice of shot and club as hole distances and directions switch about unfailingly. Trees abound and the Pentlands are often a lovely backdrop on the easterly section of the course.

Green Fees	Weekdays	Weekends	Are visitors
Round	£20	£26	welcome?
Daily	£26	£-	Yes

Nearest Airport: Edinburgh, 12.4 miles
Nearest Rail Station: Haymarket, 8.3 miles
Gazetteer Ref: p126   **Map Ref:** p157, F2

TO LOCATE THIS GOLF COURSE ON THE MAPS (p155-159) LOOK FOR THE FLAG WITH THIS PAGE NUMBER.

▼ Looking down the 18th

hidden gem

Musselburgh

Musselburgh Golf Club

Monktonhall, Musselburgh
East Lothian EH21 6SA

Advance Bookings
T: 0131 665 2005

Holes: 18
Yardage: 6725 yds
SSS: 73

HOLE	NAME	WHITE YARDS	YELLOW YARDS	PAR	STROKE INDEX
1	Willows	377	346	4	10
2	Admiral Milne	451	393	4	6
3	Whins	147	124	3	18
4	Signal Box	528	500	5	2
5	Spire	403	384	4	14
6	Shirehaugh	157	142	3	16
7	Tunnel	479	441	5/4	8
8	Railway	400	386	4	4
9	Burn	408	379	4	12
10	Monkton	445	394	4	3
11	Braid's Best	187	180	3	9
12	Firs	488	463	5/4	15
13	Old Willie	378	367	4	13
14	Dukes Dyke	419	383	4	7
15	Joogley	406	385	4	1
16	Fiery	169	154	3	17
17	Kirk	409	396	4	5
18	Old Bob	474	424	4	11

I did not visit a better prepared 18 holes last season than those presented by the green staff here. Granted, an early evening sun simply lit up the whole place, but the results of all the work on the course were plain for all to see. This is no pushover of a venue, either, with lots of long irons or fairway woods on the agenda, but beautiful putting surfaces give you every chance to recover ground lost. This hard but fair test deserves much louder applause.

Green Fees

	Weekdays	Weekends	Are visitors welcome?
Round	£20	£25	Yes
Daily	£30	£35	

Nearest Airport: Edinburgh, 16 miles
Nearest Rail Station: Musselburgh, 1.2 miles
Gazetteer Ref: p123   **Map Ref:** p157, F2

TO LOCATE THIS GOLF COURSE ON THE MAPS (p155-159) LOOK FOR THE FLAG WITH THIS PAGE NUMBER.

18th ▼

hidden gem

Kilspindie

HOLE	NAME	WHITE YARDS	YELLOW YARDS	PAR	STROKE INDEX
1	The Point	167	156	3	9
2	Kings Kist	515	490	5	3
3	Arthur's Seat	413	369	4	13
4	The Target	365	336	4	1
5	The Law	290	282	4	15
6	Green Craig	279	268	4	17
7	The Ditches	384	350	4	5
8	Gosford Bay	162	144	3	7
9	The Quarry	286	280	4	11
10	The Pond	155	145	3	10
11	The Magazine	295	266	4	8
12	The Whim	269	265	4	18
13	The Kirk	185	152	3	4
14	Dipper	339	294	4	16
15	The Graves	436	420	4	2
16	The Flagstaff	412	379	4	14
17	Craigielaw	276	259	4	6
18	Home	252	240	4/3	12

Kilspindie Golf Club

The Clubhouse, Aberlady
East Lothian EH32 0QD

Advance Bookings
T: 01875 870358

Holes: 18
Yardage: 5480 yds
SSS: 66

East Lothian has golfing jewels in abundance, but ask those who know these parts to name their favourite venue and this one will be at the top of the list. Holes one to four would have the uninitiated believe it was a Gullane or North Berwick clone. What follows thereafter is nothing more than a short, joyous romp across windswept links, with westward panoramas to Edinburgh and northwards to Fife. Better fun than this is unimaginable.

Green Fees	Weekdays	Weekends	Are visitors
Round	£25	£30	welcome?
Daily	£40	£50	Yes

Nearest Airport: Edinburgh, 25.9 miles
Nearest Rail Station: Longniddry, 4.1 miles
Gazetteer Ref: p122   **Map Ref:** p157, F2

TO LOCATE THIS GOLF COURSE ON THE MAPS (p155-159) LOOK FOR THE FLAG WITH THIS PAGE NUMBER.

▼ Short 10th

North Berwick (The Glen)

HOLE	NAME	WHITE YARDS	YELLOW YARDS	PAR	STROKE INDEX
1	The Haugh		328	4	10
2	The Rhodes		358	4	4
3	Wantin' Wa's		302	4	16
4	The Knowes		175	3	17
5	Lime Kilns		367	4	1
6	Harelaw		432	5	8
7	Tantallon		366	4	14
8	Canty Bay		350	4	6
9	Quarrel Sands		254	3	12
10	The Law		341	4	7
11	Craigleith		300	4	15
12	Bass Rock		447	4	2
13	Sea Hole		133	3	18
14	Leithies		336	4	5
15	Milsey Bay		399	4	9
16	Partan Craig		186	3	13
17	Rhodes Braes		395	4	3
18	Jacob's Ladder		365	4	11

North Berwick (The Glen)

East Links, Tantallon Terrace
North Berwick, East Lothian EH39 4LE

Advance Bookings
T: 01620 892726

Holes: 18
Yardage: 6079 yds
SSS: 69

The more modest of the two North Berwick courses, yet no other spectacular vistas on the East Lothian coastal golf trail compete with those from the Glen's upper reaches. No links on this one, just parkland – heath here and there – and it is far from a taxing test of golfing credentials. Nevertheless, should the wind be about – at this level above the sea it generally is – club choice can vary enormously. It diminishes not one whit the pleasure of playing golf here.

Green Fees	Weekdays	Weekends	Are visitors welcome?
Round	£20	£30	
Daily	£30	£35	Yes

Nearest Airport: Edinburgh, 36.4 miles
Nearest Rail Station: North Berwick, 1.2 miles
Gazetteer Ref: p123   **Map Ref:** p157, F2

TO LOCATE THIS GOLF COURSE ON THE MAPS (p155-159) LOOK FOR THE FLAG WITH THIS PAGE NUMBER.

▼ 1st green

Whitekirk

Whitekirk Golf Course

Whitekirk, North Berwick
East Lothian EH39 5PR

Advance Bookings T: 01620 870300

Holes: 18
Yardage: 6526 yds
SSS: 72

Still seen as the upstart on the East Lothian circuit, the jury is still out on the inclusion or otherwise of this great golfing test alongside the older and more revered to north and south of it. Laid out around rising ground, mainly of heath, it has no defence to the vagaries of the wind and this factor more than any other makes the test a testing one. Longish, but now mature and in lovely condition, the conquering of these eighteen is rare. Excellent clubhouse fare does compensate!

Green Fees	Weekdays	Weekends	Are visitors welcome?
Round	£18	£25	Yes
Daily	£30	£40	

Nearest Airport: Edinburgh, 37.6 miles
Nearest Rail Station: North Berwick, 4.7 miles
Gazetteer Ref: p124   **Map Ref:** p157, F2

HOLE	NAME	WHITE YARDS	YELLOW YARDS	PAR	STROKE INDEX
1	Awakener	492	481	5	5
2	Traprain	276	268	4	18
3	Garlton Tower	435	393	4	3
4	Cairn	359	344	4	13
5	Cameron's test	420	411	4	1
6	Lothian	167	160	3	14
7	Pine Wood	365	355	4	9
8	Wee One	149	139	3	17
9	New Mains	378	369	4	7
10	Dyke	360	345	4	2
11	Loch'an	389	377	4	4
12	Plantation	518	512	5	12
13	Chasing Becky	499	459	5	6
14	Becky's Strip	160	154	3	16
15	Whitekirk	572	512	5	8
16	St Baldred	358	343	4	10
17	Isle of May	220	212	3	15
18	Auldhame	409	391	4	11

7th ▼

Torrance House

HOLE	NAME	WHITE YARDS	YELLOW YARDS	PAR	STROKE INDEX
1	Mossland	478		5	10
2	Jacobs Ladder	392		4	6
3	The Braes	308		4	12
4	Crutherland	566		5	2
5	Flatt Bridge	149		3	18
6	Whitehouse	524		5	4
7	Falklands Lea	382		4	8
8	Kilbride	184		3	16
9	Laigh Croft	360		4	14
10	Round Hill	404		4	11
11	The Tor	224		3	3
12	Parkhead	332		4	9
13	Lawries Lea	481		5	13
14	Bairds Planting	362		4	7
15	The Lip	174		3	15
16	Sunnyside	468		4	1
17	Stuart of Torrance	541		5	5
18	The Yew	147		3	17

Torrance House Golf Club

Strathaven Road, East Kilbride
Lanarkshire G75 0QZ

Advance Bookings
T: 01355 248638

Holes: 18
Yardage: 6476 yds
SSS: 71

Situated to the south-east of the 'new' town of East Kilbride, the lesser known of the two courses is set in woods and parkland. Accuracy off the tee is paramount if the outcome of your visit is of a competitive nature, but for others whose enjoyment factor is uppermost in the mind, the layout and background fits the bill perfectly. It all concludes at a lovely par three, looked down upon by the House and 'The Yew'.

Green Fees	Weekdays	Weekends	Are visitors
Round	£8.90	£10.35	welcome?
Daily	£-	£-	Yes

Nearest Airport: Glasgow, 15.4 miles
Nearest Rail Station: East Kilbride, 2.4 miles
Gazetteer Ref: p133   **Map Ref:** p156, D3

TO LOCATE THIS GOLF COURSE ON THE MAPS (p155-159) LOOK FOR THE FLAG WITH THIS PAGE NUMBER.

▼ 18th green

hidden gem

Cowglen

Cowglen Golf Club

301 Barrhead Road, Glasgow
Lanarkshire G43 1AU

Advance Bookings
T: 0141 632 0556

Holes: 18
Yardage: 6079 yds
SSS: 70

HOLE	NAME	WHITE YARDS	YELLOW YARDS	PAR	STROKE INDEX
1	Farm	421	420	4	9
2	Planteau	296	265	4	7
3	Glen	317	310	4	15
4	Thorns	346	336	4	1
5	Kennishead	142	136	3	13
6	Beeches	447	433	4	3
7	South View	393	377	4	5
8	Dumgoyne	509	490	5	11
9	Copse	144	144	3	17
10	Braeface	346	334	4	12
11	Quarry	367	361	4	4
12	Racecourse	198	181	3	8
13	Mansewood	365	309	4	16
14	Pollokhead	491	477	5	2
15	Bangorshill	298	287	4	18
16	Shaws	170	162	3	14
17	Broompark	394	371	4	6
18	Eastwood	409	396	4	10

Don't let the historic associations of the name deter you from a visit here. True, a succession of fairway furrows on several holes (members assured me they were natural!) create an impression of agricultural work in the dim and distant. The over-riding memory one takes away, however, is of tree-lined fairways, a few climbs to test judgement of iron selection to elevated greens, but more than anything the fun of golf only ten minutes from the buzz of the city centre.

Green Fees	Weekdays	Weekends	Are visitors welcome?
Round	£25.50	£-	Yes, except
Daily	£-	£-	weekends

Nearest Airport: Glasgow, 9.1 miles
Nearest Rail Station: Pollockshaws West, 1 mile
Gazetteer Ref: p133   **Map Ref:** p156, D3

TO LOCATE THIS GOLF COURSE ON THE MAPS (p155-159) LOOK FOR THE FLAG WITH THIS PAGE NUMBER.

12th green ▼

Whitecraigs

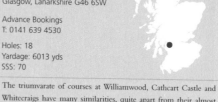

HOLE	NAME	WHITE YARDS	YELLOW YARDS	PAR	STROKE INDEX
1	Watson's First	129	124	3	12
2	Rouken Glen	370	350	4	6
3	Davieland	348	333	4	14
4	Perry Vale	430	427	4	2
5	Lomond View	160	145	3	18
6	Wolfe's Way	513	505	5	4
7	Craig End	138	130	3	16
8	Kestrel's Eyrie	345	335	4	8
9	Capelrig	410	400	4	10
10	Netherton	433	430	4	3
11	Devil's Elbow	357	345	4	11
12	The Planteau	326	324	4	7
13	Lang Wait	191	185	3	13
14	Rysland	365	355	4	1
15	West Brae	545	515	5	5
16	The Dip	150	140	3	17
17	The Beeches	254	252	4	15
18	Hame	549	492	5	9

Whitecraigs Golf Course

72 Ayr Road, Giffnock
Glasgow, Lanarkshire G46 6SW

Advance Bookings
T: 0141 639 4530

Holes: 18
Yardage: 6013 yds
SSS: 70

The triumvarate of courses at Williamwood, Cathcart Castle and Whitecraigs have many similarities, quite apart from their almost being in shouting distance of each other. Here we again see rolling fairways, lovely trees, carefully manicured hazards and lovely putting surfaces; it's perhaps only the size of the clubhouse which sets this one apart. Yet another 'Glasgow Gem' where enjoyment of the game is certain.

Green Fees	Weekdays	Weekends	Are visitors welcome?
Round	£40	£-	Yes, except
Daily	£50	£-	weekends

Nearest Airport: Glasgow, 9 miles
Nearest Rail Station: Giffnock, 2.1 miles
Gazetteer Ref: p134   **Map Ref:** p156, D3

TO LOCATE THIS GOLF COURSE ON THE MAPS (p155-159) LOOK FOR THE FLAG WITH THIS PAGE NUMBER.

▼ 18th green and clubhouse

BOARS HEAD HOTEL

4. MAIN STREET, COLMONELL, GIRVAN, AYRSHIRE KA26 ORY
TEL/FAX. 01465 - 881371 • E-Mail: alasdair@boarshead-colmonell.freeserve.co.uk
Website: www.boarshead-colmonell.freeserve.co.uk

The Hotel has six bedrooms, all en-suite,
A warm and friendly bar which has a good selection of fine malt whiskies and a pleasant dining room in which to enjoy a traditionally cooked breakfast whilst enjoying the wonderful views of the Stinchar valley including Craigneil castle.
High priority is given to relaxation and comfort in this peaceful village location.

The Golfer is well catered for with 15 Golf courses within an hours drive including the championship courses at Turnberry and Troon. Golfing holiday packages can be arranged with discounted rates available on several courses.

Bed and Breakfast from £19.50

Evening Meals available

CARLTON HOTEL

A friendly, family and child oriented hotel situated in coastal Prestwick.
37 rooms, all en-suite, with telephone, colour tv, trouser press and hairdryer. Carvery, lounge bar, residents' lounge and 100 seater restaurant.

Convenient for Troon and Prestwick Golf Courses.

187 Ayr Road, Prestwick KA9 1TP
T: 01292 476811 F: 01292 673712
e-mail hotelreservation@talk21.com

AMETHYST
HOTELS

Billy Casper

Join the **Connoisseur's Club!**

BILLY CASPER
SCOTTISH GOLF COLLECTION

Connoisseur's Club members will receive a copy of **Billy Casper's Golf Collection**, featuring 12 of Scotland's most prestigious golfing venues and associated hotels, together with a suite of discount vouchers for use on green fees, accommodation and dining. The vouchers are activated and validated by a membership card which can be used for 12 months. After the vouchers have been used the club member can carry on receiving substantial discounts for the duration of their membership.

for more information, see page 25

SAMPLE SAVINGS:
St Andrews: 50% off accommodation at the 5-star Old Course Hotel, plus 25% off green fees at the Duke's Course.

Carnoustie: 50% off accommodation at the 4-star Carnoustie Hotel, Golf Resort and Spa plus 25% off green fees at the Burnside's Course and 25% off the bill for 1-4 diners at the Dalhousie Restaurant.

Kilmarnock (Barassie)

HOLE	NAME	WHITE YARDS	YELLOW YARDS	PAR	STROKE INDEX
1	Kilmanock	506	501	5	13
2	Duncan's Pride	392	376	4	5
3	Auchengate	425	365	4	3
4	Arran	159	149	3	15
5	Railway	366	336	4	11
6	Hillhouse	154	143	3	17
7	Western	439	427	4	1
8	Dundonald	539	519	5	7
9	Gailes	383	371	4	9
10	Newmoor	357	346	4	16
11	Brodick	396	385	4	8
12	Barassie	439	387	4	2
13	Butcharts	377	355	4	14
14	Corrie	185	170	3	18
15	Adam's Gate	428	413	4	4
16	The Gap	490	475	5	12
17	Westward	406	401	4	6
18	Fullarton	376	365	4	10

Kilmarnock (Barassie) Golf Club

29 Hillhouse Road, Barassie,
Troon, Ayrshire KA10 6SY

Advance Bookings
T: 01292 313920

Holes: 18
Yardage: 6817 yds
SSS: 74

Oddly enough, Kilmarnock's golf club sits at the north-east tip of Troon, some eight miles from the town. The eagerness to enjoy these splendid – at times surprising – links is understandable although some older members still regret the passing of nine holes of the original layout to the newer short course. Nevertheless, this Open Qualifier is a stern test for even the best; those with higher handicaps may find it too demanding and opt for the wee course instead.

Green Fees	Weekdays	Weekends	Are visitors
Round	£50	£60	welcome?
Daily	£-	£-	Yes

Nearest Airport: Prestwick, 5.8 miles
Nearest Rail Station: Troon, 2.2 miles
Gazetteer Ref: p130   **Map Ref:** p156, D3

TO LOCATE THIS GOLF COURSE ON THE MAPS (p155-159) LOOK FOR THE FLAG WITH THIS PAGE NUMBER.

▼ Short 4th

Gourock

Gourock Golf Club

Cowal View, Gourock
Renfrewshire PA19 1HD

Advance Bookings
T: 01475 631001

Holes: 18
Yardage: 6408 yds
SSS: 72

At the Tail o' the Bank, this splendid creation on the hillside high above the town is quite joyful golf. Moor and heath all the way, where the variety of hole length and direction, allied to the near-certain presence of hilltop breezes, causes constant change of mind on club choice and course management. Few manage to defeat a longish and testing challenge where panoramas of the Clyde are without equal.

HOLE	NAME	WHITE YARDS	YELLOW YARDS	PAR	STROKE INDEX
1	The Gap	476		5	5
2	Cottons Way	332		4	13
3	Burn Even	368		4	1
4	Canny Noo	146		3	17
5	The Crags	340		4	15
6	Moorfoot	365		4	9
7	Millstones	185		3	11
8	Tower Hill	502		5	7
9	Mile Burn	460		4	3
10	Gully	280		4	16
11	Westward Ho!	505		5	8
12	Farm	465		4	2
13	Levan	481		5	10
14	Double Top	333		4	12
15	Cobbler	382		4	4
16	Birches	316		4	14
17	Punch Bowl	161		3	18
18	Well O Weary	415		4	6

Green Fees	Weekdays	Weekends	Are visitors welcome?
Round	£20	£27	
Daily	£27	£29	Yes

Nearest Airport: Glasgow, 20.2 miles
Nearest Rail Station: Gourock, 1.6 miles
Gazetteer Ref: p136   **Map Ref:** p156, C2

TO LOCATE THIS GOLF COURSE ON THE MAPS (p155-159) LOOK FOR THE FLAG WITH THIS PAGE NUMBER.

Short 17th ▼

Gleddoch

HOLE	NAME	WHITE YARDS	YELLOW YARDS	PAR	STROKE INDEX
1		319	309	4	11
2		181	160	3	15
3		517	435	5/4	1
4		389	379	4	9
5		438	420	4	5
6		408	398	4	3
7		145	122	3	17
8		270	265	4	18
9		341	313	4	7
10		314	304	4	10
11		524	464	5/4	4
12		172	107	3	13
13		496	395	5/4	4
14		185	165	3	14
15		372	354	4	16
16		396	379	4	8
17		423	409	4	6
18		393	354	4	12

Gleddoch Golf Club

Langbank, Port Glasgow
Renfrewshire PA14 6YE

Advance Bookings
T: 01475 540304

Holes: 18
Yardage: 6357 yds
SSS: 71

High above the village of Langbank, this beautiful mix of heath and parkland offers a golfing opportunity not to be missed as you head west down the Clyde estuary. The1970s design of Hamilton Stutt is splendid; nothing but nature's landscape has been incorporated into a stunning succession of challenges. The par threes are outstanding; the seventh is short-hole genius; the uphill fourteenth is a snorter, while the 172 yard twelfth, played through a swathe of fir trees, is unique.

Green Fees	Weekdays	Weekends	Are visitors
Round	£30	£40	welcome?
Daily	£40	£50	Yes

Nearest Airport: Glasgow, 9.8 miles
Nearest Rail Station: Paisley, 10 miles
Gazetteer Ref: p136   **Map Ref:** p156, C2

TO LOCATE THIS GOLF COURSE ON THE MAPS (p155-159) LOOK FOR THE FLAG WITH THIS PAGE NUMBER.

▼ 7th green and clubhouse

hidden **gem**

Brunston Castle

Brunston Castle Golf Club

Dailly, Girvan, Ayrshire
KA26 9GD

Advance Bookings
T: 01465 811471

Holes: 18
Yardage: 6681 yds
SSS: 72

Attracting more and more attention, particularly from visiting parties and corporate outings, the eighteen holes created from the parkland of this ancient Ayrshire estate are lovely. You need a bit of beef – it's not short – but there's bags of fairway and big, welcoming greens offer juicy targets. The course has matured well, while the surrounding scenery is ace and a majestic clubhouse suitably complements a fine development.

Green Fees	Weekdays	Weekends	Are visitors
Round	£26	£30	welcome?
Daily	£30	£45	Yes

Nearest Airport: Prestwick, 23.4 miles
Nearest Rail Station: Girvan, 6.5 miles
Gazetteer Ref: p129 **Map Ref:** p156, C5

HOLE	NAME	WHITE YARDS	YELLOW YARDS	PAR	STROKE INDEX
1	The Baillie	412	392	4	3
2	Brunston Castle	413	364	4	9
3	Doun The Water	384	364	4	13
4	The Wee Roundel	337	287	4	15
5	Drongan	192	160	3	11
6	The Inkpot	538	490	5	5
7	The Big Roundel	404	353	4	1
8	Black Bessie	177	143	3	17
9	The Fiddle	497	459	5	7
10	Milcavish	321	318	4	12
11	Ailsa View	372	323	4	2
12	Old Coach Road	430	375	4	6
13	Crown Jewel	504	494	5	14
14	Curragh	358	346	4	4
15	Cleekhimin	355	324	4	18
16	Doun 'n Roun	398	355	4	8
17	The Boggie	184	162	3	10
18	Bruxelles	386	357	4	16

TO LOCATE THIS GOLF COURSE ON THE MAPS (p155-159) LOOK FOR THE FLAG WITH THIS PAGE NUMBER.

Par 3, 5th ▼

Dunaverty

HOLE	NAME	WHITE YARDS	YELLOW YARDS	PAR	STROKE INDEX
1	Strangs	318		4	3
2	Garrach Dhu	157		3	15
3	Scott's Home	279		4	11
4	Dunaverty	177		3	18
5	Dalmore	257		4	10
6	Arthur's Seat	245		3	6
7	St. Andrews	180		3	16
8	Sanda	392		4	2
9	Punch Bowl	253		4	8
10	Mount Zion	123		3	13
11	The Cleet	266		4	9
12	Brunerican	277		4	7
13	The Cemetery	446		5	1
14	Rest and be Thankful	194		3	14
15	McNeil	352		4	5
16	Argyll	148		3	17
17	The Burn	412		4	4
18	Machribeg	323		4	12

Dunaverty Golf Club

Southend, Campbeltown
Argyll PA28 6RX

Advance Bookings
T: 01586 830677

Holes: 18
Yardage: 4799 yds
SSS: 63

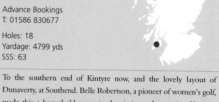

To the southern end of Kintyre now, and the lovely layout of Dunaverty, at Southend. Belle Robertson, a pioneer of women's golf, made this a household name in the sixties and seventies. You can breeze round in well under three hours, but the chances are you will set off again; it's a little course where the uniqueness of the location as well as the joy of the sport has that sort of effect on you and, boy, do these little greens sharpen your short irons!

Green Fees	Weekdays	Weekends	Are visitors welcome?
Round	£22	£25	Yes
Daily	£-	£-	

Nearest Airport: Glasgow, 139.4 miles
Nearest Rail Station: Oban, 97.5 miles
Gazetteer Ref: p127   **Map Ref:** p156, B4

TO LOCATE THIS GOLF COURSE ON THE MAPS (p155-159) LOOK FOR THE FLAG WITH THIS PAGE NUMBER.

▼ 6th, Arthur's Seat

hidden **gem**

Machrihanish

The Machrihanish Golf Club

Machrihanish, Campbeltown
Argyll PA28 6PT

Advance Bookings
T: 01586 810277

Holes: 18
Yardage: 6225 yds
SSS: 71

HOLE	NAME	WHITE YARDS	YELLOW YARDS	PAR	STROKE INDEX
1	Battery		428	4	3
2	Machrihanish		394	4	5
3	Islay		374	4	11
4	Jura		122	3	18
5	Punch Bowl		385	4	7
6	Balaclava		301	4	13
7	Bruach More		428	4	2
8	Gigha		339	4	9
9	Ranachan		353	4	15
10	Cnocmoy		503	5	10
11	Strabane		197	3	8
12	Long Hole		513	4	6
13	Kirkivan		370	4	12
14	Castlehill		438	4	1
15	The Hut		168	3	16
16	Rorke's Drift		231	3	4
17	The Burn		368	4	14
18	Lossit		313	4	17

Opinions are divided as to whether Machrihanish's distance from 'civilisation' is a blessing or a tragedy for Scottish golf. I am not going to get involved in the argument, but it remains, whatever you think, the greatest remaining natural links in Scotland. Old Tom Morris made it what it is, although even he admitted that he was presented with 'a gift from the Almighty to play golf'. The career of the links' golfer cannot be complete until he has visited.

Green Fees   Weekdays   Weekends   Are visitors welcome?
Round   £30 (fri-sun)   £40 (sat)
Daily   £50 (fri-sun)   £60 (sat)   Yes

Nearest Airport: Glasgow
Nearest Rail Station: Campbeltown
Gazetteer Ref: p127   **Map Ref:** p156, B4

TO LOCATE THIS GOLF COURSE ON THE MAPS (p155-159) LOOK FOR THE FLAG WITH THIS PAGE NUMBER.

Looking down the 10th ▼

Dollar

HOLE	NAME	WHITE YARDS	YELLOW YARDS	PAR	STROKE INDEX
1	Glen	186	196	3	7
2	Brae	80	97	3	16
3	Stable	206	254	3/4	14
4	Roundel	278	331	4	3/2
5	Prospect	285	307	4	5
6	Road	315	331	4	10
7	Scaur	299	306	4	12
8	Auld Toon	290	308	4	18
9	Castle	188	200	3	4
10	Slunk	152	153	3	11
11	Pirrock	449	449	4	1
12	Heugh	418	519	4/5	3/2
13	Loweburn	288	320	4	8
14	Westward Ho	186	302	3/4	15
15	Dip	253	288	4	17
16	Quarry	273	296	4	13
17	Macnab	287	303	4	6
18	Brewers Knowe	273	282	4	9

Dollar Golf Course

Brewlands House, Dollar
Clackmannanshire FK14 7EA

Advance Bookings T: 01259 742400

Holes: 18
Yardage: 5242 yds
SSS: 66

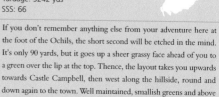

If you don't remember anything else from your adventure here at the foot of the Ochils, the short second will be etched in the mind. It's only 90 yards, but it goes up a sheer grassy face ahead of you to a green over the lip at the top. Thence, the layout takes you upwards towards Castle Campbell, then west along the hillside, round and down again to the town. Well maintained, smallish greens and above average fairway slopes and hummocks, but great fun.

Green Fees	Weekdays	Weekends	Are visitors
Round	£13.50	£22	welcome?
Daily	£17.50	£22	Yes

Nearest Airport: Edinburgh, 32.6 miles
Nearest Rail Station: Dunblane, 16.4 miles
Gazetteer Ref: p104   **Map Ref:** p157, E1

TO LOCATE THIS GOLF COURSE ON THE MAPS (p155-159) LOOK FOR THE FLAG WITH THIS PAGE NUMBER.

▼ 17th tee

Alloa (Shawpark)

Alloa Golf Club

Schawpark, Sauchie, Alloa,
Clackmannanshire FK10 3AX

Advance Bookings T: 01259
722745

Holes: 18
Yardage: 6229 yds
SSS: 70

HOLE	NAME	WHITE YARDS	YELLOW YARDS	PAR	STROKE INDEX
1	Witch's Well	333	321	4	15
2	Stey Brae	478	448	5	3
3	The Quarry	325	306	4	17
4	The Rhodos	168	155	3	13
5	White Yetts	508	495	5	7
6	Drumbeg	317	314	4	9
7	Burnee	162	148	3	11
8	Craigbank	393	371	4	1
9	Baillie's Dub	467	455	4	5
10	Brandy Hill	315	307	4	16
11	Deil's Gate	346	344	4	10
12	Mount William	428	420	4	2
13	The Spinney	313	292	4	18
14	Braid's Park	422	395	4	8
15	Seven Sisters	173	170	3	14
16	The Orchard	404	399	4	6
17	Pond's Wood	474	460	4	4
18	Beechwood	203	191	3	12

Schawpark remains one of the most under-rated courses across Central Scotland. The key to scoring success is undoubtedly being straight off the tee, as hundreds of fir trees, planted years ago to line fairways, are now mature and highly influential to the outcome on at least ten holes. It seems boring to repeat myself, but the course presentation is quite superb, while the backdrop of the Ochils completes the perfect setting for quality – and testing – golf.

Green Fees	Weekdays	Weekends	Are visitors welcome?
Round	£24	£28	Yes
Daily	£34	£38	

Nearest Airport: Edinburgh, 30.7 miles
Nearest Rail Station: Bridge of Allan, 9.3 miles
Gazetteer Ref: p103   **Map Ref:** p157, E1

TO LOCATE THIS GOLF COURSE ON THE MAPS (p155-159) LOOK FOR THE FLAG WITH THIS PAGE NUMBER.

1st ▼

hidden gem

Falkirk Tryst

HOLE	NAME	WHITE YARDS	YELLOW YARDS	PAR	STROKE INDEX
1	Londyke	325		4	9
2	Skil	188		3	17
3	Chapelburn	347		4	5
4	Post	201		3	13
5	Muirhall	337		4	11
6	Arthur's O'on	412		4	7
7	Keltor	544		5	1
8	Inches	257		4	15
9	Tents	418		4	3
10	Gap	488		5	8
11	Pavilion	245		3	10
12	Winds	298		4	16
13	Anton's Wall	162		3	18
14	Wicket	361		4	6
15	Pond	175		3	14
16	Boneyard	503		5	2
17	Road	357		4	12
18	Burnhead	435		4	4

Falkirk Tryst Golf Club

86 Burnhead Road, Stenhousemuir,
Stirlingshire FK5 4BD

Advance Bookings
T: 01324 562415

Holes: 18
Yardage: 6083 yds
SSS: 69

Flat as a pancake, yet one of the testing courses of Central Region,
an abundance of trees and above average bunker deployment creates
the challenge. No two holes go in the same direction, either, which
requires great thought on club choice especially when the wind is
about. The Tryst is not long, but you deserve a pat on the back if you
negotiate the eighteen holes to handicap.

Green Fees	Weekdays	Weekends	Are visitors welcome?
Round	£18	£-	Yes, except
Daily	£27	£-	weekends

Nearest Airport: Edinburgh, 27.2 miles
Nearest Rail Station: Larbert, 0.8 miles
Gazetteer Ref: p108   **Map Ref:** p157, E2

TO LOCATE THIS GOLF COURSE ON THE MAPS (p155-159) LOOK FOR THE FLAG WITH THIS PAGE NUMBER.

▼ 10th

Callander

Callander Golf Club

Aveland Road, Callander
Perthshire FK17 8EN

Advance Bookings
T: 01877 330090

Holes: 18
Yardage: 5151yds
SSS: 66

HOLE	NAME	WHITE YARDS	YELLOW YARDS	PAR	STROKE INDEX
1	Quarry	348	335	4	6
2	Corner	199	149	3	8
3	Tree	329	268	4	14
4	Oaks	321	270	4	12
5	Saucer	183	167	3	10
6	Dell	372	334	4	2
7	Blind	250	230	4	18
8	Burn	261	250	4	16
9	Curling House	232	217	3	4
10	Knowe	179	164	3	9
11	Beeches	179	159	3	15
12	Three Firs	404	33	4	1
13	Drumdhu	324	231	4	5
14	Dyke	224	200	3	11
15	Avenue	135	125	3	17
16	Balgibbon	365	284	4	3
17	Mount Pisgah	478	390	5	7
18	Home	333	323	4	13

Above the town, which remains one of Scotland's most visited by tourists, the Callander club enjoys tremendous popularity among members, visitors and outings alike. It's not difficult to understand; the course is not demanding in length and trees, the presence of Ben Ledi to the west and the backdrop of the hill make it extremely attractive. Kept splendidly by a hard-working green staff, it constantly earns praise from all who enjoy the challenge.

Green Fees	Weekdays	Weekends	Are visitors welcome?
Round	£18	£26	
Daily	£26	£31	Yes

Nearest Airport: Edinburgh, 44.7 miles
Nearest Rail Station: Dunblane, 12 miles
Gazetteer Ref: p106   **Map Ref:** p157, D1

TO LOCATE THIS GOLF COURSE ON THE MAPS (p155-159) LOOK FOR THE FLAG WITH THIS PAGE NUMBER.

16th green and Ben Ledi ▼

hidden gem

Anstruther

HOLE	NAME	WHITE YARDS	YELLOW YARDS	PAR	STROKE INDEX
1	Johnny Doo	259	-	4	9
2	Monument	130	-	3	17
3	Chain Road	366	-	4	1
4	Magazine	277	-	4	7
5	Rockies	215	-	3	3
6	Cuniger	137	-	3	15
7	Valley	174	-	3	11
8	East Neuk	297	-	4	5
9	The Hynd	217	-	3	13
1	Johnny Doo	259	-	4	9
2	Monument	130	-	3	17
3	Chain Road	366	-	4	1
4	Magazine	277	-	4	7
5	Rockies	215	-	3	3
6	Cuniger	137	-	3	15
7	Valley	174	-	3	11
8	East Neuk	297	-	4	5
9	The Hynd	217	-	3	13

Anstruther Golf Club

Marsfield, Shore Road
Anstruther, Fife KY10 3DZ

Advance Bookings
T: 01333 310956

Holes: 9
Yardage: 4504 metres
SSS: 63

If your golfing ambitions reach merely the relaxed or holiday level, this is for you. Nine lovely little holes on lush parkland west of the old town; no pressure frombehind and the main anxiety is whether your meanderings around the course leave time to enjoy the friendship of the club lounge afterwards!

Green Fees	Weekdays	Weekends	Are visitors welcome?
Round	£8	£12	
Daily	£10	£16	Yes

Nearest Airport: Edinburgh, 47.4 miles
Nearest Rail Station: Markinch, 19.3 miles
Gazetteer Ref: p111   **Map Ref:** p157, F1

TO LOCATE THIS GOLF COURSE ON THE MAPS (p155-159) LOOK FOR THE FLAG WITH THIS PAGE NUMBER.

▼ 3rd green

The Royal Hotel

ROYAL HOTEL, TOWNHEAD, DYSART, FIFE KY1 2XQ   TEL: 01592 654112/652109 FAX: 01592 598555

Friendly, family-run hotel, situated in the national Trust village of Dysart, overlooking the Firth of Forth. Dysart is situated halfway between Edinburgh and St Andrews, which makes us an ideal base for golfing central Scotland.

All our bedrooms have colour TV, Radio-Alarm Clock and Hospitality Tray. We also offer drying facilities in the unlikely event of rain!

With over 20 golf courses within half an hour's drive from the Hotel, we really do have an amazing selection of courses to choose from.

We will arrange the courses, fees and tee times on confirmation of your booking – all you have to do is turn up and enjoy yourself!

After a hard day of slicing, hooking and putting, enjoy a Malt Whisky or Real Ale in our comfortable lounge.

Craw's Nest

Hotel & Restaurant

Bankwell Road, Anstruther
Fife KY10 3DA

Tel: (01333) 310691
Fax: (01333) 312216
E-mail: enquiries@crawsnesthotel.co.uk
www.crawsnesthotel.co.uk

The Craw's Nest is a family run hotel situated in the heart of the East Neuk, an ideal base for inland and offshore fishing. With St Andrews just 9 miles away and over 40 courses in the area golfers are well catered for.

Come and enjoy our legendary Scottish hospitality. With 50 comfortable ensuite bedrooms and a restaurant renowned for good home cooking. The Craw's Nest is the ideal place for your next short break.

SCOTLAND
HOME OF GOLF
online

www.scotland-for-golf.com

Aberdour

HOLE	NAME	WHITE YARDS	YELLOW YARDS	PAR	STROKE INDEX
1	Bell House	159	149	3	11
2	Firs	159	156	3	13
3	Ainsley's Pier	343	307	4	6
4	Cottage	287	277	4	16
5	Oxcar	359	328	4	9
6	St Colme	365	357	4	5
7	The Dyke	163	145	3	17
8	Silver Beach	458	418	4	1
9	The Burn	394	378	4	4
10	Ash Tree	530	520	5	3
11	Manse	340	335	4	10
12	Doocot	163	158	3	14
13	Downings	251	246	4	15
14	Avenue	318	278	4	18
15	Woodside	171	161	3	8
16	Pavillion	449	382	4	2
17	Kinniker	354	349	4	7
18	Roundel	197	187	3	12

Aberdour Golf Club

Seaside Place, Aberdour
Fife KY3 0TX

Advance Bookings T: 01383
860080

Holes: 18
Yardage: 5460 yds
SSS: 66

The modesty of Aberdour's 5460 yards, together with an idyllic location, make it an obvious target for 'two-round' outings. The course handsomely rewards the expectations of the visiting golfer with a stunning array of short holes and birdiable par fours. The scenery is just a bonus. This is yet another venue where, with the sun in the morning sky, superlatives from the writer do nothing to convey the reality of being here to drink it all in personally.

Green Fees	Weekdays	Weekends	Are visitors
Round	£17	£35	welcome?
Daily	£28	£-	Yes, except Sat.

Nearest Airport: Edinburgh, 16.9 miles
Nearest Rail Station: Aberdour, 0.6 miles
Gazetteer Ref: p111   **Map Ref:** p157, E1

TO LOCATE THIS GOLF COURSE ON THE MAPS (p155-159) LOOK FOR THE FLAG WITH THIS PAGE NUMBER.

▼ Short 1st

Lundin Ladies

Lundin Ladies Golf Club

Woodlielea Road, Lundin Links
Leven, Fife KY5 6AR

Advance Bookings
T: 01333 320832

Holes: 9
Yardage: 2365 yds
SSS: 67

HOLE	NAME	WHITE YARDS	YELLOW YARDS	PAR	STROKE INDEX
1	-	327		4	3
2	-	262		4	7
3	-	355		4	1
4	-	287		4	9
5	-	309		4	5
6	-	145		3	17
7	-	234		4	11
8	-	260		4	13
9	-	186		3	15
10	-	327		4	4
11	-	262		4	8
12	-	355		4	2
13	-	287		4	10
14	-	309		4	6
15	-	145		3	18
16	-	234		4	12
17	-	260		4	14
18	-	186		3	16

Don't panic, all you gents who don't want the pressure of the big course across the road or Leven Links a couple of miles away. The name does not preclude you from a bit of fun around this little nine holer whose fame spread from the presence of the enormous standing stones on the second. It is a relaxed atmosphere, you ought to take no more than an hour and a half to scoot round, but enjoyment is certain.

Green Fees	Weekdays	Weekends	Are visitors
Round	£7.50	£9	welcome?
Daily	£12	£15	Yes

Nearest Airport: Edinburgh, 37.7 miles
Nearest Rail Station: Markinch, 7.7 miles
Gazetteer Ref: p112   **Map Ref:** p157, E1

TO LOCATE THIS GOLF COURSE ON THE MAPS (p155-159) LOOK FOR THE FLAG WITH THIS PAGE NUMBER.

2nd fairway, 1st green ▼

Dunfermline (Pitfirrane)

HOLE	NAME	WHITE YARDS	YELLOW YARDS	PAR	STROKE INDEX
1	Knowehead	283	265	4	18
2	The Paddock	208	168	3	11
3	Pitconnoquhie	475	457	5	7
4	Drummage Hill	370	334	4	4
5	The Cadger's Stane	173	156	3	15
6	The Abbey	381	348	4	1
7	Carlinthorn	480	417	5	10
8	Hardiknute	340	330	4	14
9	The Meadows	185	147	3	9
10	The Yet	378	353	4	3
11	Sunnybraes	304	265	4	17
12	Rushy park	340	286	4	13
13	Hip Hillock	163	153	3	6
14	West Lodge	381	367	4	2
15	The Pentlands	479	402	5	8
16	Myrend	156	145	3	16
17	Malcolm's Wheel	497	395	5	5
18	Halkett's Hame	528	431	5	12

Dunfermline Golf Club

Pitfirrane Crossford
Dunfermline, Fife KY12 8QW

Advance Bookings
T: 01383 729061

Holes: 18
Yardage: 6126 yds
SSS: 70

I enjoyed my first round here last year; it was a Stableford competition and news reached us on the course that some ridiculous score had been handed in. Granted, we were handicapped by rain, but how any foursome reduced this excellent parkland course to the level they did is hard to believe. It isn't too long, but drive position is crucial. The clubhouse castle is a wonderful base for the club, where hospitality of the membership is first class. Put it on the list!

Green Fees	Weekdays	Weekends	Are visitors wecome?
Round	£21	£-	Yes, except
Daily	£31	£-	weekends

Nearest Airport: Edinburgh, 16.2 miles
Nearest Rail Station: Dunfermline, 3.7 miles
Gazetteer Ref: p111 **Map Ref:** p157, E1

TO LOCATE THIS GOLF COURSE ON THE MAPS (p155-159) LOOK FOR THE FLAG WITH THIS PAGE NUMBER.

▼ The clubhouse

Falkland

Falkland Golf Club

The Myre, Falkland, Fife
KY15 7AA

Advance Bookings
T: 01337 857404

Holes: 9
Yardage: 2608 yds
SSS: 65

HOLE	NAME	WHITE YARDS	YELLOW YARDS	PAR	STROKE INDEX
1	Brig	326	308	4	5
2	Lathrisk	476	476	5	1
3	Maryfield	346	341	4	9
4	Newton	277	272	4	15
5	Barn	205	200	3	13
6	Myreside	154	149	3	17
7	Orchard	308	304	4	7
8	Lomond	148	140	3	11
9	Palace	330	320	4	3
10	Brig	322	308	4	6
11	Lathrisk	356	356	4	2
12	Maryfield	346	341	4	10
13	Newton	277	272	4	16
14	Barn	205	200	4	14
15	Myreside	154	149	3	18
16	Orchard	308	304	4	8
17	Lomond	148	140	3	12
18	Palace	330	320	4	4

Not on the calling list of many, here's a little course in central Fife which will take your mind off problems or work for a couple of hours. With the impressive East Lomond overlooking the scene and the Palace towers, tiled roofs and old buildings of the village to the west, the untaxing demands of this layout should not cause the good golfer too many problems. Be straight, though or it will cost you; but enjoy!

Green Fees	Weekdays	Weekends	Are visitors welcome?
Round	£5	£8	
Daily	£5	£8	Yes

Nearest Airport: Edinburgh, 35.9 miles
Nearest Rail Station: Ladybank, 4.7 miles
Gazetteer Ref: p112   **Map Ref:** p157, F1

TO LOCATE THIS GOLF COURSE ON THE MAPS (p155-159) LOOK FOR THE FLAG WITH THIS PAGE NUMBER.

9th ▼

Elmwood

HOLE	NAME	WHITE YARDS	YELLOW YARDS	PAR	STROKE INDEX
1		343	321	4	10
2		512	501	5	2
3		174	168	3	14
4		456	440	4	6
5		306	287	4	16
6		404	382	4	8
7		184	178	3	12
8		410	397	4	4
9		128	121	3	18
10		266	261	4	15
11		526	489	5	3
12		156	131	3	13
13		313	293	4	7
14		329	302	4	5
15		301	287	4	11
16		272	253	4	17
17		447	430	4	1
18		424	412	4	9

Elmwood Golf Course

Stratheden, Cupar
Fife KY15 5RS

Advance Bookings
T: 01334 658780

Holes: 18
Yardage: 5951 yds
SSS: 68

Just a few miles west of Cupar, this comparative newcomer to 'Pay and Play' golf in Fife is proving popular. The layout has the majority of the holes running north-east to south-west or vice versa, and although it is not a tiring course, the exposure of the location to westerly breezes can create problems. It's a fine test for new or higher handicapped players and great value for money too. A practice ground and good clubhouse complete the facilities provided.

Green Fees	Weekdays	Weekends	Are visitors free to play?
Round	£18	£22	
Daily	£27	£31	Yes

Nearest Airport: Edinburgh, 43.4 miles
Nearest Rail Station: Cupar, 3.5 miles
Gazetteer Ref: p111   **Map Ref:** p155, E7

TO LOCATE THIS GOLF COURSE ON THE MAPS (p155-159) LOOK FOR THE FLAG WITH THIS PAGE NUMBER.

▼ 18th and clubhouse

Old Course

St. Andrews Links Trust

Pilmour House, St Andrews
Fife KY16 9SF

Advance Bookings
T: 01334 466666

Holes: 18
Yardage: 6566 yds
SSS: 72

HOLE	NAME	WHITE YARDS	YELLOW YARDS	PAR	STROKE INDEX
1	Burn	376	370	4	15
2	Dyke	413	411	4	3
3	Cartgate – Out	397	352	4	13
4	Ginger Beer	464	419	4	9
5	Hole O'Cross – Out	568	514	5	1
6	Heathery – Out	412	374	4	11
7	High – Out	388	359	4	7
8	Short	175	166	3	18
9	End	352	307	4	5
10	Bobby Jones	379	318	4	10
11	High – In	174	172	3	17
12	Heathery – In	314	316	4	6
13	Hole O'Cross – In	430	398	4	12
14	Long	581	523	5	2
15	Cartgate – In	456	401	4	8
16	Corner of the Dyke	424	351	4	14
17	Road	455	455	4	4
18	Tom Morris	357	354	4	16

In the most dreadful weather ever endured by combatants in last year's Dunhill Links Championship, 1999 Open Champion Paul Lawrie twice three-putted the Road Hole, then birdied the 18th – the latter of which won him the title. Lesser mortals watching the drama nodded in recognition; they had all done it themselves (not birdied the last, perhaps, but certainly fallen foul of the 17th!) The entire Old Course experience remains unparallelled in world golf.

Green Fees	Weekdays	Weekends	Are visitors welcome?
Round	£85	£85	Yes
Low season	£60	£60	

Nearest Airport: Edinburgh, 75.2 miles
Nearest Rail Station: Leuchars, 4.8 miles
Gazetteer Ref: p113 **Map Ref:** p155, F7

TO LOCATE THIS GOLF COURSE ON THE MAPS (p155-159) LOOK FOR THE FLAG WITH THIS PAGE NUMBER.

Hell Bunker on the 14th ▼

New Course

HOLE	NAME	WHITE YARDS	YELLOW YARDS	PAR	STROKE INDEX
1	-	336		4	9
2	-	367		4	13
3	-	511		5	3
4	-	369		4	7
5	-	180		3	17
6	-	445		4	1
7	-	356		4	11
8	-	481		5	5
9	-	225		3	15
10	-	464		4	6
11	-	347		4	14
12	-	518		5	4
13	-	157		3	18
14	-	386		4	8
15	-	394		4	12
16	-	431		4	2
17	-	229		3	16
18	-	408		4	10

St. Andrews Links Trust

Pilmour House, St Andrews
Fife KY16 9SF

Advance Bookings
T: 01334 466666

Holes: 18
Yardage: 6604 yds
SSS: 72

If the trauma of an Old Course challenge is too much to face, this delightful alternative is available just across the links. While, thankfully, there are fewer tees where guesswork on drive placement is the priority, enough questions are asked of the amateur golfer's ability – particularly his long irons – to render the New a most testing experience. It's an extremely challenging links which in the opinion of many is as difficult to conquer – for different reasons – as the Old.

Green Fees	Weekdays	Weekends	Are visitors
Round	£45	£45	welcome?
Low season	£31	£31	Yes

Nearest Airport: Edinburgh, 75.2 miles
Nearest Rail Station: Leuchars, 4.8 miles
Gazetteer Ref: p113   **Map Ref:** p155, F7

TO LOCATE THIS GOLF COURSE ON THE MAPS (p155-159) LOOK FOR THE FLAG WITH THIS PAGE NUMBER.

▼ 18th green

Ladybank

Ladybank Golf Club

Annsmuir, Ladybank, Cupar
Fife KY15 7RA

Advance Bookings
T: 01337 830814

Holes: 18
Yardage: 6641 yds
SSS: 72

HOLE	NAME	WHITE YARDS	YELLOW YARDS	PAR	STROKE INDEX
1		374		4	11
2		548		5	7
3		391		4	5
4		166		3	13
5		344		4	17
6		372		4	9
7		543		5	3
8		159		3	15
9		401		4	1
10		165		3	18
11		407		4	4
12		243		3	14
13		528		5	10
14		417		4	2
15		390		4	12
16		398		4	8
17		387		4	16
18		408		4	6

You could forgive the membership here if they displayed an air of superiority to the visiting golfer. The complete opposite, in fact, is the norm. In spite of the rightful elevation of the course to the rank of an Open Qualifier – superbly designed holes with tight fairways, constant directional change, tough rough and incessant demands for forward thinking fully justify that status – it remains the most modest of clubs and a magnet for our friends from the US. It's busy!

Green Fees	Weekdays	Weekends	Are visitors welcome?
Round	£35	£40	Yes, but please
Daily	£45	£-	call first

Nearest Airport: Edinburgh, 37.7 miles
Nearest Rail Station: Ladybank, 0.9 miles
Gazetteer Ref: p111   **Map Ref:** p157, F1

TO LOCATE THIS GOLF COURSE ON THE MAPS (p155-159) LOOK FOR THE FLAG WITH THIS PAGE NUMBER.

1st green ▼

Green Hotel

HOLE	NAME	WHITE YARDS	YELLOW YARDS	PAR	STROKE INDEX
1	BLUE COURSE	162		3	11
2	-	406		4	5
3	-	546		5	17
4	-	138		3	15
5	-	305		4	9
6	-	372		4	3
7	-	343		4	7
8	-	435		4	1
9	-	402		4	13
10	-	355		4	16
11	-	501		5	10
12	-	379		4	4
13	-	350		4	2
14	-	179		3	14
15	-	550		5	8
16	-	399		4	12
17	-	166		3	18
18	-	450		4	6

Green Hotel Golf Course

Green Hotel, Kinross
Kinross-shire KY13 8AS

Advance Bookings
T: 01577 863407

Holes: 18
Yardage: 6256/6438
SSS: 73/71

Between the eastern edge of Kinross and the fisherman's dream location of Loch Leven, the parkland now owned by the Green Hotel has been sculpted to create two excellent golf courses, the 'Blue' and the 'Red'. Both layouts are excellent; the red is slightly harder than the Blue but marginally less picturesque, while the 'Island' hole has to rank as one of the most peculiar creations in Scottish golf! First class fare – as you would expect – rounds it all off.

Green Fees	Weekdays	Weekends	Are visitors
Round	£17	£27	welcome?
Daily	£27	£37	Yes

Nearest Airport: Edinburgh, 26 miles
Nearest Rail Station: Dunfermline, 12.6 miles
Gazetteer Ref: p104   **Map Ref:** p157, E1

TO LOCATE THIS GOLF COURSE ON THE MAPS (p155-159) LOOK FOR THE FLAG WITH THIS PAGE NUMBER.

▼ Green Hotel

Carnoustie Burnside

Carnoustie Golf Links

Links Parade, Carnoustie
Angus DD7 7SE

Advance Bookings
T: 01241 853789

Holes: 18
Yardage: 6020 yds
SSS: 69

I once shot 69 here; it was August, there was enormous run on baked fairways and I was really lucky. There were bad days too, but the sheer enjoyment of this brilliant understudy to its big brother cannot be underestimated. The fifth is one of Scotland's great par threes; so is the ninth (you'll tear your hair out here if your tee shot goes astray) while the finish from the fourteenth is epic. Do not be at all deflated if you can't get on the Medal Course – this is bliss.

HOLE	NAME	WHITE YARDS	YELLOW YARDS	PAR	STROKE INDEX
1	Peninsula	324		4	18
2	Ravensby	450		4	4
3	Fence	175		3	16
4	South America	460		4	2
5	Burn	158		3	10
6	Camp	348		4	14
7	Shelter	360		4	1
8	Battery	432		4	6
9	Grog	163		3	8
10	Kopje	336		4	15
11	Deil's Ha'	375		4	7
12	Heather	386		4	13
13	Punchbowl	382		4	5
14	Scoup	228		3	1
15	Sou'western	500		5	11
16	Whins	163		3	9
17	Sinkies	473		4	3
18	Lismore	307		4	17

Green Fees	Weekdays	Weekends	Are visitors welcome?
Round	£25	£40	
Daily	£25	£40	Yes

Nearest Airport: Edinburgh, 69.6 miles
Nearest Rail Station: Carnoustie, 5.5 miles
Gazetteer Ref: p137   **Map Ref:** p155, F7

TO LOCATE THIS GOLF COURSE ON THE MAPS (p155-159) LOOK FOR THE FLAG WITH THIS PAGE NUMBER.

18th green ▼

Arbroath

HOLE	NAME	WHITE YARDS	YELLOW YARDS	PAR	STROKE INDEX
1	Francie's Well	367	360	4	10
2	Balcathie	481	444	5	3
3	The Dennie	348	334	4	12
4	Lint Pot	166	153	3	16
5	Mains of Kelly	405	389	4	1
6	Inverpeffer	375	364	4	7
7	Corse Hill	159	155	3	17
8	Currie End	372	354	4	5
9	The Shelter	373	363	4	9
10	Balnirmer	407	399	4	4
11	Johnnie's Howe	326	313	4	15
12	Threap Neuk	316	290	4	11
13	Dowrie	412	368	4	2
14	The Secretary	239	200	3	14
15	Penston Burn	355	343	4	8
16	The Dunes	182	151	3	18
17	The Ditch	495	447	5	6
18	Wormie Hill	407	399	4	13

Arbroath Golf Course
Arbroath Artisan Golf Club

Elliot, Arbroath, Angus DD11 2PE

Advance Bookings
T: 01241 875837

Holes: 18
Yardage: 6185 yds
SSS: 70

It's less than ten minutes from the first tee at Carnoustie to that of the seldom-praised layout at Elliot, a mile west of Arbroath. Undoubtedly it is the proximity of the more revered challenges down the road, at Monifieth and Panmure as well as Carnoustie, which has created the deafening silence on the quality of these links. At 6185 yards, however, it is still a challenge, and one which can take on the same foreboding if the notorious North Sea winds take hold.

Green Fees	Weekdays	Weekends	Are visitors
Round	£18	£24	welcome?
Daily	£24	£32	Yes

Nearest Airport: Aberdeen, 56.7 miles
Nearest Rail Station: Arbroath, 1.9 miles
Gazetteer Ref: p137   **Map Ref:** p155, F7

TO LOCATE THIS GOLF COURSE ON THE MAPS (p155-159) LOOK FOR THE FLAG WITH THIS PAGE NUMBER.

▼ Short 16th

hidden gem

The George Hotel

Situated in the centre of Montrose, the George Hotel is a Georgian sandstone building, built in 1814. The hotel boasts beautiful quiet gardens to the rear of the hotel, used for wedding receptions and garden parties. The George Hotel is a family owned hotel, boasting a superb 'a la carte' restaurant, and a warm and friendly bar/lounge.

This is the perfect location for a stay in the Highlands – quiet but within striking distance of Aberdeen and Dundee, and the Grampians. The facilities for walking, angling, golfing, and sight seeing in the area are exceptional, with short breaks and organised golf holidays a speciality. All bedrooms in the George are en-suite, and all have satellite T.V. with free movie and sports channels, direct-dial phone, tea/coffee making facilities, and the prices include a traditional Scottish breakfast.

The hotel also boasts one of the best function suites in the area, available for weddings, conventions, exhibitions and other functions, and can cater for up to 120 people.

22 George Street, Montrose, Angus, Scotland DD10 8EW
Tel: + 44 (0)1674 675050   Fax: +44 (0)1674 671153
E-mail: reception@thegeorge-montrose.co.uk

GREY HARLINGS HOUSE
EAST LINKS, MONTROSE, ANGUS   TEL: (01674) 673980

Traditional Guest House offers a warm welcome. Quiet accommodation in comfortable well-appointed rooms, all with hospitality tray (tea, coffee, biscuits, fruit) and colour television.

Ideally situated across the links from the beach, this former clubhouse has a sunny aspect and a unique ambience. Parking is provided within the large enclosed garden.

Restaurants and bars are within a minute's walk.

Double, twin, single and family rooms are available from £20 per person B&B. En-suite or private bathroom.

BED AND BREAKFAST ON THE GOLF COURSE

MONTROSE GOLF LINKS
MONTROSE GOLF COURSES

Two Links Courses: MEDAL COURSE (Par 71, SSS 72) and BROOMFIELD COURSE (Par 66, SSS63)
MEDAL COURSE RANKED FIFTH OLDEST IN THE WORLD: 1999 OPEN QUALIFYING COURSE
Individual Round and Day Tickets Available on Both Courses: All Visitors and Parties Welcome
SPECIAL PACKAGES AVAILABLE INCLUDING CATERING AND IN CONJUNCTION WITH LOCAL HOTELS
Enquiries to: Mrs M Stewart, Secretary, Montrose Links Trust, Traill Drive, Montrose, Angus, DD10 8SW
Tel: (01674) 672932 Fax: (01674) 671800 E mail: Secretary@montroselinks.co.uk Web site: www.montroselinks.co.uk

---

The essential guide for fishing in Scotland

If you enjoy fishing, you'll love **Scotland for Fishing 2002/2003.** Edited by award-winning fisherman and journalist Mike Shepley, Scotland for Fishing contains all you need to know to get on the water at Scotland's best fishing sites.

If you order your copy direct from Pastime Publications, you can save £1 off the cover price. For just **£6.99** including post and packaging, we'll deliver the guide to your door anywhere in the UK.

Send your cheque, made payable to: Pastime Publications, Golf Reader Offer, 5 Dalgety Avenue, Edinburgh EH7 5UF, along with your address details. Then sit back and start planning your Scottish fishing holiday.

Allow 28 days for delivery.

Montrose

HOLE	NAME	WHITE YARDS	YELLOW YARDS	PAR	STROKE INDEX
1	Scurdy	391	379	4	3
2	Bents	391	378	4	7
3	Table	154	150	3	13
4	Butts	365	350	4	5
5	Hillock	292	276	4	17
6	Sandy Braes	489	479	5	15
7	Whins	368	357	4	9
8	Valley	329	299	4	11
9	Jubilee	444	420	4	1
10	Girdle	379	368	4	10
11	Mid Road	444	434	4	2
12	Pouderie	150	140	3	18
13	Gates	320	307	4	12
14	Curlie	414	401	4	6
15	Wilderness	541	516	5	16
16	Gully	235	226	3	8
17	Rashies	418	410	4	4
18	Dean's Drive	346	339	4	14

Montrose Links Trust

Traill Drive, Montrose
Angus DD10 8SW

Advance Bookings
T: 01674 672932

Holes: 18
Yardage: 6533 yds
SSS: 72

They say the golf course was created here before the town. Take that with a pinch of salt if you will, but that's the last note of amusement you'll experience on this great links. Smack up against the sand dunes, the course is suffering from the horrors of erosion by the North Sea, but there is little respite from a tremendous challenge which the locals find different every day, in terms of club choice and shot placement, not to mention coping with the trickiest of greens.

Green Fees	Weekdays	Weekends	Are visitors
Round	£28	£32	welcome?
Daily	£38	£48	Yes

Nearest Airport: Aberdeen, 2.4 miles
Nearest Rail Station: Montrose, 1.1 miles
Gazetteer Ref: p138   **Map Ref:** p155, F6

TO LOCATE THIS GOLF COURSE ON THE MAPS (p155-159) LOOK FOR THE FLAG WITH THIS PAGE NUMBER.

▼ 16th

Monifieth

Monifieth Golf Links

Princes Street, Monifieth
Angus DD5 4AW

Advance Bookings
T: 01382 532767

Holes: 18
Yardage: 6655 yds
SSS: 72

Here's another unsurpassed Angus links which justifies its ranking as an Open Qualifying course without the slightest difficulty. (Sorry – that's a contradiction in terms, but I'm sure you know what I mean.) It plays 'the other way round' as the early holes go east with the wind, while a westerly return compounds the difficulties of the finishing holes. This is a superb links – yet again – demanding the utmost respect.

HOLE	NAME	WHITE YARDS	YELLOW YARDS	PAR	STROKE INDEX
1	White Gates	312	275	4	11/14
2	Jimmy Lindsay	405	338	4	3/6
3	The Roses	419	100	3/4	17/12
4	Featherbed	445	274	4	9/4
5	South Buddon	182	296	3/4	7/18
6	Lucky Daddy	370	143	3/4	15/8
7	North Buddon	406	445	4	1/2
8	The Valley	273	339	4	5/16
9	Long Hole	536	160	3/5	13/10
10	The Rashies	360	312	4	8/7
11	Ashbank	173	294	4/3	10/15
12	Elsinore	364	379	4	2/9
13	The Pyramids	428	259	4	16/1
14	The Sandbed	143	252	4/3	14/17
15	The Plantation	370	338	4	4/5
16	Wilderness	330	143	3/4	18/11
17	Provost Stewart	424	448	4	6/3
18	Iain Hutcheon	519	328	4/5	12/13

Green Fees

	Weekdays	Weekends	Are visitors welcome?
Round	£30	£36	
Daily	£-	£-	Yes

Nearest Airport: Edinburgh, 68.5 miles
Nearest Rail Station: Monifieth, 0.3 miles
Gazetteer Ref: p138   **Map Ref:** p155, F7

TO LOCATE THIS GOLF COURSE ON THE MAPS (p155-159) LOOK FOR THE FLAG WITH THIS PAGE NUMBER.

18th green ▼

Gleneagles - Queens Course

HOLE	NAME	WHITE YARDS	YELLOW YARDS	PAR	STROKE INDEX
1	Trystin Tree		387	4	5
2	Needle's E'e		130	3	17
3	Gushet Rig		411	4	1
4	Warlock Knowe		351	4	10
5	Glower O'er'em		163	3	15
6	Drum Sichty		407	4	6
7	Westlin Wyne		476	5	8
8	Auld Fauld		310	4	12
9	Stey Brae		415	4	2
10	Pint Stoup		403	4	4
11	Muir Tap		309	4	13
12	Tinkler's Gill		407	4	3
13	Water Kelpie		132	3	18
14	Witches' Bowster		177	3	9
15	Leddy's Ain		251	4	16
16	Lovers' Gait		369	4	11
17	Hinny Mune		183	3	14
18	Queens Hame		379	4	7

The Gleneagles Hotel Golf Courses

The Gleneagles Hotel, Auchterarder,
Perthshire PH3 1NF

Advance Bookings
T: 01764 694469

Holes: 18
Yardage: 5965 yds
SSS: 70

There are many who consider the Queen's the most pleasurable of the three big tests at Gleneagles. There are, granted, plenty of questions asked but damage caused by inconsistency of direction, in particular, is perhaps more recoverable than the King's, while on the PGA it could result in write-off! The same magnificence of presentation and glorious views to Glendevon guarantee total enrapture with the third Gleneagles' challenge; it is joyful to be here anytime.

Green Fees	Weekdays	Weekends	Are visitors
Round	£75	£100	welcome?
Daily	£-	£-	Yes

Nearest Airport: Edinburgh, 40.7 miles
Nearest Rail Station: Gleneagles, 2 miles
Gazetteer Ref: p105   **Map Ref:** p155, E7

TO LOCATE THIS GOLF COURSE ON THE MAPS (p155-159) LOOK FOR THE FLAG WITH THIS PAGE NUMBER.

▼ 10th green

Taymouth Castle

E S T A T E

Enjoy Playing and Staying

Taymouth Castle Estate is a designated conservation area containing stunning highland scenery, which has Kenmore Village at its very heart, while the castle itself stands in glorious parkland grounds.

Holiday cottages are conveniently located within the castle grounds, the village of Kenmore and on the banks of the Tay. All guests, during their stay in the estate's holiday accommodation, gain **free unlimited** weekday golf at the Taymouth Castle Golf Course. There are also fishing, watersports and woodland walks, and an outstanding range of facilities and amenities nearby.

For more information call **01887 830 765** or check out our website at **www.scotland-golf.co.uk**

SCOTLAND
HOME OF GOLF
online

www.scotland-for-golf.com

Taymouth Castle

HOLE	NAME	WHITE YARDS	YELLOW YARDS	PAR	STROKE INDEX
1	Inchadney	296	261	4	14
2	Beardy's Well	306	304	4	9
3	Rhevardh	420	379	4	3
4	Surprise	170	152	3	16
5	Lawers	543	518	5	1
6	Ballivolin	365	351	4	7
7	Tomna Croiche	283	245	4	13
8	Enin	383	364	4	12
9	Sar-Mhaith	377	375	4	5
10	Snas Mhor	182	173	3	17
11	An Iomain Fhada	452	414	4	4
12	Bailie's	444	437	4	2
13	Breadalbane	298	290	4	11
14	Elbow Room	190	183	3	15
15	Beild	410	382	4	6
16	Diary	174	142	3	18
17	The Beeches	330	326	4	8
18	Castle	443	438	4	10

Taymouth Castle Golf Course

Kenmore, Perthshire
PH15 2NT

Advance Bookings
T: 01887 830228

Holes: 18
Yardage: 6066 yds
SSS: 69

It is one of the great unsolved mysteries to me that the grandeur of Taymouth Castle remains undeveloped and presumably therefore in slow decline. Fortunately the golf course in its grounds looks better with each passing season. The setting, on the flat, tree-lined parkland to the south of the Tay and east of Kenmore, is simply magnificent. While the spectacular facade of the castle lends much to the scene, the course itself deserves plaudits as a fine test.

Green Fees	Weekdays	Weekends	Are visitors
Round	£22	£26	welcome?
Daily	£-	£-	Yes

Nearest Airport: Edinburgh, 79.4 miles
Nearest Rail Station: Pitlochry, 19.9 miles
Gazetteer Ref: p107 **Map Ref:** p155, E7

TO LOCATE THIS GOLF COURSE ON THE MAPS (p155-159) LOOK FOR THE FLAG WITH THIS PAGE NUMBER.

▼ 1st green

hidden gem

Strathtay

Strathtay Golf Club

Lyon Cottage, Strathtay
Perthshire PH15 2NT

Advance Bookings
T: 01887 840211

Holes: 9
Yardage: 4082 yds
SSS: 63

HOLE	NAME	WHITE YARDS	YELLOW YARDS	PAR	STROKE INDEX
1		286		4	
2		218		3	
3		212		3	
4		155		3	
5		256		4	
6		370		4	
7		144		3	
8		288		4	
9		114		3	
10		286		4	
11		218		3	
12		212		3	
13		155		3	
14		256		4	
15		370		4	
16		144		3	
17		288		4	
18		114		3	

If the Tay is gathering impetus at Aberfeldy, a few miles east it positively thunders through Grandtully. Two hundred yards to the north, this wee Scottish gem is not for the Woods, Woosnam or Westwood of the golf scene. It is for the ultimate holiday golfer who looks for no more than fun, exercise and total friendship with the locals after the show is over. You won't find better facilities at this level of golf anywhere – the nine holes are absolutely superb.

Green Fees	Weekdays	Weekends	Are visitors
Round	£12	£12	welcome?
Weekly	£40		Yes

Nearest Airport: Edinburgh, 60.7 miles
Nearest Rail Station: Dunkeld and Birnam, 5.5 miles
Gazetteer Ref: p107   **Map Ref:** p155, E6

TO LOCATE THIS GOLF COURSE ON THE MAPS (p155-159) LOOK FOR THE FLAG WITH THIS PAGE NUMBER.

8th green and clubhouse ▼

hidden gem

Dunkeld and Birnam

HOLE	NAME	WHITE YARDS	YELLOW YARDS	PAR	STROKE INDEX
1	Strath	285	274	4	14
2	The Marshes	281	263	4	10
3	Craigvinean	140	126	3	16
4	Lowes	442	402	5/4	3
5	Craig Wood	376	373	4	6
6	Gully	303	243	4	11
7	Spoutie	271	263	4	13
8	Birk Knowe	393	336	4	1
9	Craiglush	367	367	4	8
10	Osprey	508	508	5	2
11	Newtyle	141	135	3	18
12	Lochan	274	274	4	12
13	Cally	325	325	4	9
14	Juniper Wood	417	373	4	5
15	Birnam	396	396	4	4
16	Danny's	274	274	4	7
17	Fungarth	195	193	3	15
18	Whinney Brae	123	123	3	17

Dunkeld & Birnam Golf Club

Fungarth, Dunkeld
Perthshire PH8 0HU

Advance Bookings
T: 01350 727524

Holes: 18
Yardage: 5508 yds
SSS: 67

Recently upgraded to 18 holes, this lovely little club enjoys a perfect setting in the hillside north-east of the town. The rolling new fairways and presence of water hazards add another dimension, while the proximity of the Loch of the Lowes means that an abundance of birdies (of the feathered variety) is ever in sight or earshot. The prevalent breeze will be influential, but my guess is that, when mature, the contrast between new and old will be highly poular.

Green Fees	Weekdays	Weekends	Are visitors
Round	£20	£25	welcome?
Daily	£28	£35	Yes

Nearest Airport: Edinburgh, 57.1 miles
Nearest Rail Station: Dunkeld and Birnam, 2.2 miles
Gazetteer Ref: p106   **Map Ref:** p155, E7

TO LOCATE THIS GOLF COURSE ON THE MAPS (p155-159) LOOK FOR THE FLAG WITH THIS PAGE NUMBER.

▼ 10th green

Stonehaven

Stonehaven Golf Club

Cowie, Stonehaven
Kincardineshire AB39 3RH

Advance Bookings
T: 01569 762124

Holes: 18
Yardage: 5103 yds
SSS: 65

The continuing popularity of this idyllic place for leisurely golf remains unbeatable. Set on the clifftops north of the town, with unrivalled panoramas of the North Sea, the short parkland challenge of just over 5000 yards is always in beautiful condition and is the perfect springboard to a golfing tour of the north-east. There are very few restrictions to availability for play, while the club's friendly spirit is simply the best.

Green Fees	Weekdays	Weekends	Are visitors welcome?
Round	£15	£22	
Daily	£20	£25	Yes

Nearest Airport: Aberdeen, 18.1 miles
Nearest Rail Station: Stonehaven, 3 miles
Gazetteer Ref: p117   **Map Ref:** p155, G6

HOLE	NAME	WHITE YARDS	YELLOW YARDS	PAR	STROKE INDEX
1	Ruthery	305	300	4	15
2	Fault	203	198	3	3
3	Kingsacre	331	326	4	7
4	Garron	364	359	4	5
5	Jake's View	376	376	4	9
6	Glack	190	171	3	13
7	Skatie Brow	170	165	3	11
8	Ridges	159	132	3	18
9	Cowie	398	391	4	2
10	Slughead	329	294	4	10
11	Denhead	272	257	4	17
12	Logie	416	396	4	1
13	Red Man	252	247	4/3	14
14	Auld House	169	149	3	12
15	Gully Cup	161	156	3	6
16	Rashes	482	447	5/4	16
17	Laird's View	315	268	4	8
18	Home	211	172	3	4

TO LOCATE THIS GOLF COURSE ON THE MAPS (p155-159) LOOK FOR THE FLAG WITH THIS PAGE NUMBER.

2nd tee ▼

Hazelhead

HOLE	NAME	WHITE YARDS	YELLOW YARDS	PAR	STROKE INDEX
1	Larches	309		4	15
2	Hazeldene	396		4	1
3	Heather	366		4	7
4	Mound	326		4	9
5	Garden	174		3	17
6	Muirhead	400		4	3
7	Beeches	386		4	5
8	Whins	309		4	13
9	Road	186		3	11
10	Count'swells	383		4	4
11	Lochnager	392		4	8
12	Wardhead	195		3	14
13	The Shelter	379		4	6
14	Plantation	430		4	2
15	Smithfield	546		5	12
16	Woodside	166		3	18
17	Blackhill	476		5	16
18	Hazelhead	385		4	10

Hazelhead Golf Course

Hazelhead, Aberdeen
Aberdeenshire AB15 8BD

Advance Bookings
T: 01224 321830

Holes: 18
Yardage: 5673 yds
SSS: 70

The two courses which make up Aberdeen City Council's parkland (rather than links) challenges, are excellent tests of accuracy. Number One is the longer of the two, and failure to capitalise on a front nine some 500 yards shorter than the inward half will cost you dear. Lots of trees create a fine backdrop to play, as well as forcing the golfer to keep the ball in play to avoid severe problems.

Green Fees	Weekdays	Weekends	Are visitors
Round	£9	£25	welcome?
Daily	£-	£-	Yes

Nearest Airport: Aberdeen, 5.7 miles
Nearest Rail Station: Aberdeen, 3.6 miles
Gazetteer Ref: p114   **Map Ref:** p155, G5

TO LOCATE THIS GOLF COURSE ON THE MAPS (p155-159) LOOK FOR THE FLAG WITH THIS PAGE NUMBER.

▼ 18th green

Inchmarlo (The Laird's Course)

Inchmarlo Golf Centre

Inchmarlo, Banchory
Aberdeenshire AB31 4BQ

Advance Bookings
T: 01330 822557

Holes: 18
Yardage: 6218
Par: 71

HOLE	NAME	WHITE YARDS	YELLOW YARDS	PAR	STROKE INDEX
1	Queen's Drive	284	259	4	11
2	Hollies	174	170	3	15
3	Crow's Nest	295	288	4	13
4	Loch Hope	555	527	5	1
5	Standing Stones	424	401	4	5
6	Massie's Well	395	379	4	7
7	Craiglea	496	468	5	3
8	Poplars	174	168	3	17
9	Glencommon	299	299	4	9
10	Wellburn	339	315	4	10
11	The Firs	107	101	3	18
12	Auldeer	473	442	4	2
13	The Beech	422	398	4	8
14	Jampots	549	518	5	4
15	Brathens	184	176	3	16
16	The Copse	298	290	4	6
17	Garden Wood	320	315	4	14
18	Scotty View	405	383	4	12

Just west of Banchory, this recently completed golfing development is capitalising on the burgeoning popularity of golf in Aberdeenshire. The little course is an absolute gem, with every test of skill you can imagine built into the design – and plenty of water too! The big course promises to be a real cracker when it matures but the whole complex has created a first class alternative for golf in Deeside.

Green Fees	Weekdays	Weekends	Are visitors
Round	£20	£25	welcome?
Daily	£-	£-	Yes

Nearest Airport: Aberdeen, 19.4 miles
Nearest Rail Station: Aberdeen, 18.8 miles
Gazetteer Ref: p115 **Map Ref:** p155, F5

TO LOCATE THIS GOLF COURSE ON THE MAPS (p155-159) LOOK FOR THE FLAG WITH THIS PAGE NUMBER.

6th green ▼

hidden **gem**

Aboyne

HOLE	NAME	WHITE YARDS	YELLOW YARDS	PAR	STROKE INDEX
1	Road	236	227	3	12
2	Dyke	379	361	4	6
3	Formaston	380	366	4	8
4	Teuchit	160	158	3	18
5	Planteau	395	386	4	2
6	Grants Lochrie	245	322	4	14
7	Auld Line	483	470	5	4
8	Mortlich	166	148	3	16
9	Loch	389	385	4	10
10	Bonnyside	499	426	4	11
11	Valley	388	353	4	5
12	Lochnagar	178	157	3	15
13	Fernie Brae	377	367	4	1
14	Burn	180	165	3	13
15	Ladywell	377	355	4	7
16	Darach Mor	431	400	4	3
17	Queens Hill	351	341	4	17
18	Hame	230	220	3	9

Aboyne Golf Club

Formaston Park, Aboyne
Aberdeenshire AB34 5HP

Advance Bookings
T: 01339 886328

Holes: 18
Yardage: 5910 yds
SSS: 68

The lovely eighteen holes here have long been held as the most pleasant of all the Deeside clubs. I visited last on the most glorious of April mornings; an overnight ground frost contrasted with the emergent greens of spring, while the early rays of sunshine lit up every fairway furrow, slopes and slants on greens and the mists which crept across the surface of the loch were stunning. It is just the prettiest course and a regular stop for the visiting golfer.

Green Fees	Weekdays	Weekends	Are visitors welcome?
Round	£19	£23	Yes
Daily	£25	£30	

Nearest Airport: Aberdeen, 28 miles

Nearest Rail Station: Aberdden, 30 miles

Gazetteer Ref: p114   **Map Ref:** p155, F5

TO LOCATE THIS GOLF COURSE ON THE MAPS (p155-159) LOOK FOR THE FLAG WITH THIS PAGE NUMBER.

▼ Frost on the 10th

Banchory

Banchory Golf Club

Kinneskie Road, Banchory
Aberdeenshire AB31 5TA

Advance Bookings
T: 01330 822447

Holes: 18
Yardage: 5775 yds
SSS: 68

HOLE	NAME	WHITE YARDS	YELLOW YARDS	PAR	STROKE INDEX
1	St Ternan	315	315	4	10
2	Mavisbank	224	220	3	6
3	Hallow	125	125	3	18
4	Fernbank	444	430	4	2
5	Tor-na-Coille	354	289	4	12
6	Inchmarlo	485	465	5/4	8
7	Major	188	170	3	14
8	Roe's Pot	326	312	4	4
9	Lairds Cast	155	134	3	16
10	Oaks	514	501	5	13
11	Firs	353	342	4	9
12	The Wood	183	173	3	5
13	Sandy Haven	420	376	4	1
14	Paul Lawrie	302	292	4	15
15	Bohore	521	491	5	7
16	Doocot	88	80	3	17
17	Doctor	430	412	4	3
18	Kinneskie	354	354	4	11

Not a million miles behind the offerings along the Dee at Aboyne is the slightly shorter – but no less attractive – layout at Banchory. The unique hexagonal clubhouse overlooks the course as it spreads itself a 'long a narrowish stretch of land between the town and the river. Accuracy is paramount, particularly off the tee, while a quality short game will bring its rewards.

Green Fees	Weekdays	Weekends	Are visitors welcome?
Round	£20	£23	Yes, with restrictions
Daily	£28	Weekly £80	on Tues & weekends

Nearest Airport: Aberdeen, 18.8 miles
Nearest Rail Station: Aberdeen, 18 miles
Gazetteer Ref: p115   **Map Ref:** p155, F5

TO LOCATE THIS GOLF COURSE ON THE MAPS (p155-159) LOOK FOR THE FLAG WITH THIS PAGE NUMBER.

13th green ▼

Moray (Lossiemouth)

HOLE	NAME	WHITE YARDS	YELLOW YARDS	PAR	STROKE INDEX
1	Hillocks	367	-	4	10
2	Pitgaveny	325	-	4	14
3	King o' the Castle	419	-	4	2
4	Junction	132	-	3	16
5	Jimmy Neil	371	-	4	5
6	JR Robertson	100	-	3	18
7	Covesea	422	-	4	7
8	Skerries	412	-	4	3
9	Ca Canny	364	-	4	12
10	Bents	325	-	4	9
11	Ben Rinnes	151	-	3	17
12	Altyre	433	-	4	4
13	Auld Dyke	340	-	4	11
14	Dinna Top	512	-	5	1
15	Boyd Anderson	405	-	4	6
16	The Rock	328	-	4	13
17	Caesar's Grave	181	-	3	15
18	The Mound	417	-	4	8

Moray Golf Club

Stotfield, Lossiemouth
Morayshire IV31 6QS

Advance Bookings
T: 01343 813330

Holes: 18
Yardage: 6643 yds
SSS: 73

One of the great northern links venues, the Moray Club offers two majestic courses for the enthusiasts of seaside golf. If you are in search of a score, rather than a hard challenge, opt for the 6000 yards of the New, as you will do well to play to handicap on the 6500 yards of the Old. A combination of links, hazards, the extra length and, of course, seaside breezes, make life very difficult. It's a great course, with the eighteenth ranked one of Scotland's best finishing holes.

Green Fees	Weekdays	Weekends	Are visitors
Round	£35	£45	welcome?
Daily	£50	£65	Yes

Nearest Airport: Inverness, 36.2 miles
Nearest Rail Station: Elgin, 6.5 miles
Gazetteer Ref: p119 **Map Ref:** p155, F3

TO LOCATE THIS GOLF COURSE ON THE MAPS (p155-159) LOOK FOR THE FLAG WITH THIS PAGE NUMBER.

▼ Short 1st

Duff House Royal

Duff House Royal Golf Club

The Barnyards, Banff
Banffshire AB45 3SX

Advance Bookings
T: 01261 812062

Holes: 18
Yardage: 6161 yds
SSS: 70

HOLE	NAME	WHITE YARDS	YELLOW YARDS	PAR	STROKE INDEX
1	Doune	314	310	4	13
2	Barnyards	366	356	4	8
3	Gaveny	392	377	4	3
4	Alexandra	367	362	4	10
5	Corskie	330	309	4	12
6	Fife	139	131	3	18
7	Island	460	449	4	1
8	Dane's Dyke	381	373	4	6
9	Kirkside	172	161	3	16
10	Lochlaverock	403	390	4	9
11	Orchard	214	201	3	15
12	Planteau	498	489	5	2
13	Duff	175	178	3	17
14	Plantation	434	425	4	7
15	Connaught	468	459	4	5
16	Venus	242	234	3	14
17	Bridge	262	448	4	4
18	Airlie	344	339	4	11

The town of Banff has long been a favourite holiday destination. The French design of Duff House drew many a visitor, while the parkland of the local golf club laid out between it and the Findhorn attracted the enthusiasts of golf. The house dominates proceedings, but a splendidly maintained and lush challenge keeps the mind on the job in hand, never more so than where trees or the river bound the holes, while the 'short' sixteenth is a truly superb par three.

Green Fees	Weekdays	Weekends	Are visitors welcome?
Round	£18	£24	
Daily	£25	£30	Yes

Nearest Airport: Aberdeen, 40.4 miles
Nearest Rail Station: Keith, 20.6 miles
Gazetteer Ref: p117   **Map Ref:** p155, F4

TO LOCATE THIS GOLF COURSE ON THE MAPS (p155-159) LOOK FOR THE FLAG WITH THIS PAGE NUMBER.

16th green ▼

Inverness

HOLE	NAME	WHITE YARDS	YELLOW YARDS	PAR	STROKE INDEX
1	Culcabock	308	301	4	14
2	Quarry	179	141	3	18
3	Drakies	487	444	5/4	10
4	Whins	463	444	4	2
5	Pump	478	464	5/4	8
6	Wyvis	313	291	4	12
7	Spion Kop	197	169	3	4
8	Meadows	373	343	4	6
9	Kellys Copse	208	179	3	16
10	Kingsmills	406	405	4	3
11	Seven Sisters	423	394	4	11
12	Kessock Bridge	394	339	4	13
13	Diriebught	190	154	3	15
14	Midmills	475	435	4	1
15	Curling Point	188	147	3	7
16	Leys	380	356	4	9
17	Ridge	333	326	4	17
18	Deoch an Dorvis	461	446	4	5

Inverness Golf Club

Culcabock Road, Inverness
Inverness-shire IV2 3XQ

Advance Bookings
T: 01463 239882

Holes: 18
Yardage: 6256 yds
SSS: 70

Splendid parkland, regularly punctuated by trees with the presence of water to cause a bit of head scratching here and there, are the major characteristics of this very pleasant City of Inverness course. There is the need, too, to take advantage of the shorter outward nine as the stiffer inward half demands more of your long game. An impressive clubhouse majestically completes the provision of a first class venue for the sport in the capital of the Highlands.

Green Fees	Weekdays	Weekends	Are visitors
Round	£29	£39	welcome?
Daily	£29	£39	Yes

Nearest Airport: Inverness, 1.9 miles
Nearest Rail Station: Inverness, 2.4 miles
Gazetteer Ref: p120   **Map Ref:** p155, E4

TO LOCATE THIS GOLF COURSE ON THE MAPS (p155-159) LOOK FOR THE FLAG WITH THIS PAGE NUMBER.

▼ Short 9th

Golspie

Golspie Golf Club

Ferry Road, Golspie
Sutherland KW10 6ST

Advance Bookings
T: 01408 633266

Holes: 18
Yardage: 5836 yds
SSS: 68

James Braid's indelible trade mark is all over this course, from devious pot bunker placement to subtle tee and green design. The early and late sections of the course feature wide open links where improvisation and forethought are as important as ever, while the southern and more heathy part puts the emphasis on accuracy. There are some lovely holes, with the short tenth surely ranking as one of Scotland's most picturesque – and hazardous – par threes.

HOLE	NAME	WHITE YARDS	YELLOW YARDS	PAR	STROKE INDEX
1	Backies		386	4	6
2	Kirk		165	3	14
3	Shore		352	4	8
4	Gully		522	5	4
5	Sahara		287	4	11
6	Saucer		146	3	16
7	Fleet		279	4	18
8	Wood		400	4	5
9	Paradise		408	4	1
10	Lochy		140	3	17
11	Tinker's Camp		323	4	12
12	Table		323	4	9
13	Cup		311	4	15
14	Fields		409	4	2
15	Tattie Pits		410	4	7
16	Cairngorms		167	3	10
17	Sahara Back		212	3	13
18	Drum Brae		437	4	3

Green Fees

	Weekdays	Weekends
Round	£20	£20
Daily	£25	£25

Are visitors welcome?
Yes

Nearest Airport: Inverness, 56.6 miles
Nearest Rail Station: Golspie, 0.6 miles
Gazetteer Ref: p122   **Map Ref:** p155, E3

TO LOCATE THIS GOLF COURSE ON THE MAPS (p155-159) LOOK FOR THE FLAG WITH THIS PAGE NUMBER.

Short 2nd ▼

Tain

HOLE	NAME	WHITE YARDS	YELLOW YARDS	PAR	STROKE INDEX
1	Road	382	371	4	11
2	River	391	351	4	6
3	Knowe	435	416	4	1
4	Long	542	532	5	5
5	Quaich	181	167	3	17
6	Bunker	309	309	4	16
7	Morich	377	369	4	7
8	Short	189	179	3	13
9	Mafeking	355	349	4	9
10	Garden	403	380	4	3
11	Alps	380	374	4	4
12	Plaids	386	372	4	12
13	Kelpie	501	492	5	14
14	Well	438	397	4	2
15	Braehead	346	330	4	15
16	Kelag	147	139	3	18
17	Black Bridge	215	211	3	8
18	Home	427	371	4	10

Tain Golf Club

Chapel Road, Tain, Ross-shire
IV19 1JE

Advance Bookings
T: 01862 892314

Holes: 18
Yardage: 6404 yds
SSS: 71

Dornoch, Brora, Golspie, Tain – and now the Carnegie Club at Skibo – make up a formidable quintet of links venues which will keep visiting golfers enthralled. A terrific opening hole promises birdie or bogey; thereafter, rolling and at times tight fairways put the emphasis on accuracy from the tee, while the longer par fours can all too easily cost shots if the long game fails you. The trio of finishing holes – the seventeenth is outstanding – ranks with the country's best.

Green Fees	Weekdays	Weekends	Are visitors
Round	£30	£36	welcome?
Daily	£36	£46	Yes

Nearest Airport: Inverness, 40.9 miles
Nearest Rail Station: Tain, 0.5 miles
Gazetteer Ref: p121   **Map Ref:** p155, E3

TO LOCATE THIS GOLF COURSE ON THE MAPS (p155-159) LOOK FOR THE FLAG WITH THIS PAGE NUMBER.

▼ 1st

The Lochcarron Hotel
Wester Ross

For a friendly holiday, with a touch of true Scottish hospitality.

Situated on the picturesque shore of Loch Carron amidst the rugged grandeur of Wester Ross, The Lochcarron Hotel has been tastefully developed from a former Highland Inn of long standing.

Boats, canoes, fishing tackle and dinghies are available for hire locally and Lochcarron has a nine-hole golf course, with reduced fees for hotel guests.

To find out more about The Lochcarron Hotel, visit our website at www.lochcarronhotel.com

The Lochcarron Hotel, Main Street, Lochcarron, Wester Ross, IV54 8YS
Tel: 01520 722226 – Fax: 01520 722612

Join the **Connoisseur's Club!**

Connoisseur's Club members will receive a copy of **Billy Casper's Golf Collection**, featuring 12 of Scotland's most prestigious golfing venues and associated hotels, together with a suite of discount vouchers for use on green fees, accommodation and dining. The vouchers are activated and validated by a membership card which can be used for 12 months. After the vouchers have been used the club member can carry on receiving substantial discounts for the duration of their membership.

for more information, see page 25

SAMPLE SAVINGS:
St Andrews: 50% off accommodation at the 5-star Old Course Hotel, plus 25% off green fees at the Duke's Course.

Carnoustie: 50% off accommodation at the 4-star Carnoustie Hotel, Golf Resort and Spa plus 25% off green fees at the Burnside's Course and 25% off the bill for 1-4 diners at the Dalhousie Restaurant.

Strathpeffer

HOLE	NAME	WHITE YARDS	YELLOW YARDS	PAR	STROKE INDEX
1	Castle Leod	297		4	
2	Dyke	257		4	
3	Pavilion	199		3	
4	Cairn	211		3	
5	Short	120		3	
6	Fence	183		3	
7	Rockies	287		4	
8	Terrace	316		4	
9	Long	430		4	
10	High	162		3	
11	Kinellan	231		3	
12	Flagstaff	279		4	
13	Valley	306		4	
14	Target	151		3	
15	Ord	419		4	
16	Ulladale	369		4	
17	Strath	271		4	
18	Home	306		4	

Strathpeffer Spa Golf Club

Strathpeffer, Ross-shire IV14 9AS

Advance Bookings
T: 01997 421219

Holes: 18
Yardage: 4792 yds
SSS: 64

The beauty of this Victorian town up the valley from Dingwall is legend. The fun of its golf course in the hills above has perhaps not quite earned that status, but you will go far to find sheer enjoyment of the game which rivals this. A downward plunge from the first tee is followed by a steady climb over the next eight holes to the high point of the course. Spectacular views abound, heathy fairways are springy and greens are near-perfect.

Green Fees	Weekdays	Weekends	Are visitors welcome?
Round	£16	£16	
Daily	£20	£21	Yes

Nearest Airport: Inverness, 25.8 miles
Nearest Rail Station: Dingwall, 5.3 miles
Gazetteer Ref: p121   **Map Ref:** p155, D4

TO LOCATE THIS GOLF COURSE ON THE MAPS (p155-159) LOOK FOR THE FLAG WITH THIS PAGE NUMBER.

▼ Looking down the 2nd

hidden gem

Fortrose and Rosemarkie

Fortrose & Rosemarkie Golf Club

Ness Road East, Fortrose
Ross-shire IV10 8SE

Advance Bookings
T: 01381 620529

Holes: 18
Yardage: 5875 yds
SSS: 69

HOLE	NAME	WHITE YARDS	YELLOW YARDS	PAR	STROKE INDEX
1	Fort George	331		4	13
2	The Dyke	412		4	3
3	The Cup	314		4	9
4	The Lighthouse	455		5	1
5	Icehouse	132		3	15
6	Rosehaugh	469		5	17
7	Ormond Hill	309		4	11
8	Chanonry	389		4	5
9	The Ness	196		3	7
10	Feu Road	322		4	8
11	Dalcross	381		4	10
12	Culloden	394		4	2
13	Quigish	308		4	6
14	Bonfire Hill	267		4	18
15	Target	293		4	16
16	Coignach Odheur	336		4	14
17	Clay pots	355		4	4
18	Fiery Hillock	212		3	12

The thinning spit of links which thrusts into the Moray Firth from these 'twin' towns is the setting for the Black Isle's golfing gem. Split down the middle by the road to Chanonry Point lighthouse, the course is subjected to near permanent winds which sweep up – or down – the Firth. It's a fascinating challenge, with but two par threes offering a change to an almost exact north/south direction of play. 'Beat the breeze, beat the course', the locals will tell you.

Green Fees	Weekdays	Weekends	Are visitors welcome?
Round	£30	£35	
Daily	£33	£38	Yes

Nearest Airport: Inverness, 20.1 miles
Nearest Rail Station: Muir of ord, 15.1 miles
Gazetteer Ref: p120   **Map Ref:** p155, E4

TO LOCATE THIS GOLF COURSE ON THE MAPS (p155-159) LOOK FOR THE FLAG WITH THIS PAGE NUMBER.

3rd green ▼

hidden gem

Glencruitten

HOLE	NAME	WHITE YARDS	YELLOW YARDS	PAR	STROKE INDEX
1		432	397	4/5	
2		163	149	3	
3		160	151	3	
4		271	266	4	
5		148	139	3	
6		215	199	3/4	
7		205	193	3/4	
8		263	239	4	
9		187	165	3	
10		141	127	3	
11		205	177	3	
12		373	332	4	
13		176	168	3	
14		310	303	4	
15		151	143	3	
16		313	313	4	
17		180	151	3	
18		357	321	4	

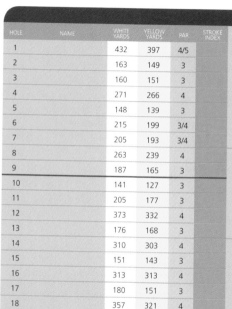

Glencruitten Golf Course

Glencruitten Road, Oban, Argyll
PA34 4PU

Advance Bookings
T: 01631 562868

Holes: 18
Yardage: 4452 yds
SSS: 63

A unique golfing experience is guaranteed at this thoroughly entertaining – and regularly frustrating – little course in the hillside to the south-east of Oban. A fairly stiff opening gives way to a succession of quaint par threes and short par fours which weave in and out and round about, subjecting your club choice to the highest imaginable examination. Get that right, hit straight and a flattering score is within reach. On the other hand . . .

Green Fees	Weekdays	Weekends	Are visitors
Round	£17	£18	welcome?
Daily	£-	£-	Yes

Nearest Airport: Glasgow, 89.5 miles
Nearest Rail Station: Oban, 0.8 miles
Gazetteer Ref: p128   **Map Ref:** p154, C7

TO LOCATE THIS GOLF COURSE ON THE MAPS (p155-159) LOOK FOR THE FLAG WITH THIS PAGE NUMBER.

▼ Looking down to the clubhouse

hidden **gem**

Millport

Millport Golf Club

Golf Road, Millport, Isle of Cumbrae, Ayrshire KA28 0HB

Advance Bookings
T: 01475 530311

Holes: 18
Yardage: 5828 yds
SSS: 69

Once the destination of holidaying Glaswegians in their thousands, the island of Cumbrae, and Millport in particular, are nowadays much quieter in the summer, but the reputation of the golf course remains. It stretches northwards for close on two miles on a ribbon of heath beneath the high ground north-west of the town. Tight fairways abound, the wind can blow but the hole names are splendid and it's a great location. Well worth making the ferry crossing.

HOLE	NAME	WHITE YARDS	YELLOW YARDS	PAR	STROKE INDEX
1	Sheuchans	307		4	16
2	Mountstuart	323		4	7
3	Whale's Back	402		4	2
4	Deil's Cast	162		3	17
5	Tairge	227		3	13
6	Bogie	312		4	8
7	Cobbler	373		4	5
8	Muirfield	303		4	15
9	Quaich	313		4	12
10	Plateau	345		4	10
11	Gawn's glen	384		4	4
12	Doo's Nest	159		3	18
13	Coney Lee	449		4	1
14	Stey Brae	342		4	6
15	Westward Ho!	418		4	9
16	Gully	160		3	14
17	Gowk Stane	449		4	3
18	Home	400		4	11

Green Fees	Weekdays	Weekends	Are visitors welcome?
Round	£20	£25	
Daily	£20	£25	Yes

Nearest Airport: Prestwick by ferry
Nearest Rail Station: Largs by ferry
Gazetteer Ref: p139   **Map Ref:** p156, C3

TO LOCATE THIS GOLF COURSE ON THE MAPS (p155-159) LOOK FOR THE FLAG WITH THIS PAGE NUMBER.

Short 4th and 5th tee ▼

hidden **gem**

Shiskine

HOLE	NAME	WHITE YARDS	YELLOW YARDS	PAR	STROKE INDEX
1	Road Hole	389	374	4	5
2	Twa'Burns	400	366	4	1
3	Crows Nest	135	117	3	9
4	The Shelf	148	141	3	11
5	The Point	247	200	3	7
6	Shore Hole	281	273	4	3
7	Himalayas	170	161	3	10
8	Hades	253	224	4	6
9	Druadoon	509	476	5	2
10	Paradise	167	161	3	12
11	The Hallows	222	210	3	4
12	Kilmory	129	120	3	8

Shiskine Golf and Tennis Club

Blackwaterfoot, Isle of Arran
KA27 8HA

Advance Bookings
T: 01770 860226

Holes: 12
Yardage: 2990 yds
SSS: 42

The club at Shiskine, at Blackwaterfoot on Arran, is renowned not only for the uniqueness of its twelve hole layout, but also for the golfing masses who make this lovely links a 'must' for a golfing break. The views across to Kintyre and Knapdale are ever-present, and to the Irish coast when visibility permits, are a gift from nature. The modest challenge of a par 63 belies blind shots galore, water hazards and gorse; it is wonderful to play.

Green Fees	Weekdays	Weekends	Are visitors
Round	£13	£17	welcome?
Daily	£18	£25	Yes

Nearest Airport: Prestwick by ferry
Nearest Rail Station: Ardrossan by ferry
Gazetteer Ref: p138   **Map Ref:** p156, C3

TO LOCATE THIS GOLF COURSE ON THE MAPS (p155-159) LOOK FOR THE FLAG WITH THIS PAGE NUMBER.

▼ 7th green

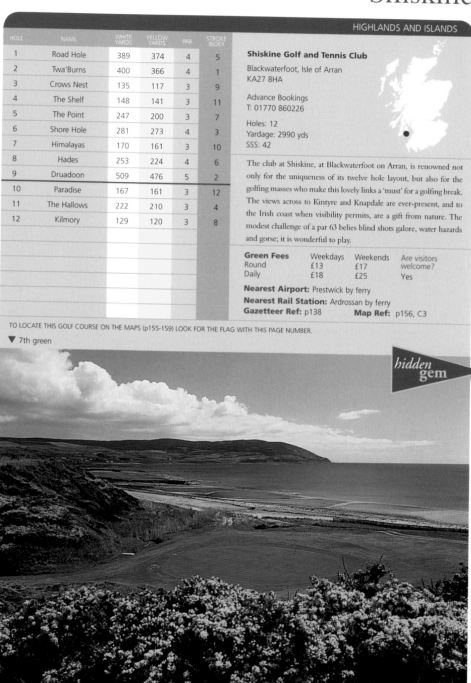

hidden **gem**

Machrie

Islay Golf Club
The Machrie Hotel & Golf Club

Port Ellen, Isle of Islay PA42 7AN

Advance Bookings
T: 01496 302310 (Hotel)

Holes: 18
Yardage: 6225 yds
SSS: 70

Steeped in romance and history, the most southerly Hebridean Isle also boasts one of the great natural Scottish links courses. The name derives from Gaelic, meaning 'land behind the beach' and that is exactly where this wonderful seaside golfing experience has been created. Big dunes, tough marram grass, hidden greens – and, inevitably, the near-permanent breeze – combine to provide one of the real 'hidden gems' of Scottish golf.

Green Fees	Weekdays	Weekends	Are visitors
Round	£35	£35	welcome?
Daily	£-	£-	Yes

Nearest Airport: Prestwick by ferry
Nearest Rail Station: Ardrossan by ferry
Gazetteer Ref: p139   **Map Ref:** p156, A3

HOLE	NAME	WHITE YARDS	YELLOW YARDS	PAR	STROKE INDEX
1	Kilbrannan		262	4	3
2	The Hummocks		162	3	9
3	Windy Knowe		160	3	17
4	Auchengallon		281	4	13
5	The Grid		162	3	11
6	The Glaick		254	4	15
7	Ard Bheinn		267	4	5
8	Crown Green		220	4	1
9	The Road Hole		239	4	7
10	Kilbrannan		262	4	4
11	The Hummocks		162	3	10
12	Windy Knowe		160	3	18
13	Auchengallon		281	4	14
14	The Grid		162	3	12
15	The Glaick		254	4	16
16	Ard Bheinn		267	4	6
17	Crown Green		220	4	2
18	The Road Hole		239	4	8

TO LOCATE THIS GOLF COURSE ON THE MAPS (p155-159) LOOK FOR THE FLAG WITH THIS PAGE NUMBER.

Looking to the 15th ▼

Advertise here to reach over 20,00 golfers worldwide

Gazeteer of Scotland's Golf Clubs

A guide to using our Gazetteer Section

Scotland has seen many changes in boundaries over the years; we have had County boundaries, District boundaries and Regional boundaries. While our featured courses section is broken down by Regional boundaries, the number of entries in the Gazetteer section makes this rather difficult for the reader to find courses in close proximity when arranging a tour. We have therefore gone back to the old county system to assist you in your search. We have broken Scotland down into nine regions and the Scottish Islands, and listed our twenty-nine counties against them on this page to help you along.

KEY TO FACILITIES AVAILABLE

Caddy Cars	CC	Buggy Hire	BH		
Practice Green	PG	Pro Shop	PS		
Car Parking	CP	Driving Range	DR		
Caddies	C	Club Hire	CH		
Bar	B	Dining	D		

Berwickshire

Hirsel Golf Club
Kelso Road, Coldstream
Berwickshire TD12 4NJ
Advance Bookings **T**: 01890 882678
Holes: 18
Yardage: 6092 yds
SSS: 70

Duns Golf Club
Hardens Road, Duns
Berwickshire TD11 3NR
Advance Bookings **T**: 01361 882194
Holes: 18
Yardage: 6209 yds
SSS: 70

Eyemouth Golf Club
Gunsgreenhill, Eyemouth
Berwickshire TD14 5SF
Advance Bookings **T**: 01890 750004
Holes: 18
Yardage: 6520 yds
SSS: 72

Lauder Golf Club
Galashiels Road, Lauder
Berwickshire TD2 6RA
Advance Bookings **T**: 01578 722526
Holes: 9
Yardage: 3001 yds
Par: 71
SSS: 69

Peebleshire

Innerleithen Golf Club
Leithen Water, Innerleithen
Peeblesshire EH44 6HZ
Advance Bookings Phone: 01896 830951
Holes: 9
Yardage: 6066 yds
SSS: SSS69

Peebles Golf Club
Kirkland Street, Peebles
Peeblesshire EH45 8EU
Advance Bookings **T**: 01721 720197
Holes: 18
Yardage: 5636 yds
SSS: 70

West Linton Golf Club

Medwyn Road, West Linton
Peeblesshire EH46 7HN
Advance Bookings **T**: 01968 660970
Club Established: 1890
Email: secretarywlgc@btinternet.com
Website: www.wlgc.co.uk
Clubhouse **T**: 01968 660463
Secretary: A. J. Mitchell
T: 01968 660970
Pro: Ian Wright
T: 01968 660256
Visitor Restrictions: Yes
Concessions Available: No
Regular Closures: No

FACILITIES AVAILABLE:

CC BH PG PS CP B D

COURSE 1: WEST LINTON

Holes: 18
Yardage: 6132 yds
Par: 69
SSS: 70
Designed by: James Braid

Fees:	Round	Daily
Weekdays:	£20	£30
Weekends:	£30	N/A

Roxburghshire

Minto Golf Club

Denholm, Hawick
Roxburghshire TD9 8SH
Advance Bookings **T**: 01450 870220
Holes: 18
Yardage: 5542 yds
Par: 69
SSS: 67   **SEE PAGE 28**

Jedburgh Golf Club

Dunion Road, Jedburgh
Roxburghshire TD8 6TA
Advance Bookings **T**: 01835 863587
Holes: 9
Yardage: 5492 yds
SSS: 67   **SEE PAGE 27**

Kelso Golf Club

Abbot Seat Road, Kelso
Roxburghshire TD5 7SL
Advance Bookings **T**: 01573 223009

Hawick Golf Club

Vertish Hill, Hawick
Roxburghshire TD9 0NY
Advance Bookings **T**: 01450 372293
Club Established: 1873
Email: thesecretary@
hawickgolfclub.psnet.co.uk
Website: www.ukgolfer.com/hawick
Clubhouse **T**: 01450 372293
Secretary: Mr Jack Harley
T: 01450 374947
Visitor Restrictions: Sat/Sun not
before 10.30am
Concessions Available:
Packages on request
Regular Closures: No

FACILITIES AVAILABLE:

CC PG PS CP B D

COURSE 1: VERTISH

Holes: 18
Yardage: 5933ds
Par: 68
SSS: 69

Fees:	Round	Daily
Weekdays:	£21.00	£21.00
Weekends:	£26.00	£26.00

The Vertish is a taxing par 68
with a number of long par 4's.
The course usually attracts
visitors to return.

Melrose Golf Club

The Clubhouse, Dingleton Road
Melrose, Roxburghshire
TD6 9HS
Advance Bookings **T**: 01896 822855
Holes: 9
Yardage: 5579 yds
SSS: 68

The Roxburghe Golf Course

Kelso, Roxburghshire
TD5 8JZ
Advance Bookings **T**: 01573 450331
Holes: 18
Yardage: 6925
SSS: 74   **SEE PAGE 30**

Newcastleton Golf Club

Holm Hill, Newcastleton
Roxburghshire TD9 0QD
Advance Bookings **T**: 013873 75257
Holes: 9
Yardage: 5748 m
SSS: 68

St. Boswells Golf Club

Braehead, St. Boswells
Roxburghshire TD6 0DE
Advance Bookings **T**: 01835 823527
Holes: 9
Yardage: 5250 yds
SSS: 65   **SEE PAGE 29**

Selkirkshire

Galashiels Golf Club

Ladhope Recreation Ground
Galashiels, Selkirkshire TD1 2BF
Advance Bookings **T**: 01896 753724
Holes: 18
Yardage: 5185 yds
SSS: 66

Torwoodlee Golf Club

Edinburgh Road, Galashiels
Selkirkshire TD1 2NE
Advance Bookings **T**: 01896 752260
Holes: 18
Yardage: 6200 yds
Par: 70
SSS: 69

Selkirk Golf Club

Selkirk Hills, Selkirk
Selkirkshire TD7 4NW
Advance Bookings **T**: 01750 20621
Holes: 9
Yardage: 5636 yds
Par: 68
SSS: 67

Clackmannanshire

Alloa Golf Club

Schawpark, Sauchie, Alloa,
Clackmannanshire FK10 3AX
Advance Bookings T: 01259 722745
Holes: 18
Yardage: 6229 yds
SSS: 71   **SEE PAGE 60**

Central

Braehead Golf Club
Cambus, Alloa
Clackmannanshire FK10 2NT
Advance Bookings **T**: 01259 725766
Holes: 18
Yardage: 6086 yds
SSS: 69

Tulliallan Golf Club
Alloa Road, Kincardine, Alloa
Clackmannanshire FK10 4BB
Advance Bookings **T**: 01259 730396
Clubhouse **T**: 01324 485420
Secretary: Steven Kelly (Golf Pro)
T: 01259 730798
Visitor Restrictions: Yes
Holes: 18
Yardage: 5965 yds
SSS: 69

Fees:	Round
Weekdays:	£15
Weekends:	£25

Alva Golf Club
Beauclerc Street, Alva
Clackmannanshire FK12 5LH
Advance Bookings **T**: 01259 760431
Holes: 9
Yardage: 2423 yds
SSS: 64

Dollar Golf Course
Brewlands House, Dollar
Clackmannanshire FK14 7EA
Advance Bookings **T**: 01259 742400
Holes: 18
Yardage: 5242 yds
SSS: 66   **SEE PAGE 59**

Muckhart Golf Club
Muckhart, Dollar
Clackmannanshire FK14 7JH
Advance Bookings **T**: 01259 781423
Holes: 18
Yardage: 6034 yds
SSS: 70

Tillicoultry Golf Course
Alva Road, Tillicoultry
Clackmannanshire FK13 6BL
Advance Bookings **T**: 01259 750124
Holes: 9
Yardage: 2633 yds
SSS: 66

Kinross-shire

Bishopshire Golf Course
Kinnesswood, Kinross
Kinross-shire KY13 9HX
Advance Bookings **T**: 01592 780203
Holes: 9
Yardage: 4700 (for 18)
Par: 64
SSS: 64

Green Hotel Golf Course
Green Hotel, Kinross
Kinross-shire KY13 8AS
Advance Bookings **T**: 01577 863407
Holes: 18
Yardage: 6256/6438
SSS: 73/71   **SEE PAGE 73**

Milnathort Golf Club Ltd
South Street, Milnathort
Kinross-shire KY13 9XA
Advance Bookings **T**: 01577 864069
Holes: 9
Yardage: 5702 yds
SSS: 69

Perthshire

Aberfeldy Golf Club
Taybridge Road, Aberfeldy
Perthshire PH15 2BH
Advance Bookings **T**: 01887 820535
Club Established: 1895
Email: abergc@supanet.co.uk
Website: www.aberfeldygolf.co.uk
Clubhouse **T**: 01887 820535
Secretary: P.M. Wolley
T: 01887 829422
Visitor Restrictions: None

Holes: 18
Yardage: 5283 yds
Par: 68
SSS: 66

Fees:	Round	Daily
Weekdays:	£16	£21
Weekends:	£26	£29

Blair Atholl Golf Club
Invertilt Road, Blair Atholl
Perthshire PH18 5TG
Advance Bookings **T**: 01796 481407
Holes: 9
SSS: SSS68

Alyth Golf Club
Alyth, Blairgowrie
Perthshire PH11 8HF
Advance Bookings **T**: 01828 632268
Holes: 18
Yardage: 6205 yds
SSS: 71

Auchterarder Golf Club
Orchil Road, Auchterarder
Perthshire PH3 1LS
Advance Bookings **T**: 01764 662804
Holes: 18
Yardage: 5778 yds
SSS: 68

Strathmore Golf Centre
Leroch, Alyth
Perthshire PH11 8NZ
Advance Bookings **T**: 01828 633322
Club Established: 1996
Website: www.strathmoregolf.com
Clubhouse **T**: 01828 633372
Secretary: Jane Taylor
T: 01828 633372
Fax: 01828 633533
Pro: Colin Smith
T: 01828 633322
Fax: 01828 633533
Visitor Restrictions: None
Concessions Available: None
Regular Closures: None

FACILITIES AVAILABLE:

CC   B   DR   PG   PS   CP   CH   B   D

COURSE 1: BANNALEROCH

Holes: 18
Yardage: 6454 yds
Designed by: John Salveson

Fees:	Round	Daily
Weekdays:	£22	£25
Weekends:	£33	£37.50

COURSE 2: LEITFIE LINKS

Holes: 9
Yardage: 1719
Par: 29
SSS: 29

Fees:	Daily
Weekday	£8
Weekends	£10

Scenic panoramic parkland courses
which are a test to the good golfer
and forgiving to the less good.

The Gleneagles Hotel Golf Courses

SEE PAGE 79

The Gleneagles Hotel,
Auchterarder, Perthshire
PH3 1NF
Advance Bookings **T**: 01764 694469
Email: visitor.golf@gleneagles.com
Website: www.gleneagles.com
Secretary: Dorothy M Welsh
Visitor Restrictions: No

FACILITIES AVAILABLE:

CC DR PG PS CP C CH B D

COURSE 1: KING'S COURSE

Holes: 18
Yardage: 6790 yds
Par: 70
SSS: 73
Designed by: James Braid

Blairgowrie Golf Club

Golf Course Road, Rosemount
Blairgowrie, Perthshire
PH10 6LG
Advance Bookings **T**: 01250 872622
Club Established: 1889
Clubhouse **T**: 01250 872383
Secretary: John Simpson
T: 01250 872622
Fax: 01250 875451
Pro: Charles Dernie
T: 01250 873116

FACILITIES AVAILABLE:

CC BH C PG PS CP CH B D

COURSE 1: LANSDOWNE COURSE

Holes: 18
Yardage: 6895 yds
Par: 72
SSS: 74
Designed by:
Dave Thomas/Peter Alliss

Dalmunzie Golf Course

Glenshee, Blairgowrie
Perthshire PH10 7QG
Advance Bookings **T**: 01250 885224
Club Established: 1948
Email: dalmunzie@aol.com
Visitor Restrictions: Yes
Concessions Available: Under 14
£5.Weekly Family £75

COURSE 2: QUEENS COURSE

Holes: 18
Yardage: 5965 yds
Par: 68
SSS: 70
Designed by: James Braid

COURSE 3: THE WEE COURSE

Holes: 9
Yardage: 1481
Par: 27

COURSE 4: THE PGA CENTENARY COURSE

Holes: 18
Yardage: 6551yds
Par: 72
SSS: 73
Designed by: Jack Nicklaus

Fees:	Round	Daily
Weekdays:	£40	£40
Weekends:	£70	£70

COURSE2: ROSEMOUNT COURSE

Holes: 18
Yardage: 6588 yds
Par: 72
SSS: 73
Designed by: James Braid

Fees:	Round	Daily
Weekdays:	£50	£50
Weekends:	£70	£70

COURSE 3: WEE COURSE

Holes: 9
Yardage: 4614 yds
SSS: 65
Designed by: Tom Morris/Peter Chalmers

Fees:	Round	Daily
Weekends:	£20	£20

FACILITIES AVAILABLE:

CP CH B D

Holes: 9
Yardage: 2099 yds
Par: 30
SSS: 60

Fees:	Round
Weekends:	£11

Glenisla Golf Centre

Pitcrocknie, Alyth
Blairgowrie, Perthshire PH11 8JJ
Advance Bookings **T**: 01828 632445
Club Established: 1998
Email: info@golf-glenisla.co.uk
Website: www.golf-glenisla.co.uk
Clubhouse **T**: 01828 632445
Fax: 01828 633749
Visitor Restrictions: Welcome 7 days call for availability
Concessions Available: Juniors 50%, Perthshire Green Card

FACILITIES AVAILABLE:

CC BH C PG PS CP CH B D

COURSE 1: GLENISLA GOLF COURSE

Holes: 18
Yardage: 6402 yds
Par: 71
SSS: 71
Designed by: Tony Wardle

Fees:	Round	Daily
Weekdays:	£22	£27
Weekends:	£33	£40

Recently voted one of Scotland's favourite courses, Glenisla is set amidst 180 acres of beautiful undulating parkland in Perthshire. Open all year, this quality golfing venue, which features over 40 bunkers and 5 water hazards, provides a superb challenge to golfers of all abilities and also offers the option to stay and play at the centre's delightful on-site B&B or self catering cottage. The superbly appointed, fully licensed clubhouse offers extensive facilities.

Comrie Golf Club

Laggan Braes, Comrie
Perthshire PH6 2LR
Advance Bookings **T**: 01786 880727
Holes: 9
Yardage: 6016 yds
Par: 70
SSS: 70

Central

Callander Golf Club

Aveland Road, Callander
Perthshire FK17 8EN
Club Established: 1890
Email: callandergc@nextcall.net
Clubhouse **T**: 01877 330090
Secretary: Mrs Sandra Smart
T: 01877 330090
Fax: 01877 330062
Pro: Allan Martin
T: 01877 330975
Visitor Restrictions: Handicap
certificates required Wed & Sun

FACILITIES AVAILABLE:

PG PS CP CH B D

COURSE 1: CALLANDER

Holes: 18
Yardage: 4447yds
Par: 63
SSS: 62
Designed by: Tom Morris/W. Fernie

Fees:	Round	Daily
Weekdays:	£18	£26
Weekends:	£26	£31

Callander golf club is a
picturesque, undulating parkland
course set in the heart of the
Trossachs.

SEE PAGE 62

Crieff Golf Club Ltd

Perth Road, Crieff
Perthshire PH7 3LR
Advance Bookings **T**: 01764 652909
Club Established: 1891
Email: bookings@crieffgolf.co.uk
Website: www.crieffgolf.co.uk
Clubhouse **T**: 01764 652397
Secretary: J S Miller
T: 01764 652397
Fax: 01764 653803
Pro: David Murchie
T: 01764 652909
Fax: 01764 655096
Visitor Restrictions: None
Concessions Available: No

FACILITIES AVAILABLE:

CC BH PG PS CP CH B D

COURSE 1: FERNTOWER COURSE

Holes: 18
Yardage: 6427 yds
Par: 71
SSS: 72
Designed by: James Braid

Fees:	Round	Daily
Weekdays:	£20/£26	£25/£35
Weekends:	£33/£42	

COURSE2: DORNOCK COURSE

Holes: 9
Yardage: 4744
Par: 64
SSS: 63
Designed by: James Braid

Fees:	Round	Daily
Weekdays:	£14	£14

Set in the dramatic countryside of
Perthshire. Crieff Golf Club
offers a most enjoyable days
golfing. The Ferntower course
has hosted various Championships throughout the years and
has magnificent views over the
Strathearn Valley. The short nine
hole Dornock course provides an
interesting challenge on a more
modest scale. The Club welcomes
visitors all the year round.

Crieff Hydro Golf Course

Crieff Hydro Hotel, Crieff
Perthshire PH7 3LQ
Advance Bookings **T**: 01764 652909
Holes: 9
Yardage: 2366
Par: 64
SSS: 64

Foulford Inn Golf Course

Crieff, Perthshire PH7 3LN
Advance Bookings **T**: 01764 652407
Holes: 9
Yardage: 916 yds
SSS: 27

Muthill Golf Club

Peat Road, Crieff,
Perthshire PH5 2DA
Advance Bookings **T**: 01764 681523
Holes: 9
Yardage: 2350 yds
SSS: 63

Dunblane New Golf Club

Perth Road, Dunblane
Perthshire FK15 0LJ
Advance Bookings **T**: 01786 821521
Holes: 18
Yardage: 5536 yds
SSS: 67

Dunkeld & Birnam Golf Club

Fungarth, Dunkeld
Perthshire PH8 0HU
Advance Bookings **T**: 01350 727524
Holes: 18
Yardage: 5508 yds
SSS: 67   **SEE PAGE 83**

Kenmore Golf Course

Mains of Taymouth, Kenmore
Perthshire EH15 2HN
Advance Bookings **T**: 01887 830226
Email: info@taymouth.co.uk
Website: www.taymouth.co.uk
Clubhouse **T**: 01887 830226
Visitor Restrictions: None
Concessions Available: Yes

FACILITIES AVAILABLE:

CC BH C PG PS CP CH B D

COURSE 1: KENMORE

Holes: 9
Yardage: 3026 yds
Par: 70
SSS: SSS69
Designed by: Robert Menzies

Fees:	Round	Daily
Weekdays:	£9(9)	£10(9)
	£13(18)	£14(18)
Weekends:	£16	£18

Set in magnificent highland
Perthshire Kenmore is a true
gem. Superb fairways and first
class greens – a good test of golf.

Strathtay Golf Club
Lorne Cottage, Dalguise
Dunkeld, Perthshire
PH8 0JX
Advance Bookings **T**: 01350 727797
Holes: 9
Yardage: 2041 yds
SSS: SSS63   **SEE PAGE 82**

Taymouth Castle Golf Course
Kenmore, Perthshire
PH15 2NT
Advance Bookings **T**: 01887 830228
Holes: 18
Yardage: 6066 yds
SSS: 69   **SEE PAGE 81**

Killin Golf Club
The Golf House, Killin
Perthshire FK21 8TX
Advance Bookings **T**: 01567 820312
Holes: 9
Yardage: 5066 yds
SSS: 65

King James VI Golf Club
Moncreiffe Island
Perth, Perthshire PH2 8NR
Advance Bookings **T**: 01738 632460
Club Established: 1858
Clubhouse **T**: 01738 625170
Secretary: Helen Blair
T: 01738 445132
Fax: 01738 445132
Pro: Andrew Crerar
T: 01738 632460
Visitor Restrictions: No visitors on Saturdays

FACILITIES AVAILABLE:

CC BH PG PS B D

COURSE 1: KING JAMES V1

Holes: 18
Yardage: 5664 yds
SSS: 68
Designed by: Old Tom Morris

Fees:	Round	Daily
Weekdays:	£18	£20
Weekends:	£25	£30

Dunning Golf Club
Rollo Park, Station Road
Dunning, Perth, Perthshire
PH2 0RH
Advance Bookings **T**: 01764 684747
Holes: 9
Yardage: 4836 yds
SSS: 63

Murrayshall Golf Club
Murrayshall Country House
Hotel, Scone, Perth
Perthshire PH2 7PH
Advance Bookings **T**: 01738 551171
Holes: 18
Yardage: 6043 yds
SSS: 70

North Inch Golf Club
North Inch (off Hay Street)
Perth, Perthshire PH1 5HT
Advance Bookings **T**: 01738 636481
Holes: 18
Yardage: 4936 metres
SSS: 63

The Craigie Hill Golf Club
Cherrybank, Perth, Perthshire
PH2 0NE
Advance Bookings **T**: 01738 622644
Club Established: 1911
Clubhouse **T**: 01738 624377
Secretary: Andrew Tunnicliffe
T: 01738 620829
Fax: 01738 620829
Pro: Ian Muir
T: 01738 622644
Visitor Restrictions: Saturdays

FACILITIES AVAILABLE:

CC PG PS CP CH B D

COURSE 1: CRAIGIE HILL GOLF CLUB

Holes: 18
Yardage: 5386 yds
SSS: 67

Fees:	Round
Weekdays:	£18
Weekends:	£30

A challenging golf course with panoramic views over Perth and the hills beyond. Playing to one's handicap is a real achievement.

Pitlochry Golf Course Ltd
Golf Course Road, Pitlochry
Perthshire PH16 5Q7
Advance Bookings **T**: 01796 472792
Holes: 18
Yardage: 5811 yds
SSS: 69

St. Fillans Golf Club
South Lochearn Road, St. Fillans
Perthshire PH6 2NJ
Advance Bookings **T**: 01764 685312
Holes: 9
Yardage: 5628 yds
SSS: 67

Stirlingshire

Buchanan Castle Golf Club
Drymen, Stiringshire
G63 0HY
Advance Bookings **T**: 01360 660369
Holes: 18
Yardage: 6086 yds
SSS: 69

Aberfoyle Golf Club
Braeval, Aberfoyle
Stirlingshire FK8 3UY
Advance Bookings **T**: 01877 382493
Holes: 18
Yardage: 5204 yds
SSS: 66

Bonnybridge Golf Club
Larbert Road, Bonnybridge
Stirlingshire FK4 1NY
Advance Bookings **T**: 01324 812822
Holes: 9
Yardage: 6058 yds
SSS: 69

Bridge of Allan Golf Club
Sunnylaw, Bridge of Allan
Stirlingshire FK9 4LY
Advance Bookings **T**: 01786 832332
Holes: 9
Yardage: 4932 yds
SSS: 65

Grangemouth Golf Course

Polmonthill by Falkirk,
Stirlingshire FK2 OYA
Advance Bookings **T**: 01324 503840
Club Established: 1974
Clubhouse **T**: 01324 711500
Secretary: Ian Hutton
T: 01324 712585
Fax: 01324 717087
Pro: Greg McFarlane
T: 01324 503840
Fax: 01324 503841
Visitor Restrictions: Not Sat 8am -
4pm
Concessions Available: Pensioners £5
M/W Juniors £5
Regular Closures: 25 Dec, 1 Jan

FACILITIES AVAILABLE:

CC PG PS CP B D

COURSE 1: GRANGEMOUTH GOLF CLUB

Holes: 18
Yardage: 6400
Par: 71
SSS: 70

Fees:	Round	Daily
Weekdays:	£14	£17.50
Weekends:	£20	£25

Grangemouth is a parkland
course with views over the Firth
of Forth. In a good test of golf
the 7th a par 3 over water and the
8th a testing dog leg par four
could be considered the feature
holes.

Strathendrick Golf Club

Drymen, Stirlingshire G83 8AA
Advance Bookings **T**: 01360 660695
Holes: 9
Yardage: 5116 yds
SSS: 65

Carmuirs Golf Course

136 Stirling Road, Camelon
Falkirk, Stirlingshire FK2 7YP
Advance Bookings **T**: 01324 639573
Holes: 18
Yardage: 6282yds
Par: 71
SSS: 70

Falkirk Golf Club

Carmuirs, 136 Stirling Road
Falkirk, Stirlingshire FK2 7YP
Advance Bookings **T**: 01324 611061
Email: falkirkcarmuirsgolfclub.co.uk
Clubhouse **T**: 01324 611061
Secretary: Mr John Elliot
T: 01324 611061
Fax: 01324 639573
Pro: Stewart Craig
T: 01324 612219
Visitor Restrictions: Yes

COURSE 1: CARMUIRS

Holes: 18
Yardage: 6290 yds
Par: 71
SSS: 70

Fees:	Round	Daily
Weekdays:	£20	£30
Weekends:	£30	£40

Polmont Golf Club Ltd.

Manuel Rigg, Maddiston
Falkirk, Stirlingshire FK2 0LS
Advance Bookings **T**: 01324 711277
Holes: 9
Yardage: 6603 yds
SSS: 70

Kilsyth Lennox Golf Club

Tak-Ma-Doon Road, Kilsyth
Stirlingshire G65 0HX
Advance Bookings **T**: 01236 824115
Holes: 18
Yardage: 5940 yds
SSS: 70

Glenbervie Golf Club

Stirling Road, Larbert
Stirlingshire FK5 4SJ
Advance Bookings **T**: 01324 562605
Holes: 18
Yardage: 6234 yds
SSS: 71

Campsie Golf Club

Crow Road, Lennoxtown
Stirlingshire G66 7HX
Advance Bookings **T**: 01360 310244
Holes: 18
Yardage: 5509 yds
SSS: 68

Falkirk Tryst Golf Club

86 Burnhead Road,
Stenhousemuir, Stirlingshire
FK5 4BD
Advance Bookings **T**: 01324 562415
Holes: 18
Yardage: 6083 yds
SSS: 69   SEE PAGE 61

Stirling Golf Club

Queen's Road, Stirling
Stirlingshire FK8 3AA
Advance Bookings **T**: 01786 473801
Holes: 18
Yardage: 6400 yds
SSS: 71

Dumfrieshire

Dumfries and County Golf Club

Nunfield, Edinburgh Road
Dumfries, Dumfrieshire
DG1 1JX
Advance Bookings **T**: 01387 268918
Club Established: 1913
Email: dumfriescounty
@netscapeonline.co.uk
Website: dumfriesandcounty-
gc.fsnet.co.uk
Clubhouse **T**: 01387 249921
Secretary: Brian R.M. Duguid
T: 01387 253585
Fax: 01387 253585
Pro: Stuart Syme
T: 01387 268918
Fax: 01387 268918
Visitor Restrictions: Yes
Concessions Available: No

FACILITIES AVAILABLE:

CC PG PS CP CH B D

COURSE 1: DUMFRIES AND COUNTY

Holes: 18
Yardage: 5928 yds
Par: 69
SSS: 69
Designed by: W. Fernie

Fees:	Round	Daily
Weekdays:	£26	£26
Weekends:	£26	

Excellent parkland course
renowned for its fine greens,
situated close to Dumfries town
centre and bordering the river Nith.

Powfoot Golf Club

Powfoot, Annan
Dumfrieshire DG12 5QE
Advance Bookings **T**: 01461 700276
Holes: 18
Yardage: 6010 yds
SSS: 70

Crichton Golf Club

Bankend Road, Dumfries
Dumfrieshire DG1 4TH
Advance Bookings **T**: 01387 247894
Holes: 9
Yardage: 2976 yds
SSS: 69

Dumfries and Galloway Golf Club

2 Laurieston Avenue
Dumfries
Dumfrieshire
DG2 7NY
Advance Bookings **T**: 01387 253582
Club Established: 1880
Clubhouse **T**: 01387 263848
Secretary: T.M. Ross
T: 01387 263848
Fax: 01387 263848
Pro: Joe Fergusson
T: 01387 256902
Fax: 01387 270297
Visitor Restrictions: Yes

FACILITIES AVAILABLE:

CC PP PS CP CH B D

Holes: 18
Yardage: 6309 yds
Par: 70
SSS: 71

Fees:	Round	Daily
Weekdays:	£26	£32
Weekends:	£26	£32

SEE PAGE 36

Pines Golf Centre

Lockerbie Road, Dumfries
Dumfrieshire DG1 3PF
Advance Bookings **T**: 01387 247444

Southerness Golf Club

Southerness, Dumfries
Dumfrieshire DG2 8AZ
Advance Bookings **T**: 01387 880677
Holes: 18
Yardage: 6564 yds
SSS: 73

SEE PAGE 33

Cally Palace Hotel Golf Club

Gatehouse of Fleet, Dumfrieshire
DG7 2DL
Advance Bookings **T**: 01557 814341
Holes: 18
Yardage: 5802 yds
Par: 70

Langholm Golf Course

Whitaside, Langholm
Dumfrieshire DG13 0JS
Advance Bookings **T**: 01387 381247
Holes: 9
Yardage: 3090 yds
SSS: 70

Hoddom Castle Golf Club

Hoddom Castle, Hoddom Bridge
Lockerbie, Dumfrieshire
DG11 1AS
Advance Bookings **T**: 01576 300251
Holes: 9
Yardage: 2274yds
SSS: 66

Lochmaben Golf Club

Castlehillgate, Lochmaben
Lockerbie, Dumfrieshire
DG11 1NT
Advance Bookings **T**: 01387 810552
Holes: 18
Yardage: 5357 yds
Par: 67
SSS: 66

Lockerbie Golf Club

Corrie Road, Lockerbie
Dumfrieshire, DG11 2NP
Advance Bookings **T**: 01576 203363
Holes: 18
Yardage: 5614 yds
SSS: 67

Moffat Golf Club

Coatshill, Moffat
Dumfrieshire, DG10 9SB
Advance Bookings **T**: 01683 220020
Holes: 18
Yardage: 5218 yds
SSS: 67

Sanquhar Golf Course

Blackaddie Road, Sanquhar
Dumfrieshire DG4 6JZ
Advance Bookings **T**: 01659 50577
Holes: 9
Yardage: 5594 yds
SSS: 68

Thornhill Golf Club

Blacknest, Thornhill
Dumfrieshire DG3 5DW
Advance Bookings **T**: 01848 330546
Holes: 18
Yardage: 6085 yds
SSS: 70

Kirkudbrightshire

Colvend Golf Club

Sandyhills,
Colvend by Dalbeattie
Kirkcudbrightshire DG5 4PY
Advance Bookings **T**: 01556 630398
Holes: 18
Yardage: 4716 yds
SSS: 67   **SEE PAGE 35**

Dalbeattie Golf Club

Off Maxwell Park
Dalbeattie
Kirkcudbrightshire
DG5 4LS
Advance Bookings **T**: 01556 610311
Club Established: 1894
Email: arthurhowatson@aol.com
Clubhouse **T**: 01556 611421
Secretary: Arthur Howatson
T: 01506 610311
Fax: 01506 610311
Visitor Restrictions: None except open
competitions
Concessions Available: Certain hotels
& Tourist board vouchers

FACILITIES AVAILABLE:

BH PG DR CP B D

Holes: 9
Yardage: 5710
Par: 68
SSS: 68

Fees:	Round	Daily
Weekdays:	£15	£15
Weekends:	£15	£15

Castle Douglas Golf Course

Abercromby Road,
Castle Douglas
Kirkcudbrightshire DG7 1BA
Advance Bookings **T**: 01556 502801
Holes: 9
Yardage: 5408 yds
SSS: 66

Gatehouse Golf Club

Laurieston Road, Gatehouse of
Fleet, Castle Douglas
Kirkcudbrightshire DG7 2BE
Advance Bookings **T**: 01557 814766
Holes: 9
Yardage: 2521 yds
SSS: 66   **SEE PAGE 31**

Kirkcudbright Golf Club

Stirling Crescent
Kirkcudbrightshire DG6 4EZ
Advance Bookings **T**: 01557 330314
Club Established: 1893
Email: david@kircudbrightgolf.co.uk
Website: www.kircudbrightgolf.co.uk
Clubhouse **T**: 01557 330314
Secretary: Mr Dave MacKenzie
T: 01557 330314
Fax: 01557 330314
Visitor Restrictions: Yes

FACILITIES AVAILABLE:

CC BH PG CP CH B D

Holes: 18
Yardage: 5739 yds
Par: 69
SSS: 69

New Galloway Golf Club

New Galloway
Kirkcudbrightshire
DG7 3RN
Advance Bookings **T**: 01644 450685
Holes: 9
Yardage: 2529 yds
SSS: 65

Wigtownshire

St. Medan Golf Club

Monreith, Port William
Newton Stewart, Wigtownshire
DG8 8NJ
Advance Bookings **T**: 01988 700358
Club Established: 1905
Clubhouse **T**: 01988 700358
Secretary: D Ronald Graham
Visitor Restrictions: Visitors welcome
all week
Regular Closures: Wed from
4pm Fri pm

FACILITIES AVAILABLE:

CC PG CP CH B D

COURSE 1: ST. MEDAN GOLF CLUB

Holes: 9
Yardage: 2227 yds
SSS: 63
Designed by: James Braid

Fees:	Round	Daily
Weekdays:	£15	£15
Weekends:	£20	£20

Testing 9 hole course with
unparalleled views of Luce Bay.
Catering and bar available from
April to September.

Portpatrick Golf Club

Golf Course Road, Portpatrick
Wigtownshire DG9 8TB
Advance Bookings **T**: 01776 810273
Club Established: 1903
Email:
enquiries@portpatrickgolfclub.com
Website:
www.portpatrickgolfclub.com
Clubhouse **T**: 01776 810273
Secretary: Mr J A Horberry
T: 01776 810273
Fax: 01776 810811
Visitor Restrictions: Yes
Concessions Available: Various local
hotels & Bunkered
Regular Closures: No

Dunskey – Links type course set
on cliffs above the picturesque
village of Portpatrick and
acclaimed 'the best kept secret in
South West Scotland'. Dinvin –
Par 3 hones the short game and is
ideal for 'holiday' golfers.

Wigtownshire County Golf Club

Mains of Park, Glenluce
Newton Stewart, Wigtownshire
DG8 0NN
Advance Bookings **T**: 01581 300420
Club Established: 1894
Email: enquiries
@wigtonshirecountygolfclub.com
Website:
www.wigtonshirecountygolfclub.com
Clubhouse **T**: 01581 300420
Secretary: Mr R McKnight (The
Secretary)
T: 01581 300420
Fax: 01581 300420
Regular Closures: No

FACILITIES AVAILABLE:

CC BH PG CP CH B D

COURSE 1: WIGTONSHIRE COUNTY

Holes: 18
Yardage: 5847 yds
Par: 70
SSS: 68
Designed by: C Hunter/W G
Cunningham

Fees:	Round	Daily
Weekdays:	£20	£22
Weekends:	£26	£28

FACILITIES AVAILABLE:

CC BH PG PS CP CH B D

COURSE 1: DUNSKEY

Holes: 18
Yardage: 5908
Par: 70
SSS: 69
Designed by: Wm Hunter (Prestwick)

Fees:	Round	Daily
Weekdays:	£24	£30
Weekends:	£36	£40

COURSE 2: DINVIN

Holes: 9
Yardage: 1504
Par: 27
SSS: 27
Designed by: Dunskey Estates

Fees:	Round	Daily
Weekdays:	£10 (18)	£10 (18)
Weekends:	£15	£15

Newton Stewart Golf Club

Kirroughtree Avenue, Minnigaff
Newton Stewart, Wigtownshire
DG8 6PF
Advance Bookings **T**: 01671 402172
Holes: 18
Yardage: 5900 yds
SSS: 70

Wigtown & Bladnoch Golf Club

Wigtown, Newton Stewart
Wigtownshire DG8 9EF.
Advance Bookings **T**: 01988 403354
Holes: 9
Yardage: 2521 metres
SSS: 67

Stranraer Golf Club

Creachmore, Leswalt
Stranraer, Wigtownshire
DG9 0LF
Advance Bookings **T**: 01776 870245
Holes: 18
Yardage: 6308 yds
SSS: 72

Fife

Aberdour Golf Club

Seaside Place, Aberdour
Fife KY3 0TX
Advance Bookings **T**: 01383 860080
Holes: 18
Yardage: 5460 yds
Par: 67
SSS: 66   **SEE PAGE 65**

Anstruther Golf Club

Marsfield, Shore Road
Anstruther, Fife KY10 3DZ
Advance Bookings **T**: 01333 310956
Secretary: Graham Simpson
Fax: 01333 312283

FACILITIES AVAILABLE:

CC PG CP B D

Holes: 9
Yardage: 4504 metres
Par: 62
SSS: 63
Fees: Round   Daily
Weekdays: £14 9/9 £16 10/9
                              SEE PAGE 63

Burntisland Golf House Club

Dodhead, Burntisland
Fife KY3 9LQ
Advance Bookings **T**: 01592 874093
Holes: 18
Yardage: 5897 yds
SSS: 70

Balbirnie Park Golf Club

Balbirnie Park, Markinch
by Glenrothes, Fife KY7 6NR
Advance Bookings **T**: 01592 612095
Holes: 18
Yardage: 6210 yds
SSS: 70

Auchterderran Golf Club

Woodend Road, Cardenden
Fife KY5 0NH
Holes: 9
Yardage: 5250 yds
SSS: 66

Charleton Golf Club

Colinsburgh, Fife KY9 1HG
Advance Bookings **T**: 01333 340505
Holes: 18
Yardage: 6149 yds
Par: 72
SSS: 70

Cowdenbeath Golf Club

Seco Place, Cowdenbeath
Fife KY4 8PD
Advance Bookings **T**: 01383 511918
Holes: 9
Yardage: 3261 yds
SSS: 70

Dora Golf Course

Seco Place, Cowdenbeath
Fife KY4 9AD
Advance Bookings **T**: 01383 511918
Holes: 18
Yardage: 6202
Par: 70
SSS: 70

Crail Golfing Society

Balcomie Club House, Fifeness
Crail, Fife KYl0 3XN
Advance Bookings **T**: 01333 450686
Holes: 18
Yardage: 5922 yds
Par: 69
SSS: 69

Cupar Golf Club

Hilltarvit, Cupar, Fife KY15 5JT
Advance Bookings **T**: 01334 653549
Holes: 9
Yardage: 5074 yds
SSS: 65

Elmwood Golf Course

Stratheden, Cupar
Fife KY15 5RS
Advance Bookings **T**: 01334 658780
Holes: 18
Yardage: 5951 yds
Par: 70
SSS: 68   **SEE PAGE 69**

Ladybank Golf Club

Annsmuir, Ladybank, Cupar
Fife KY15 7RA
Advance Bookings **T**: 01337 830814
Holes: 18
Yardage: 6601 yds
SSS: 72   **SEE PAGE 72**

Canmore Golf Club

Venturefair Avenue, Dunfermline
Fife KY12 0PE
Advance Bookings **T**: 01383 724969
Holes: 18
Yardage: 5376 yds
SSS: 66

Dunfermline Golf Club

Pitfirrane Crossford
Dunfermline, Fife KY12 8QW
Advance Bookings **T**: 01383 729061
Holes: 18
Yardage: 6126 yds
SSS: 70   **SEE PAGE 67**

Fife

Pitreavie (Dunfermline) Golf Club

Queensferry Road, Dunfermline
Fife, KY11 5PE
Advance Bookings **T**: 01383 722591
Holes: 18
Yardage: 6086 yds
SSS: 69

Elie Golf Club

Golf Course Lane, Elie, Fife
KY9 1AS
Advance Bookings **T**: 01333 330301
Holes: 18
Yardage: 6241 yds
SSS: 70

Falkland Golf Club

The Myre, Falkland, Fife
KY7 7AA
Advance Bookings **T**: 01337 857404
Holes: 9
Yardage: 2608 yds
SSS: 66   **SEE PAGE 68**

Glenrothes Golf Club

Golf Course Road, Glenrothes
Fife KY6 2LA
Advance Bookings **T**: 01592 758686
Holes: 18
Yardage: 6444 yds
Par: 71
SSS: 71

Leslie Golf Club

Balsillie Laws, Leslie
Glenrothes, Fife KY6 3EZ
Advance Bookings **T**: 01592 620040
Holes: 9
Yardage: 4940 yds
Par: 62
SSS: 65

Kinghorn Municipal Golf Club

Macduff Crescent, Kinghorn
Fife KY3 9RE
Advance Bookings **T**: 01592 890345
Holes: 18
Yardage: 4969 yds
SSS: 66

Dunnikier Park Golf Course

Dunnikier Way, Kirkcaldy
Fife KY1 3LP
Advance Bookings **T**: 01592 261599
Holes: 18
Yardage: 6601 yds
SSS: 72

Kirkcaldy Golf Club

Balwearie Road, Kirkcaldy
Fife KY2 5LT
Advance Bookings **T**: 01592 205240
Email: enquiries
@kircaldygolfclub.sol.co.uk
Secretary: Mr A Thomson
Pro Shop **T**: 01592 203258
Visitor Restrictions: Yes

FACILITIES AVAILABLE:

CC BH PG PS CP CH B D

Holes: 18
Yardage: 6038 yds
SSS: 69

Fees:	Round	Daily
Weekdays:	£22	£28
Weekends:	£28	£36

Leven Links Golf Course

The Promenade, Leven
Fife KY8 4HS
Advance Bookings **T**: 01333 428859
Email: secretary@levenlinks.com
Secretary: Sandy Herd
T: 01333 428859
Fax: 01333 428859
Visitor Restrictions: No visitors on
Saturdays

FACILITIES AVAILABLE:

CC PG CP B D

COURSE 1: LEVEN LINKS

Holes: 18
Yardage: 6436 yds
SSS: 70

Fees:	Round	Daily
Weekdays:	£30	£35
Weekends:	£40	£50

True seaside course, Leven is a
final qualifying course when the
Open Championship is held at St
Andrews.

St Michaels Golf Club

Leuchars, Fife
KY16 0DX
Advance Bookings **T**: 01334 839365
Holes: 18
Yardage: 5563 yds
SSS: 67

Lundin Ladies Golf Club

Woodlielea Road, Lundin Links
Leven, Fife KY5 6AR
Club Established: 1891
Email: lundinladies
@asmadasafish.com
Clubhouse **T**: 01333 320832
Secretary: Mrs Marion Mitchell
T: 01333 320832
Visitor Restrictions: Not Wed
April/August inclusive
Concessions Available: Yes for Juniors
Regular Closures: Xmas Day

FACILITIES AVAILABLE:

BH C PG CP

COURSE 1: LUNDIN LADIES

Holes: 9
Yardage: 2365 yds
Par: 68
SSS: 67
Designed by: James Braid

Fees:	Round	Daily
Weekends:	£12	£15

Parkland course with famous
standing stones on the second
fairway. Despite its name both
ladies and gentlemen visitors are
very welcome. Bookings are not
usually necessary. Reduced green
fees for juniors. Tea and coffee
facilities are available. Caddies by
prior arrangement only.
                        SEE PAGE 68

Scoonie Golf Club

North Links, Leven
Fife KY8 4SP
Advance Bookings **T**: 01333 307007
Holes: 18
Yardage: 4967 metres
SSS: 65

Lochgelly Golf Course
Lochgelly Golf Club

Cartmore Road, Lochgelly
Fife KY5 9PB
Advance Bookings **T**: 01592 780174
Holes: 18
Yardage: 5454
Par: 68
SSS: 67

Lochmore Meadows
Golf Course

Lochmore Meadows Country
Park, Crosshill, Lochgelly
Fife KY5 8BA
Advance Bookings **T**: 01592 414318
Holes: 9
Yardage: 6482
Par: 71
SSS: 71

Lundin Golf Club

Golf Road, Lundin Links
Fife KY8 6BA
Advance Bookings **T**: 01333 320202
Club Established: 1868
Email: secretary@lundingolfclub.co.uk
Website: www.lundingolfclub.co.uk
Clubhouse **T**: 01333 320202
Secretary: D.R. Thomson
T: 01333 320202
Fax: 01333 329743
Pro: David Webster
T: 01333 320081
Fax: 01333 329743
Visitor Restrictions: Yes
Concessions Available: No
Regular Closures: No

FACILITIES AVAILABLE:

CC PG PS CP B D

COURSE 1: LUNDIN

Holes: 18
Yardage: 6394 yds
SSS: 71
Designed by: James Braid

Fees:	Round	Daily
Weekdays:	£32	£40
Weekends:	£40	

Saline Golf Club

Kinneddar Hill, Saline
Fife KY12 9LT
Advance Bookings **T**: 01383 852591
Holes: 9
Yardage: 5302 yds
SSS: 66

St. Andrews Links Trust

Pilmour House, St Andrews
Fife KY16 9SF
Advance Bookings **T**: 01334 466666

OLD COURSE

Holes: 18
Yardage: 6566 yds
Par: 72
SSS: 72   SEE PAGE 70

NEW COURSE

Holes: 18
Yardage: 6604 yds
Par: 71
SSS: 72   SEE PAGE 71

EDEN COURSE

Holes: 18
Yardage: 6112 yds
Par: 70
SSS: 70

JUBILEE COURSE

Holes: 18
Yardage: 6805 yds
Par: 72
SSS: 73

STRATHTYRUM COURSE

Holes: 18
Yardage: 5094 yds
Par: 69
SSS: 70

BALGOVE COURSE

Holes: 9
Yardage: 1530 yds
Par: 30

Drumoig Golf Club
& Hotel

Drumoig, Leuchars, St. Andrews
Fife KY16 0BE
Advance Bookings **T**: 01382 541800
Holes: 18
Yardage: 7006 yds
SSS: 73

Duke's Course

Craigton, St Andrews, Fife
KY16 8NS
Advance Bookings **T**: 01334 474371
Holes: 18
Yardage: 7271
Par: 72

Kingsbarns Golf Club

Kingsbarns, St. Andrews
Fife KY16 8QD
Advance Bookings **T**: 01334 460860
Holes: 18
Yardage: 6174
Par: 72

Scotscraig Golf Club

Golf Road, Tayport, Fife
DD6 9DZ
Advance Bookings **T**: 01382 552515
Club Established: 1817
Email: scotscraig@scottishgolf.com
Clubhouse **T**: 01382 552701
Secretary: Barrie D Liddle
T: 01382 552515
Fax: 01382 553130
Pro: Stuart Campbell
T: 01382 552855
Visitor Restrictions: Mon/Fri 9.30-4.30
Sat/Sun 10-11 2.30-4.
Concessions Available: Discounts
Parties 12+
Regular Closures: None

FACILITIES AVAILABLE:

CC BH C PG PS CP CH B D

COURSE 1: SCOTSCRAIG

Holes: 18
Yardage: 6550 yds
Par: 71
SSS: 72
Designed by: James Braid

Fees:	Round	Daily
Weekdays:	£35	£40
Weekends:	£35	£40

Scotscraig is only 15 minutes
from the Old Course at St
Andrews and is regularly used as
a full qualifying course for the
Open Championship. Links
championship course.

Fife – Grampian & Moray

St Andrews Bay
Golf Resort & Spa, St Andrews
Fife KY16 8PN
Advance Bookings **T**: 01334 837000
Holes: 18
Yardage: 7026 yds
Par: 72

Thornton Golf Club
Station Road, Thornton, Fife
KY1 4DW
Advance Bookings **T**: 01592 771111
Holes: 18
Yardage: 6177 yds
SSS: 69

Aberdeenshire
Auchmill Golf Course
Bonnyview Road, Aberdeen
Aberdeenshire AB16 7FQ
Advance Bookings **T**: 01224 714577
Holes: 18
Yardage: 5082 yds
Par: 70
SSS: 68

Balnagask Golf Course
St Fitticks Road, Aberdeen
Aberdeenshire AB11 8TN
Advance Bookings **T**: 01224 876407
Holes: 18
Yardage: 5472 yds

Bon Accord Golf Club
19 Golf Road, Aberdeen
Aberdeenshire AB24 5QB
Advance Bookings **T**: 01224 633464
Holes: 18
Yardage: 6270 yds
SSS: 69

Caledonian Golf Club
20 Golf Road, Aberdeen
Aberdeenshire AB24 5QB
Advance Bookings **T**: 01224 632269
Holes: 18
Yardage: 6437 yds
SSS: 69

Craibstone Golf Centre
Craibstone Estate, Bucksburn
Aberdeen, Aberdeenshire
AB21 9YA
Advance Bookings **T**: 01224 716777
Email: smay@ab.sac.ac.uk
Website: www.craibstone.com
Clubhouse **T**: 01224 716777
Secretary: Susan May
T: 01224 711195
Fax: 01224 711298
Visitor Restrictions: None

FACILITIES AVAILABLE:

CC PG PG CP CH B D

COURSE 1: CRAIBSTONE

Holes: 18
Yardage: 5613 yds
Par: 68
SSS: 69
Designed by: Greens of Scotland

Fees:	Round	Daily
Weekdays:	£16	£20
Weekends:	£24	£30

Parkland course with stunning
views over Aberdeen. Large
undulating greens give a test of
golf to all levels. Visitors can play
seven days a week with a seven
day booking system in place.

Deeside Golf Club
Bieldside, Aberdeen
Aberdeenshire AB15 9DL
Advance Bookings **T**: 01224 869457
Holes: 18
Yardage: 6237 yds
SSS: SSS70

Hazlehead Golf Course
Hazlehead, Aberdeen
Aberdeenshire AB15 8BD
Advance Bookings **T**: 01224 321830
Holes: 18
Yardage: 5673 yds
Par: 70
SSS: 70   **SEE PAGE 85**

Kings Links Golf Course
Golf Road, Aberdeen
Aberdeenshire AB24 1RZ
Advance Bookings **T**: 01224 632269
Holes: 18
Yardage: 6270 yds
SSS: 70

Murcar Golf Club
Bridge of Don, Aberdeen
Aberdeenshire AB23 8BD
Advance Bookings **T**: 01224 704354
Holes: 18
Yardage: 6287 yds
SSS: 71

Northern Golf Club
22 Golf Road, Aberdeen
Aberdeenshire AB24 3BQ
Advance Bookings **T**: 01224 522000
Holes: 18
Yardage: 6270 yds
SSS: 69

Peterculter Golf Club
Burnside Road, Peterculter
Aberdeen, Aberdeenshire
AB14 0LN
Advance Bookings **T**: 01224 735245
Holes: 18
Yardage: 5601 yds
SSS: 69

Royal Aberdeen Golf Club
Links Road, Bridge of Don
Aberdeen, Aberdeenshire
AB23 8AT
Advance Bookings **T**: 01224 702221
Holes: 18
Yardage: 6403 yds
SSS: 71

Aboyne Golf Club
Golf Road, Aboyne
Aberdeenshire AB34 5HP
Advance Bookings **T**: 01339 886328
Holes: 18
Yardage: 5910 yds
SSS: 69   **SEE PAGE 87**

Tarland Golf Club
Aberdeen Road, Tarland
Aboyne, Aberdeenshire
AB34 4TB
Advance Bookings **T**: 013398 81413
Holes: 9
Yardage: 5888 yds
SSS: 68

114 SCOTLAND **HOME OF GOLF**

Alford Golf Club

Montgarrie Road, Alford
Aberdeenshire AB33 8AE
Advance Bookings **T**: 019755 62178
Email: golf@alford.co.uk
Website: http://golf.alford.co.uk
Clubhouse **T**: 019755 62178
Secretary: John Pennet
T: 019755 62178
Fax: 019755 62178

FACILITIES AVAILABLE:

CC PG PS CP CH B D

COURSE 1: ALFORD GOLF CLUB

Holes: 18
Yardage: 5483 yds
SSS: 65

Fees:	Round	Daily
Weekdays:	£13	£20
Weekends:	£19	£26

Ballater Golf Club

Victoria Road, Ballater
Aberdeenshire AB35 5QX
Advance Bookings **T**: 01339 755567
Holes: 18
Yardage: 5638 yds
SSS: 67

East Aberdeenshire Golf Course

Millden, Balmedie
Aberdeenshire AB23 8YY
Advance Bookings **T**: 01358 742111
Email: info@e-aberdeenshire.co.uk
Secretary: Mr Forrest
Fax: 01343 742123

FACILITIES AVAILABLE:

CC BH PG PS CP CH B D

COURSE 1: EAST ABERDEENSHIRE

Holes: 18
Yardage: 6276 yds
Par: 71
SSS: 71

Fees:	Round	Daily
Weekdays:	£15	£20
Weekends:	£25	£30

Banchory Golf Club

Kinneskie Road, Banchory
Aberdeenshire AB31 5TA
Advance Bookings **T**: 01330 822447
Club Established: 1905
Email: info@banchorygolfclub.co.uk
Website:
www.banchorygolfclub.co.uk
Clubhouse **T**: 01330 822365
Secretary: Bill Crighton
T: 01330 822365
Fax: 01330822491
Pro: David Naylor
T: 01330 822447
Fax: 01330 822447
Visitor Restrictions: Spaces limited
Tues & Weekends
Concessions Available: Parties over 12
-10% discount

FACILITIES AVAILABLE:

CC BH PG PS CP CH B D

COURSE 1: BANCHORY

Holes: 18
Yardage: 5775 yds
Par: 69
SSS: 68

Fees:	Round	Daily
Weekdays:	£20	£23
Weekends:	£28	N/A

Banchory is where Open winner
Paul Lawrie began his career. The
picturesque par 69 course is set
above the banks of the river Dee
on Royal Deeside and offers a
challenge to golfers of all
standards.

SEE PAGE 88

Inchmarlo Golf Centre

Inchmarlo, Banchory
Aberdeenshire AB31 4BQ
Advance Bookings **T**: 01330 822557
Holes: 18
Yardage: 6198
Par: 71   SEE PAGE 86

Cruden Bay Golf Club

Aulton Road, Cruden Bay
Aberdeenshire AB42 0NN
Advance Bookings **T**: 01779 812285
Holes: 18
Yardage: 6395 yds
Par: 70
SSS: 72

Braemar Golf Course

Cluniebank Road, Braemar
Aberdeenshire AB35 5XX
Advance Bookings **T**: 013397 41618
Club Established: 1902
Clubhouse **T**: 013397 41618
Secretary: John Pennet
T: 01224 704471
Fax: 013397 41400

FACILITIES AVAILABLE:

CC PG CP CH PS B D

Holes: 18
Yardage: 4916 yds
SSS: 64

Fees:	Round	Daily
Weekdays:	£16	£19
Weekends:	£21	£24

McDonald Golf Club

Hospital Road, Ellon
Aberdeenshire AB41 9AW
Advance Bookings **T**: 01358 720576
Holes: 18
Yardage: 5986 yds
Par: 70
SSS: 69

Fraserburgh Golf Club

Fraserburgh, Aberdeenshire
AB43 8TL
Advance Bookings **T**: 01346 518287
Holes: 18
Yardage: 6278 yds
Par: 70
SSS: 68

Inverallochy Golf Course

Whitelink, Inverallochy
Fraserburgh, Aberdeenshire
AB43 8XY
Advance Bookings **T**: 01346 582000
Holes: 18
Yardage: 5244 yds
SSS: 66

Huntly Golf Club

Cooper Park, Huntly
Aberdeenshire AB54 4SH
Advance Bookings **T**: 01466 792643
Holes: 18
Yardage: 5899 yds
SSS: 66

Grampian & Moray

Insch Golf Club
Golf Terrace, Insch
Aberdeenshire AB52 6JY
Advance Bookings **T**: 01464 820363
Holes: 18
Yardage: 5395 yds
SSS: 66

Inverurie Golf Club
Blackhall Road, Inverurie
Aberdeenshire AB51 5JB
Advance Bookings **T**: 01467 620193/
620207
Club Established: 1923
Email:
administrator@inveruriegc.co.uk
Website: www.inveruriegc.co.uk
Clubhouse Phone: 01467 624080
Secretary: Ms B Rogerson
Phone: 01467 624080
Fax: 01467 621051
Pro: Mr M Lees
Phone: 01467 620193
Fax: 01467 620193

FACILITIES AVAILABLE:

CC CP CH PS B D

Holes: 18
Yardage: 5711 yds
SSS: 68

Fees:	Round	Daily
Weekdays:	£14	£18

This parkland course has an open
varied start and a picturesque tree
lined section to finish.

Old Meldrum Golf Club
Kirk Brae, Old Meldrum
Inverurie, Aberdeenshire
AB51 0DJ
Advance Bookings **T**: 01651 872648
Holes: 18
Yardage: 5988 yds
SSS: 69

Kemnay Golf Club
Monymusk Road, Kemnay
Aberdeenshire AB51 5RA
Advance Bookings **T**: 01467 642060
Holes: 18
Yardage: 6342 yds
SSS: 71

Kintore Golf Club
Balbithan Road, Kintore
Aberdeenshire, AB51 0UR
Advance Bookings **T**: 01467 632631
Holes: 18
Yardage: 6019 yds
Par: 70
SSS: 69

Longside Golf Club
Westend, Longside
Aberdeenshire AB42 7XJ
Advance Bookings **T**: 01779 821558
Holes: 18
Yardage: 5215 yds
SSS: 66

Newburgh-on-Ythan Golf Club
Beach Road, Newburgh
Aberdeenshire AB41 6BE
Advance Bookings **T**: 01358 789058
Holes: 18
Yardage: 6162 yds
Par: 72
SSS: 70

Newmachar Golf Club
Swailend, Newmachar
Aberdeenshire AB21 7UU
Advance Bookings **T**: 01651 863002
Holes: 18
Yardage: 6628 yds
Par: 72
SSS: 74

Meldrum House
Meldrum House Estate
Oldmeldrum, Aberdeenshire
AB51 0AE
Advance Bookings **T**: 01651 873553
Holes: 18
Yardage: 6379 yds
Par: 70
SSS: 72

Peterhead Golf Club
Riverside Drive, Peterhead
Aberdeenshire AB42 1LT
Advance Bookings **T**: 01779 472149
Holes: 18
Yardage: 6173 yds
Par: 70
SSS: 71

Portlethen Golf Club
Badentoy Road, Portlethen
Aberdeenshire AB12 4YA
Advance Bookings **T**: 01224 781090
Holes: 18
Yardage: 6707 yds
SSS: 72

Rosehearty Golf Club
Mason's Arms Hotel, Rosehearty
Aberdeenshire AB43 7JJ
Advance Bookings **T**: 01346 571250
Holes: 9
Yardage: 4394 yds
SSS: 62

Dunecht House Golf Course
Dunecht, Skene, Aberdeenshire
AB32 7AW
Advance Bookings **T**: 01330 860223
Holes: 9
Yardage: 3135 yds
Par: 70
SSS: 70

Turriff Golf Club
Rosehall, Turriff, Aberdeenshire
AB53 4HD
Advance Bookings **T**: 01888 562982
Holes: 18
Yardage: 6107 yds
SSS: 69

Westhill Golf Club (1977)
Westhill Heights, Westhill
Aberdeenshire AB32 6RY
Advance Bookings **T**: 01224 742567
Holes: 18
Yardage: 5849 yds
SSS: 69

Banffshire

Buckpool Golf Club
Barhill Road, Buckie
Banffshire AB56 1DU
Advance Bookings **T**: 01542 832236
Holes: 18
Yardage: 6257 yds
SSS: 70

Strathlene Golf Club

Portessie, Buckie, Banffshire
AB56 2DJ
Advance Bookings **T**: 01542 831798
Holes: 18
Yardage: 5977 yds
SSS: 69

Dufftown Golf Club

Methercluny, Tomintoul Road
Dufftown, Banffshire AB55 4BS
Advance Bookings **T**: 01340 820325
Holes: 18
Yardage: 5308 yds
SSS: 67

Duff House Royal Golf Club

The Barnyards, Banff
Banffshire AB45 3SX
Advance Bookings **T**: 01261 812062
Club Established: 1910
Email: enquiries@banffgolf.co.uk
Website:
www.theduffhouseroyalgolfclub.co.uk
Clubhouse **T**: 01261 812062
Secretary: Mrs Jan Corbett
T: 01261 812062
Fax: 01261 812224
Pro: R.S. Strachan
T: 01261 812075
Visitor Restrictions: Some Weekends
Concessions Available: Yes on
application

FACILITIES AVAILABLE:

CC PG CP CH PS B D

Course 1: Duff House Royal
Holes: 18
Yardage: 6161 yds
Par: 68
SSS: 70
Designed by: Dr Alister MacKenzie

Fees:	Round	Daily
Weekdays:	£18	£25
Weekends:	£24	£30

Beautiful parkland course
designed by Dr Alister
MacKenzie of Augusta fame.
Large two tiered greens are a
feature of the course.

SEE PAGE 90

Keith Golf Course

Fife Park, Keith, Banffshire
AB55 5DF
Advance Bookings **T**: 01542 882469
Holes: 18
Yardage: 5802 yds
Par: 69
SSS: 68

Royal Tarlair Golf Club

Buchan Street, Macduff
Banffshire AB44 1TA
Advance Bookings **T**: 01261 832897
Holes: 18
Yardage: 5866 yds
SSS: 68

Cullen Golf Club

The Links, Cullen, Buckie
Banffshire AB56 2UU
Advance Bookings **T**: 01542 840685
Club Established: 1870
Email: www.cullengolfclub.co.uk
Clubhouse **T**: 01542 840685
Secretary: Mr Ian Findlay
T: 01542 840685
Concessions Available: No

FACILITIES AVAILABLE:

PG CP B D

COURSE 1: CULLEN GOLF CLUB

Holes: 18
Yardage: 4610 yds
Par:
SSS: SSS62

Fees:	Round	Daily
Weekdays:	£12	£16
Weekends:	£18	£22

Situated on the delightful Bay Of
Cullen, this seaside course,
dotted with rocky outcrops and
bound by natural hazards, will be
enjoyed by all standards of golfer.

Kincardineshire

Stonehaven Golf Club

Cowie, Stonehaven
Kincardineshire AB39 3RH
Advance Bookings **T**: 01569 762124
Club Established: 1888
Clubhouse **T**: 01569 762124
Secretary: W A Donald
T: 01569 762124
Fax: 01569 765973
Visitor Restrictions: Welcome M/F
9.30-4.00 Sat 4+ Sun 9.30+

FACILITIES AVAILABLE:

CC PG CP CH B D

COURSE 1: STONEHAVEN

Holes: 18
Yardage: 5103 yds
Par: 66
SSS: 65
Designed by: A. Simpson

Fees:	Round	Daily
Weekdays:	£15	£22
Weekends:	£20	£25

SEE PAGE 84

Torphins Golf Club

Torphins, Banchory
Kincardineshire AB31 4JU
Advance Bookings **T**: 01339 882115
Holes: 9
Yardage: 4738 yds
SSS: 64

Auchenblae Golf Club

Auchenblae, Laurencekirk
Kincardineshire AB30 1AA
Advance Bookings **T**: 01561 320002
Holes: 9
Yardage: 2226 yds
SSS: 30

Morayshire

Garmouth & Kingston Golf Club

Garmouth, Fochabers
Morayshire IV32 7LE
Advance Bookings **T**: 01343 870388
Holes: 18
Yardage: 5935 yds
Par: 69
SSS: 69

Grampian & Moray

Elgin Golf Club

Hardhillock, Birnie Road
Elgin, Morayshire
IV30 3SX
Advance Bookings **T**: 01343 542338
Club Established: 1906
Email: secretary@elgingolfclub.com
Website: www.elgingolfclub.com
Clubhouse **T**: 01343 542338
Secretary: David Black
T: 01343 542338
Fax: 01343 542341
Pro: Kevin Stables
T: 01343 542884
Visitor Restrictions: Yes
Concessions Available: Yes

FACILITIES AVAILABLE:

CC BH C DR PG PS CP CH B D

COURSE 1: HARDHILLOCK

Holes: 18
Yardage: 6401 yds
SSS: 71
Designed by: John MacPherson

Fees:	Round	Daily
Weekdays:	£25	£25
Weekends:	£30	£30

Craggan Golf Course

Craggan Farm, Grantown-on-Spey
Morayshire PH26 3NT
Advance Bookings **T**: 01479 872120
Secretary **T**: 01479 872120
Fax: 01479 872325

FACILITIES AVAILABLE:

CP B D

COURSE 1: CRAGGAN

Holes: 18
Yardage: 2159
Par: 54
SSS:
Designed by:

Fees:	Round	Daily
Weekdays:		
Weekends:	£10	£10

Par three course on the western
outskirts of Grantown on Spey.

Grantown on Spey Golf Club

Golf Course Road
Grantown-on-Spey
Morayshire PH26 3HY
Advance Bookings **T**: 01479 872079
Email: secretary
@grantownonspeygolfclub.co.uk
Website: www.grantownonspey-
golfclub.co.uk
Clubhouse **T**: 01479 872079
Secretary: James S Macpherson
T: 01479 872079
Fax: 01479 873725
Visitor Restrictions: Yes

FACILITIES AVAILABLE:

CC BH PG PS CH B D

Holes: 18
Yardage: 5710 yds
SSS: 68

Fees:	Round
Weekdays:	£20
Weekends:	£20

Hopeman Golf Club

The Clubhouse, Hopeman
Morayshire, IV30 5YA
Advance Bookings **T**: 01343 830578
Club Established: 1906
Email: Hopemangc@aol.com
Website: www.hopeman-golf-
club.co.uk
Clubhouse **T**: 01343 830578
Secretary: Jim Fraser
T: 01343 830578
Fax: 01343 830152
Visitor Restrictions: Yes
Concessions Available: Yes
Regular Closures: No

FACILITIES AVAILABLE:

CC BH PG PS CP B D

COURSE 1: HOPEMAN

Holes: 18
Yardage: 5590 yds
Par: 68
SSS: 67
Fees: on application

The superb views over the Moray
Firth, where occasionally
dolphins can be sighted, are an
additional bonus at this excellent
golfing location.

Spey Bay Golf Club

Spey Bay Hotel, Spey Bay
Fochabers, Morayshire
IV32 7PJ
Advance Bookings **T**: 01343 820424
Holes: 18
Yardage: 6092 yds
SSS: 69

The Nairn Golf Club

Seabank Road, Nairn
Morayshire IV12 4HB
Advance Bookings **T**: 01667 453208
Club Established: 1887
Email: bookings@nairngolf.co.uk
Website: www.nairngolf.co.uk
Clubhouse **T**: 01667 453208
Secretary **T**: 01667 453208
Fax: 01667 456328
Pro: Robin P Fyfe
T: 01667 452787
Fax: 01667 451315
Visitor Restrictions: Some Sat/Sun
Concessions Available: £50 round in
April

FACILITIES AVAILABLE:

CC C DR PG PS CP CH B D

COURSE 1: NAIRN CHAMPIONSHIP
(BLUE TEES)

Holes: 18
Yardage: 6745 yds
Par: 72
SSS: 74
Designed by: Archie Simpson, Old
Tom Morris & James Braid

Fees:	Round	Daily
Weekdays:	£70	£70
Weekends:	N/A	N/A

This traditional Scottish golf
links course was created on the
shores of the Moray Firth from a
wilderness of whins and heather,
and tests the talents of
professional and amateur alike.
Founded in 1887 and extended
by Archie Simpson, Old Tom
Morris and James Braid it is now
one of the best courses in the
UK, hosting the 37th Walker Cup
in 1999. Nairn Members have
attained the highest honour in
golf, that of becoming the
Capatin of the Royal and Ancient
Golf Club of St Andrews.

Kinloss Country Golf Course

Kinloss, Forres, Morayshire
IV36 0UB
Advance Bookings **T**: 01343 850242
Holes: 9
Yardage: 2535 yds
Par: 68

Forres Golf Club

Muiryshade, Forres
Morayshire IV36 0RD
Advance Bookings **T**: 01309 672250
Holes: 18
Yardage: 6236 yds
SSS: 70

Moray Golf Club

Stotfield, Lossiemouth
Morayshire IV31 6QS
Advance Bookings **T**: 01343 812018
Holes: 18
Yardage: 6990 yds
Par: 71
SSS: 73   **SEE PAGE 89**

Nairn Dunbar Golf Club

Lochloy Road, Nairn
Morayshire IV12 5AE
Advance Bookings **T**: 01667 452741
Holes: 18
Yardage: 6720 yds
SSS: 73

Rothes Golf Club

Blackhall, Rothes
Morayshire AB38 7AN
Advance Bookings **T**: 01340 831443
Holes: 18
Yardage: 4972 yds
SSS: 64

Caithness

Wick Golf Club

Reiss, Caithness
Caithness KW1 4RW
Advance Bookings **T**: 01955 602726
Holes: 18
Yardage: 5796 yds
SSS: 69

Lybster Golf Club

Main Street, Lybster
Caithness KW1 6BL
Advance Bookings **T**: 01593 721308
Holes: 9
Yardage: 1929 yds
SSS: 61

Reay Golf Club

Reay, Thurso, Caithness
KW14 7RE
Advance Bookings **T**: 01847 811288
Club Established: 1893
Email: info@reaygolfclub.co.uk
Website: www.reaygolfclub,co.uk
Clubhouse **T**: 01847 811288
Secretary: Bill McIntosh
T: 01847 894189 or 07702 568333
Fax: 01847 894189
Visitor Restrictions: None
Concessions Available: Various 2 for 1

FACILITIES AVAILABLE:

CC BH PG CP CH B D

COURSE 1: REAY

Holes: 18
Yardage: 5831 yds
Par: 69
SSS: 69
Designed by: Original 12 holes by
James Braid

Fees:	Round	Daily
Weekdays:	£20	£20
Weekends:	£20	£20

Most northerly 18 hole seaside
links on the British mainland.
Visitors welcome all year.

Thurso Golf Club

Newlands of Geise, Thurso
Caithness KW14 7LF
Advance Bookings **T**: 01847 893807
Holes: 18
Yardage: 5828 yds
SSS: 69

Inverness-shire

Traigh Golf Course

Traigh, Arisaig
Inverness-shire PH39 4NT
Advance Bookings **T**: 01687 450337
Holes: 9
Yardage: 2456 yds
SSS: 65

Boat of Garten Golf Club

Nethybridge Road
Boat of Garten, Inverness-shire
PH24 3BQ
Advance Bookings **T**: 01479 831282
Holes: 18
Yardage: 5866 yds
SSS: 69

Aigas Golf Course

by Beauly, Inverness-shire IV4 7AD
Advance Bookings **T**: 01463 782942
Holes: 9
Yardage: 2439 yds
SSS: 64

Carrbridge Golf Club

Inverness Road, Carrbridge
Inverness-shire PH23 3AU
Advance Bookings **T**: 01479 841623
Email: enquiries@carrbridgegolf.com
Website: www.carrbridgegolf.com
Secretary: Mrs Anne Baird
Visitor Restrictions: Yes
Holes: 9
Yardage: 5400 yds
Par: 72
SSS: 68

Fort Augustus Golf Club

Markethill, Fort Augustus
Inverness-shire PH32 4DP
Advance Bookings **T**: 01320 366309
Holes: 9
Yardage: 5454 yds
SSS: 67

Fort William Golf Club

North Road, Torlundy
Fort William, Inverness-shire
PH33 6SN
Advance Bookings **T**: 01397 704464
Holes: 18
Yardage: 6217 yds
SSS: 71

Torvean Golf Club

Glenurquhart Road, Inverness
Inverness-shire IV3 8JN
Advance Bookings **T**: 01463 225651
Holes: 18
Yardage: 5784 yds
SSS: 68

Highlands

Kingussie Golf Club

Gynack Road, Kingussie
Inverness-shire PH21 1LR
Advance Bookings **T**: 01540 661600
Holes: 18
Yardage: 5555 yds
SSS: 68

Inverness Golf Club

Culcabock Road, Inverness
Inverness-shire IV2 3XQ
Advance Bookings **T**: 01463 239882
Club Established: 1883
Email: igc@freeuk.com
Website:
www.invernessgolfclub.co.uk
Clubhouse **T**: 01463 233422
Secretary: J S Thomson
T: 01463 239882
Fax: 01463 239882
Pro: A.P.Thomson
T: 01463 231989
Fax: 01463 243464
Visitor Restrictions: Limited times
Thurs/Sat
Concessions Available: Yes
Regular Closures: No

FACILITIES AVAILABLE:

CC C PG PS CP CH B D

COURSE 1: INVERNESS

Holes: 18
Yardage: 6256 yds
Par: 69
SSS: 70
Designed by: Unknown/redesigned by
James Braid

Fees:	Round	Daily
Weekdays:	£29	£29
Weekends:	£39	£39

Situated one mile from the city
centre this well maintained
parkland course is an excellent
test of golf for all categories of
golfer.

SEE PAGE 91

Newtonmore Golf Club

Golf Course Road, Newtonmore
Inverness-shire PH20 1AT
Advance Bookings **T**: 01540 673878
Holes: 18
Yardage: 6029 yds
Par: 70
SSS: 68

Spean Bridge Golf Club

2 Aonachan Gardens, Spean Bridge,
Inverness-shire PH34 4ET
Advance Bookings **T**: 01397 703379
Holes: 9
Yardage: 2203 yds
SSS: 62

Loch Ness Golf Course

Fairways Leisure, Castle Heather
Inverness, Inverness-shire
IV2 6AA
Advance Bookings **T**: 01463 713335
Club Established: 1996
Email: info@golflochness.com
Website: www.golflochness.com
Clubhouse **T**: 01463 713335
Secretary: Neil D Hampton
T: 01463 713335
Fax: 01463 712695
Pro: Martin Piggott
T: 01463 713334
Fax: 01463 712695
Visitor Restrictions: No
Concessions Available: Yes
Greenfeesavers, 2 Fore 1
Regular Closures: No

FACILITIES AVAILABLE:

CC BH C DR PG PS CP CH B D

COURSE 1: LOCH NESS GOLF COURSE

Holes: 18
Yardage: 6772 yds
Par: 73
SSS: 72
Designed by: Caddies GC Design

Fees:	Round	Daily
Weekends:	£25	£30

Located on the South West
outskirts of Inverness, the generous
fairways and large greens make this
challenging parkland course
suitable for golfers of all abilities.

Abernethy Golf Club

Nethy Bridge, Inverness-shire
PH25 3EB
Advance Bookings **T**: 01479 821305
Email: info@abernethygolfclub.com
Website: www.abernethygolfclub.com
Secretary: Mr Bob Robbie
T: 01479 821305
Fax: 01479 821305

FACILITIES AVAILABLE:

CH D CC

Holes: 9
Yardage: 2519
Par: 66
SSS: 66

Fees:	Round	Daily
Weekends:	£13	£16

Ross-shire

Fortrose & Rosemarkie Golf Club

Ness Road East, Fortrose
Ross-shire IV10 8SE
Advance Bookings **T**: 01381 620529
Email: secretary@fortrosegolfclub.co.uk
Website: www.fortrosegolfclub.co.uk
Clubhouse **T**: 01381 620529
Secretary: Mr William Baird
T: 01381 620529
Fax: 01381 621328

FACILITIES AVAILABLE:

CC BH PG PS CP CH D B

COURSE 1: FORTROSE & ROSEMARKIE

Holes: 18
Yardage: 5875 yds
SSS: 69
Designed by: James Braid

Fees:	Round	Daily
Weekdays:	£22	£27
Weekends:	£33	£38

This private club welcomes
visitors to the course with sea on
three sides of the peninsula and
bottle nose dolphins in the firth.

SEE PAGE 96

Alness Golf Club

Ardross Road, Alness
Ross-shire IV17 0QA
Advance Bookings **T**: 01349 883877
Holes: 18
Yardage: 4886 yds
SSS: 64

Gairloch Golf Club
Gairloch, Ross-shire IV21 2BQ
Advance Bookings **T**: 01445 712407
Holes: 9
Yardage: 4250 yds
SSS: 63

Invergordon Golf Club
King George Street, Invergordon
Ross-shire IV18 0BA
Advance Bookings **T**: 01349 852715
Holes: 18
Yardage: 6020 yds
SSS: 69

Lochcarron Golf Club
Lochcarron, Ross-shire IV54 8YA
Advance Bookings **T**: 01520 766211
Holes: 9
Yardage: 1789 yds
SSS: 60

Muir of Ord Golf Club
Great North Road, Muir of Ord
Ross-shire IV6 7SX
Advance Bookings **T**: 01463 870825
Holes: 18
Yardage: 5557 yds
Par: 68
SSS: 68

Stromness Golf Club
Ness, Stromness, Ross-shire
KW16 3DL
Advance Bookings **T**: 01856 850772
Holes: 18
Yardage: 4762 yds
SSS: 68

Strathpeffer Spa Golf Club
Strathpeffer, Ross-shire IV14 9AS
Advance Bookings **T**: 01997 421219
Holes: 18
Yardage: 4792 yds
SSS: 64 **SEE PAGE 95**

Tarbat Golf Club
Portmahomack, Tain
Ross-shire IV20 1YB
Advance Bookings **T**: 01862 871236
Holes: 9
Yardage: 2990 yds
Par: 31
SSS: 66

Tain Golf Club
Chapel Road, Tain, Ross-shire
IV19 1JE
Advance Bookings **T**: 01862 892314
Club Established: 1890
Email: info@tain-golfclub.co.uk
Website: www.tain-golfclub.co.uk
Clubhouse **T**: 01862 892314
Secretary: Mrs Kathleen Ross
T: 01862 892314
Fax: 01862 892099
Pro Shop **T**: 01862 893313
Visitor Restrictions: No
Concessions Available: on application

FACILITIES AVAILABLE:

CC BH C PG PS CP CH B D

COURSE 1: TAIN GOLF CLUB

Holes: 18
Yardage: 6404 yds
SSS: 71
Designed by: Old Tom Morris

Fees:	Round	Daily
Weekdays:	£30	£36
Weekends:	£36	£46

First class, Old Tom Morris
designed links course with
outstanding views. Visitors and
parties are always welcome.

SEE PAGE 93

Sutherland

Brora Golf Club
Golf Road, Brora, Sutherland
KW9 6QS
Advance Bookings **T**: 01408 621417
Club Established: 1891
Email: secretary@broragolf.co.uk
Website: www.broragolf.co.uk
Secretary: Mr James Fraser
T: 01408 621417
Fax: 01408 622157

FACILITIES AVAILABLE:

CC BH PG PS CP CH B D

COURSE 1: BRORA

Holes: 18
Yardage: 6110 yds
Par: 69
SSS: 69

Fees:	Round	Daily
Weekdays:	£25	£30
Weekends:	£35	£40

Bonar Bridge-Ardgay Golf Club
Migdale Road, Bonar Bridge
Sutherland IV24 3EJ
Advance Bookings **T**: 01863 766199
Holes: 9
Yardage: 5284 yds
SSS: 66

Royal Dornoch Golf Club
Golf Road, Dornoch
Sutherland IV25 3LW
Advance Bookings **T**: 01862 810219
Email: rdgc@royaldornoch.com
Website: www.royaldornoch.com
Clubhouse **T**: 01862 811220
Secretary: John Duncan
T: 01862 811220
Fax: 01862 810792
Pro: Andrew Skinner
T: 01862 810902
Visitor Restrictions: Yes
Regular Closures: Tournament week
2 August

FACILITIES AVAILABLE:

CC BH C PG PS CP CH B D

COURSE 1: CHAMPIONSHIP COURSE

Holes: 18
Yardage: 6514 yds
Par: 70
SSS: 73
Designed by: Old Tom Morris/
J Sutherland

Fees:	Round	Daily
Weekdays:	£60	£70
Weekends:	TBC	TBC

COURSE 2: STRUIE COURSE

Holes: 18
Yardage: 5438 yds
Par: 69
SSS: 66

Fees:	Round	
Weekdays:	£18.00	
Weekends:	£25.00	

The Championship Course, rated
9th amongst Britain's courses is a
classic links of rare subtlety in a
splendid setting. Golfers will find
the target well presented,
although rarely easy to reach. A
second Par 69 links, The Struie,
provides another enjoyable
experience suitable to all abilities.

Carnegie Club
Skibo Castle, Dornoch
Sutherland IV25 3RQ
Advance Bookings **T**: 01862 894600
Holes: 18
Yardage: 6671 yds
SSS: 72

Durness Golf Club
Durness, Sutherland IV27 4PN
Advance Bookings **T**: 01971 511364
Holes: 9
Yardage: 5555 yds
SSS: 69

Golspie Golf Club
Ferry Road, Golspie
Sutherland KW10 6ST
Advance Bookings **T**: 01408 633266
Holes: 18
Yardage: 5836 yds
SSS: 68

Helmsdale Golf Club
Golf Road, Helmsdale
Sutherland KW8 6JA
Advance Bookings **T**: 01431 821650
Holes: 2 x 9
Yardage: 3720 yds
SSS: SSS60

East Lothian

Luffness New Golf Club
The Clubhouse, Aberlady
East Lothian EH32 0QA
Advance Bookings **T**: 01620 843336
Holes: 18
Yardage: 6122 yds
SSS: 70

Dunbar Golf Club
East Links, Dunbar
East Lothian EH42 1LL
Advance Bookings **T**: 01368 862317
Holes: 18
Yardage: 6404 yds
SSS: 71

Winterfield Golf Club
St. Margarets, Back Road
Dunbar, East Lothian EH42 1XE
Advance Bookings **T**: 01368 862280
Holes: 18
Yardage: 5155 yds
Par: 65
SSS: 64

Craigielaw Golf Club
Aberlady, East Lothian EH32 0PY
Advance Bookings **T**: 01875 870801
Club Established: 2001
Email: info@craigielawgolfclub.com
Website: www.craigielawgolfclub.com
Clubhouse **T**: 01875 870802
Manager: Alan L Aitkin
T: 01875 870801
Fax: 01875 870620
Pro: Derek Scott
T: 01875 870 800
Fax: 01875 870620
Visitor Restrictions: Club
Competitions

FACILITIES AVAILABLE:

CC CP BH C DR PG PS B D

COURSE 1: CRAIGIELAW

Holes: 18
Yardage: 6601 yds
Par: 71
SSS: 71
Designed by: Tom McKenzie of
Donald Steel & Co

Fees:	Round	Daily
Weekdays:	£35	£45
Weekends:	£50	£60

Inspired by the great links
courses of Britain, particularly
those on land which are less
dominated by dunes, Cragielaw is
equal to many of the finest
examples of such courses which
are conveniently located nearby
in the East Lothian area.

Gifford Golf Club
Calroust, Tweeddale Avenue
Gifford, East Lothian EH41 4QN
Advance Bookings **T**: 01620 810267
Holes: 9
Yardage: 6243 yds
Par: 71
SSS: 70

Kilspindie Golf Club
The Clubhouse, Aberlady
East Lothian EH32 0QD
Advance Bookings **T**: 01875 870358
Club Established: 1867
Email: kilspindie@btconnect.com
Clubhouse **T**: 01875 870216
Secretary: P B Casely
T: 01875 870358
Pro Shop **T**: 01875 870216
Visitor Restrictions: No
Concessions Available: No
Regular Closures: No

FACILITIES AVAILABLE:

CC BH C PG PS CP CH B D

COURSE 1: KILSPINDIE

Holes: 18
Yardage: 5480 yds
SSS: 66

Fees:	Round	Daily
Weekdays:	£27.50	£33
Weekends:	£44	£55

SEE PAGE 45

Castle Park Golf Club
Gifford, East Lothian EH41 4PL
Advance Bookings **T**: 01620 810733
Website:
www.castleparkgolfclub.co.uk
Secretary: Stuart Fortune
Fax: 01620 810723
Pro **T**: 01368 862872

FACILITIES AVAILABLE:

CC PG B DR CP B D

COURSE 1: CASTLE PARK

Holes: 9
Yardage: 5266
SSS: 68

Fees:	Round
Weekdays:£12.00/£14.00	
Weekends:£18.00/£22.00	

In May 2002 Castle Park will
open a second nine holes which
should turn the course from a
great 'fun for a visit' course to an
18 hole gem. The new course
will measure 6121yds (72) medal,
5848 (71) yellow markers and
5551yds (72) for ladies. Castle
Park offers a range of packages
for outings or parties.

Gullane Golf Course

Gullane, East Lothian EH31 2BB
Advance Bookings **T**: 01620 842255
Email: bookings@gullanegolfclub.com
Website: www.gullanegolfclub.com
Pro Shop **T**: 01620 843111
Visitor Restrictions: Yes

FACILITIES AVAILABLE:

CC PG PS CP B D

COURSE 1: GULLANE NO 1 GOLF COURSE

Holes: 18
Yardage: 6466 yds
SSS: 72

Fees:	Round	Daily
Weekdays:	£65	£80
Weekends:	£90	N/A

COURSE 2: GULLANE NO 2 GOLF COURSE

Holes: 18
Yardage: 6244yds
SSS: 70

Fees:	Round	Daily
Weekdays:	£29	£35
Weekends:	£41	£50

COURSE 3: GULLANE NO 3 GOLF COURSE

Holes: 18
Yardage: 5252yds
SSS: 66

Fees:	Round	Daily
Weekdays:	£17	£24
Weekends:	£25	£33

Honourable Company of Edinburgh Golfers

Muirfield, Gullane
East Lothian EH31 2EG
Advance Bookings **T**: 01620 842123
Holes: 18
Yardage: 6601 yds
SSS: 73

Haddington Golf Club

Amisfield Park, Haddington
East Lothian EH41 4PT
Advance Bookings **T**: 01620 823627
Holes: 18
Yardage: 6317 yds
SSS: 70

North Berwick (The Glen)

East Links, Tantallon Terrace
North Berwick, East Lothian
EH39 4LE
Advance Bookings **T**: 01620 892221
Holes: 18
Yardage: 6079 yds
SSS: 69   SEE PAGE 47

The North Berwick Golf Club

Beach Road, North Berwick
East Lothian EH39 4BB
Advance Bookings **T**: 01620 895040
Holes: 18
Yardage: 6420 yds
SSS: 71

Musselburgh Golf Club

Monktonhall, Musselburgh
East Lothian EH21 6SA
Advance Bookings **T**: 0131 665 2005
Club Established: 1938
Email: secretary
@themusselburghgolfclub.com
Website:
www.themusselburghgolfclub.com
Clubhouse **T**: 0131 653 2591
Secretary: G Finlay
T: 0131 665 2005
Pro: Fraser Mann
T: 0131 665 7055
Fax: 0131 665 7055
Visitor Restrictions: Yes

FACILITIES AVAILABLE:

CC B PG PS CP CH B D

COURSE 1: MONKTONHALL

Holes: 18
Yardage: 6725 yds
Par: 71
SSS: 73
Designed by: James Braid

Parkland course which has hosted
the Scottish Amateur and
Professional Championships.

SEE PAGE 44

Longniddry Golf Club

Links Road, Longniddry
East Lothian EH32 0NL
Advance Bookings **T**: 01875 852141
Holes: 18
Yardage: 6260 yds
Par: 68
SSS: 70

Musselburgh Links

The Old Golf Course
10 Balcarres Road, Musselburgh
East Lothian EH21 7SB
Advance Bookings **T**: 0131 665 5438
Email:
info@musselburgholdlinks.co.uk
Website:
www.musselburgholdlinks.co.uk
Clubhouse **T**: 0131 665 6981
Secretary: Mr Lionel Freedman
T: 0131 665 4861
Visitor Restrictions: Yes
Concessions Available: £4.50
Child/OAP

FACILITIES AVAILABLE:

PG CP CH B D

COURSE 1: MUSSELBURGH LINKS, THE
OLD GOLF COURSE

Holes: 9
Yardage: 2808
Par: 34
SSS: 34

Fees:	Round	Daily
Weekdays:	£8.00	£8.00

Dating back to at least 1567
Musselburgh Links, The Old
Course is the oldest playing golf
course in the world. Host to six
open championships between
1874 & 1889 and the first ladies
competition in 1811. Step back in
time by playing its nine holes
with hickory clubs, which are
available for hire.

Royal Musselburgh Golf Club

Preston Grange House
Prestonpans, East Lothian
EH32 9RP
Advance Bookings **T**: 01875 810276
Holes: 18
Yardage: 6237 yds
SSS: 70

Lothians

Whitekirk Golf Course

Whitekirk, North Berwick
East Lothian EH39 5PR
Advance Bookings **T**: 01620 870300
Club Established: 1995
Email: countryclub@whitekirk.com
Website: www.whitekirk.com
Clubhouse **T**: 01620 870300
Secretary: David Brodie
Phone: 01620 870300
Fax: 01620 870330
Pro: Paul Wardell
Phone: 01620 870300
Fax: 01620 870330
Visitor Restrictions: Not before 10 am Sat/Sun
Concessions Available: Juniors Half Price

FACILITIES AVAILABLE:

CC BH DR PG PS CP CH B D

COURSE 1: WHITEKIRK

Holes: 18
Yardage: 6526 yds
SSS: 72

Fees:	Round	Daily
Weekdays: £20	£30
Weekends: £28	£45

Whitekirk is a heathland style course with panoramic views around the East Lothian coastline. It is a challenging course for all levels of golfer. Groups are welcome and a variety of packages are offered.

SEE PAGE 48

Midlothian

Newbattle Golf Club Ltd

Abbey Road, Dalkeith
Midlothian EH22 3AD
Advance Bookings **T**: 0131 663 2123
Holes: 18
Yardage: 6012 yds
SSS: 70

Braid Hills Golf Course

Braid Hills Approach, Edinburgh
Midlothian EH10 6JZ
Advance Bookings **T**: 0131 447 6666
Holes: 2 x 18
Yardage: 6172 / 4832 yds
Par: 70/65
SSS: 68/63

Broomieknowe Golf Club

36 Golf Course Road, Bonnyrigg
Midlothian EH19 2HZ
Advance Bookings **T**: 0131 663 9317
Club Established: 1805/1806
Email: administrator@broomieknowe.com
Website: www.broomieknowe.com
Clubhouse **T**: 0131 663 7844
Secretary: John Fisher
T: 0131 663 9317
Fax: 0131 663 2152
Pro: Mark Patchett
T: 0131 660 2035
Visitor Restrictions: Yes

FACILITIES AVAILABLE:

CC BH PG PS CP CH B D

COURSE 1: BROOMIEKNOWE

Holes: 18
Yardage: 6150 yds
Par: 70
SSS: 70
Designed by: Ben Sayers & James Braid

Fees:	Round	Daily
Weekdays:	£19	£25
Weekends:	£25.00	N/A

Situated on high ground but not hilly and providing beautiful views of the Firth of Forth and Moorfoot Hills, Broomieknowe is an excellent test of golf.

Bruntsfield Links

32 Barnton Avenue
Davidsons Mains, Edinburgh
Midlothian EH4 6JH
Advance Bookings **T**: 0131 3362006
Holes: 18
Yardage: 6407 yds
SSS: 71

Carricknowe Golf Club

27 Glendevon Park, Edinburgh
Midlothian EH12 5XA
Advance Bookings **T**: 0131 337 2217
Holes: 18
Yardage: 6500 yds
SSS: 68

Baberton Golf Club

50 Baberton Avenue
Juniper Green, Edinburgh
Midlothian EH14 5DU
Advance Bookings **T**: 0131 453 4911
Club Established: 1893
Email:
babertongolfclub@btinternet.com
Website: www.baberton.co.uk
Secretary: Mr B. M. Fluckhart
T: 0131 453 4911
Fax: 0131 453 4678
Pro: Ken Kelly
T: 0131 453 3555
Visitor Restrictions: No visitor before 4pm Sat

FACILITIES AVAILABLE:

CC PG CH PS CP B D

COURSE 1: BABERTON

Holes: 18
Yardage: 6129 yds
Par: 69
SSS: 70
Designed by: Willie Park Jnr

Fees:	Round	Daily
Weekdays:	£22	£30
Weekends:	£32	£35

Challenging but fair test to all handicap level of golfers with majestic views of the Pentland Hills, Forth Bridges, Edinburgh Castle and the Edinburgh skyline.

Craigentinny Golf Course

Craigentinny Avenue, Edinburgh
Midlothian EH7 6RG
Advance Bookings **T**: 0131 554 7501
Holes: 18
Yardage: 5418 yds
Par: 67
SSS: 65

Craigmillar Park Golf Club

1 Observatory Road, Edinburgh
Midlothian EH9 3HG
Advance Bookings **T**: 0131 667 0047
Holes: 18
Yardage: 5851 yds
SSS: 69

Lothianburn Golf Club

106a Biggar Road, Edinburgh
Midlothian EH10 7DU
Advance Bookings **T**: 0131 445 5067
Club Established: 1893
Clubhouse **T**: 0131 445 2206
Secretary: W F A Jardine
T: 0131 445 6057
Pro: Kurt Mungall
T: 0131 445 2288
Fax: 0131 445 2288
Visitor Restrictions: Weekends can be difficult
Concessions Available: Discounts for groups 16+
Regular Closures: None

FACILITIES AVAILABLE:

CC PG PS CH B D

COURSE 1: LOTHIANBURN

Holes: 18
Yardage: 5662
Par: 71
SSS: 68
Designed by: James Braid

Fees:	Round	Daily
Weekdays:	£16.50	£22.50
Weekends:	£22.50	£27.50

Excellent greens, magnificent views, comfortable clubhouse, Good professional teacher, Friendly people – what more could anyone want!

Duddingston Golf Club

137-139 Duddingston Road West
Edinburgh, Midlothian
EH15 3QD
Advance Bookings **T**: 0131 661 7688
Holes: 18
Yardage: 6420 yds
SSS: 71 SEE PAGE 42

Kingsknowe Golf Club Ltd

326 Lanark Road, Edinburgh
Midlothian EH14 2JD
Advance Bookings **T**: 0131 441 1144
Holes: 18
Yardage: 5979 yds
SSS: 69

Liberton Golf Club

297 Gilmerton Road, Edinburgh
Midlothian EH16 5UJ
Advance Bookings **T**: 0131 664 3009
Holes: 18
Yardage: 5299 yds
SSS: 66

Murrayfield Golf Club

43 Murrayfield Road, Edinburgh
Midlothian EH12 6EU
Advance Bookings **T**: 0131 337 3478
Holes: 18
Yardage: 5765 yds
Par: 70
SSS: 69

Merchants of Edinburgh Golf Club

10 Craighill Gardens, Edinburgh
Midlothian EH10 5PY
Advance Bookings **T**: 0131 447 1219
Club Established: 1907
Email: admin@merchantsgolf.com
Website: www.merchantsgolf.com
Clubhouse **T**: 0131 447 1219
Secretary: John Elvin
T: 0131 447 1219
Fax: 0131 466 9833
Pro: Neil Colquhoun
T: 0131 447 8709
Fax: 0131 447 8709
Visitor Restrictions: Bookings 48hrs in advance
Concessions Available: Yes
Regular Closures: No

FACILITIES AVAILABLE:

CC BH PG PS CP CH B D

COURSE 1: MERCHANTS OF EDINBURGH GOLF CLUB

Holes: 18
Yardage: 4889 yds
Par: 65
SSS: 64

Fees:	Round	Daily
Weekdays:	£16	£24
Weekends:	£20	N/A

The Merchants is a short but very interesting parkland course. There are no par 5's and seven par 3's. The course boasts a unique natural setting and offers magnificent views.

Mortonhall Golf Club

231 Braid Road, Edinburgh
Midlothian EH10 6PB
Advance Bookings **T**: 0131 4472411
Holes: 18
Yardage: 6548 yds
SSS: 72

Portobello Golf Club

Stanley Street, Edinburgh
Midlothian EH15 1JJ
Advance Bookings **T**: 0131 669 4361
Holes: 9
Yardage: 2400 yds
SSS: 32

Prestonfield Golf Club

6 Priestfield Road North
Edinburgh, Midlothian
EH16 5HS
Advance Bookings **T**: 0131 667 9665
Holes: 18
Yardage: 6214 yds
Par: 70
SSS: 70 SEE PAGE 41

Ravelston Golf Club

24 Ravelston Dykes Road
Edinburgh, Midlothian EH4 5NZ
Advance Bookings **T**: 0131 343 2177
Holes: 9
Yardage: 5200 yds
SSS: 65

Royal Burgess Golfing Society

181 Whitehouse Road, Edinburgh
Midlothian EH4 6BY
Advance Bookings **T**: 0131 339 2075
Holes: 18
Yardage: 6494 yds
SSS: 71

Silverknowes Golf Club (Private)

Silverknowes Parkway, Edinburgh
Midlothian EH4 5ET
Advance Bookings **T**: 0131 336 5359
Holes: 18
Yardage: 6298 yds
Par: 71
SSS: 70

Lothians

Swanston Golf Club

111 Swanston Road, Edinburgh
Midlothian EH10 7DS
Advance Bookings **T**: 0131 445 2239
Holes: 18
Yardage: 5024 yds
SSS: 66

Torphin Hill Golf Club

Torphin Road, Edinburgh
Midlothian EH13 0PL
Advance Bookings **T**: 0131 441 1100
Holes: 18
Yardage: 5020 yds
SSS: 66

Marriott Dalmahoy Hotel & Country Club

Kirknewton, Midlothian
EH27 5EB
Advance Bookings **T**: 0131 333 1845
Holes: 18
Yardage: 6677 yds
Par: 72
SSS: 72

Vogrie Golf Course

Vogrie Estate Country Park
Gorebridge, Midlothian
EH23 4NU
Advance Bookings **T**: 01875 821716
Holes: 9
Yardage: 2530
SSS: 33

Kings Acre Golf Course

Lasswade, Midlothian EH18 1AU
Advance Bookings **T**: 0131 663 3456
Holes: 18
Yardage: 5935 yds
SSS: 70

Melville Golf Course

Melville Golf Centre, Lasswade
Midlothian EH18 1AN
Advance Bookings **T**: 0131 663
8038/0131 654 0224
Secretary: Mr MacFarlane
Pro **T**: 0131 663 8138
Visitor Restrictions: Yes
Holes: 18
Yardage: 4580 yds
Par: 66
SSS: 62
Fees: Round
Weekdays: £12/£16

Glencorse Golf Club

Milton Bridge, Midlothian
EH26 0RD
Advance Bookings **T**: 01968 677177
Holes: 18
Yardage: 5205 yds
SSS: 66   SEE PAGE 43

Ratho Park Golf Club

Ratho, Newbridge, Midlothian
EH28 8NX
Advance Bookings **T**: 0131 333 2566
Holes: 18
Yardage: 5900 yds
SSS: 68

Dundas Parks Golf Club

South Queensferry, Midlothian
EH30 9SS
Advance Bookings **T**: 0131 331 3179
Holes: 9
Yardage: 6024 yds
SSS: 70   SEE PAGE 40

West Lothian

Bathgate Golf Course

Edinburgh Road, Bathgate
West Lothian EH48 1BA
Advance Bookings **T**: 01506 630505
Club Established: 1892
Email: bathgate.golfclub@lineone.net
Clubhouse **T**: 01506 652232
Secretary: W.A. Osborne
T: 01506 630505
Fax: 01506 636775
Pro: S. Strachan
T: 01506 630553
Visitor Restrictions: limited at weekend

FACILITIES AVAILABLE:

CC BH PG PS CP CH B D

COURSE 1: BATHGATE

Holes: 18
Yardage: 6325 yds
SSS: 70
Designed by: Wm Park Jnr

Fees:	Round	Daily
Weekdays:	£17	£33
Weekends:	£22	£33

Greenburn Golf Club

60 Greenburn Gardens, Whitburn
Bathgate, West Lothian EH47 8NL
Advance Bookings **T**: 01501 770292
Holes: 18
Yardage: 6000 yds
SSS: 69

Niddry Castle Golf Club

Castle Road, Winchburgh
Broxburn, West Lothian
EH52 6RQ
Advance Bookings **T**: 01506 891097
Holes: 9
Yardage: 5514 yds
SSS: 67

Uphall Golf Club

Uphall, Broxburn, West Lothian
EH52 6JT
Advance Bookings **T**: 01506 856404
Holes: 18
Yardage: 5592 yds
SSS: 67

Linlithgow Golf Club

Braehead, Linlithgow
West Lothian EH49 6QF
Advance Bookings **T**: 01506 842585
Holes: 18
Yardage: 5729 yds
SSS: 68   **SEE PAGE 37**

West Lothian Golf Club

Airngath Hill by Linlithgow
Linlithgow, West Lothian
EH49 7RH
Advance Bookings **T**: 01506 826030
Holes: 18
Yardage: 6578 yds
SSS: 71

Pumpherston Golf Club

Drumshoreland Road
Pumpherston, Livingston
West Lothian
EH53 0LF
Advance Bookings **T**: 01506 432869
Club Established: 1895
Website:
www.pumpherstongolfclub.com
Clubhouse **T**: 01506 432869
Secretary: Mr I McArthur
T: 01506 432869
Fax: 01506 438250
Visitor Restrictions: None

FACILITIES AVAILABLE:

PG CP B D

COURSE 1: PUMPHERSTON GOLF COURSE

Holes: 18
Yardage: 6004 yds
Par: 70
SSS: 69
Designed by: Glen Andrews

Fees:	Round	Daily
Weekdays:	£18	£22
Weekends:	£25	£33

New undulating parkland course
with landscaped contours. Trees
and ponds are used to create an
interesting challenge to all classes
of golfer.

SEE PAGE 39

Deer Park Golf & Country Club

Golf Course Road
Knightsridge West, Livingston
West Lothian EH54 8AB
Advance Bookings **T**: 01506 431037
Holes: 18
Yardage: 6688 yds
SSS: 72   **SEE PAGE 38**

Harburn Golf Club

West Calder, West Lothian
EH55 8RS
Advance Bookings **T**: 01506 871131
Club Established: 1933
Secretary: J. McLinden
T: 01506 871131
Fax: 01506 870286
Pro: Mr S Mills
T: 01506 871582
Visitor Restrictions: Yes
Concessions Available: Yes
Regular Closures: No

FACILITIES AVAILABLE:

CC BH PG CP CH B D

COURSE 1: HARBURN GOLF CLUB

Holes: 18
Yardage: 5921 yds
Par: 69
SSS: 69

Fees:	Round	Daily
Weekdays:	£18	£23
Weekends:	£25	£34

Situated 14 miles west of
Edinburgh. Parkland course in
quiet rural surroundings.
Comfortable clubhouse offering
extensive bar menu.

Polkemmet Country Park

West Lothian Council
Park Centre, Whitburn
West Lothian EH47 0AD
Advance Bookings **T**: 01501 743905
Holes: 9
Yardage: 2969 metres

Argyll

Dunaverty Golf Club

Southend, Campbeltown
Argyll PA28 6RX
Advance Bookings **T**: 01586 830677
Holes: 18
Yardage: 4799 yds
SSS: 63   **SEE PAGE 57**

The Machrihanish Golf Club

Machrihanish, Campbeltown
Argyll PA28 6PT
Advance Bookings **T**: 01586 810277
Club Established: 1876
Email: secretary@machgolf.com
Website: www.machgolf.com
Clubhouse **T**: 01586 810213
Secretary: Anna Anderson
T: 01586 810213
Fax: 01586 810221
Pro: Ken Campbell
T: 01586 810277
Visitor Restrictions: Yes

FACILITIES AVAILABLE:

CC C PG PS CP B D

COURSE 1: MACHRIHANISH

Holes: 18
Yardage: 6225 yds
SSS: 71

Fees:	Round	Daily
Weekdays:	£30(Sun/Fri)	£40(Sat)
Weekends:	£50(Sun/Fri)	£60(Sat)

SEE PAGE 58

Craignure Golf Club

Scallastle, Craignure, Argyll
PA65 6AY
Advance Bookings **T**: 01680 300402
Holes: 9
Yardage: 5233 yds
SSS: 66

Blairmore & Strone Golf Club

High Road, Blairmore, Dunoon
Argyll PA23 8JJ
Advance Bookings **T**: 01369 840676
Holes: 9
Yardage: 2112 yds
Par: 62
SSS: 62

Strathclyde

Cowal Golf Club
22 Ardenslate Road, Dunoon
Argyll PA23 8NN
Advance Bookings **T**: 01369 705673
Holes: 18
Yardage: 6063 yds
SSS: 70

Dunoon Golf Course
Ardenslate Road, Dunoon
Argyll PA23 8NN
Advance Bookings **T**: 01369 705673
Holes: 18
Yardage: 6063 yds
Par: 70
SSS: 70

Dalmally Golf Club
Orchy Bank, Dalmally, Argyll
PA33 1AS
Advance Bookings **T**: 01838 200370
Club Established: 1987
Email: aj.burke@talk21.com
Website: www.loch-
awe.com/golfclub/
Secretary: A J Burke
T: 01838 200370
Visitor Restrictions: 18/18.30pm
Mon/Tue 9/9.30 13/13.30 Sun
Concessions Available: None
Regular Closures: None

FACILITIES AVAILABLE:

CP CH B

COURSE 1: DALMALLY

Holes: 9
Yardage: 2264 yds
Par: 64
SSS: 63
Designed by: C. Macfarlane-Barron

Fees:	Round	Daily
Weekdays:	£10	£10
Weekends:	£10	£10

Flat parkland course bounded by
the river Orchy and surrounded
by mountains. Many bunkers and
water hazards. A very interesting
test of golf.

Innellan Golf Club
Knockamillie Road, Innellan
Argyll PA23 7SG
Advance Bookings **T**: 01369 703242
Holes: 9
Yardage: 2342 yds
SSS: 64

Inveraray Golf Club
North Cromalt
Lochgilphead Road, Inveraray
Argyll PA32 8XT
Advance Bookings **T**: 01499 302079
Holes: 9
Yardage: 2753 yds
SSS: SSS68

Carradale Golf Course
Carradale, Kintyre, Argyll
PA28 6RY
Advance Bookings **T**: 01583 431378
Holes: 9
Yardage: 2387 yds
SSS: 64

Lochgilphead Golf Club
Blarbuie Road, Lochgilphead
Argyll PA31 8LE
Advance Bookings **T**: 01546 602340
Holes: 9
Yardage: 4484 yds
Par: 63
SSS: 63

Drimsynie Golf Course
Lochgoilhead, Argyll PA24 8AD
Advance Bookings **T**: 01301 703247
Holes: 9
Yardage: 1817 yds
SSS: 60

Glencruitten Golf Course
Glencruitten Road, Oban, Argyll
PA34 4PU
Advance Bookings **T**: 01631 562868
Holes: 18
Yardage: 4452 yds
SSS: 63 SEE PAGE 97

Bute Golf Club
Sithean, Academy Road
Rothesay, Argyll PA20 0BG
Advance Bookings **T**: 01700 504369
Holes: 9
Yardage: 2497 yds
SSS: 64

Tarbert Golf Club
Kilberry Road, Tarbert, Argyll
PA29 6XX
Advance Bookings **T**: 01880 820565
Holes: 9
Yardage: 4744 yds
SSS: 64

Taynuilt Golf Club
Laroch, Taynuilt, Argyll PA35 1JE
Advance Bookings **T**: 01866 822429
Holes: 9
Yardage: 4302 yds
SSS: 61

Kyles of Bute Golf Club
The Moss, Kames, Tighnabruaich
Argyll PA21 2EE
Advance Bookings **T**: 01700 811603
Club Established: 1906
Secretary: Dr Jeremy Thomson
T: 01700 811603
Visitor Restrictions: Sunday am
Concessions Available: Yes

FACILITIES AVAILABLE:

CP CH

Holes: 9
Yardage: 4778 yds
Par: 66
SSS: 64

Fees:	Round	Daily
Weekdays:	£8	£10
Weekends:	£8	£10

Tobermory Golf Club
Erray Road, Tobermory, Argyll
PA75 6PS
Advance Bookings **T**: 01688 302238
Holes: 9
Yardage: 4890
SSS: 64

Ayrshire

Belleisle Golf Club

Belleisle Park, Ayr, Ayrshire
KA7 4DU
Advance Bookings **T**: 01292 441258
Holes: 18
Yardage: 6431 yds
SSS: 64

Dalmilling Municipal Golf Club

Westwood Avenue, Ayr, Ayrshire
KA8 0QY
Advance Bookings **T**: 01292 263893
Holes: 18
Yardage: 5724 yds
SSS: 68

Beith Golf Club

Bigholm Road, Beith, Ayrshire
KA15 2JR
Advance Bookings **T**: 01505 503166
Holes: 18
Yardage: 5641 yds
SSS: 68

Loudoun Gowf Club

Edinburgh Road, Galston
Ayrshire KA4 8PA
Advance Bookings **T**: 01563 821993
Holes: 18
Yardage: 6016 yds
SSS: 69

Brunston Castle Golf Club

Dailly, Girvan, Ayrshire
KA26 9GD
Advance Bookings **T**: 01465 811471
Holes: 18
Yardage: 6681 yds
SSS: 72   **SEE PAGE 56**

Girvan Golf Club

Golf Course Road, Girvan
Ayrshire KA26 9HW
Advance Bookings **T**: 01465 714346
Holes: 18
Yardage: 5064 yds
SSS: 64

Glasgow Gailes Golf Club

Gailes, Irvine, Ayrshire KA11 5AE
Advance Bookings **T**: 01294 311258
Holes: 18
Yardage: 6513 yds
SSS: 72

Irvine Golf Club

Sandy Road, Bogside, Irvine
Ayrshire KA12 8SN
Advance Bookings **T**: 01294 275979
Holes: 18
Yardage: 6408 yds
SSS: 71

Ravenspark Golf Course

13 Kidsneuk, Irvine, Ayrshire
KA12 8SR
Advance Bookings **T**: 01294 271293
Holes: 18
Yardage: 6543 yds
SSS: 71

Western Gailes Golf Club

Gailes, Irvine, Ayrshire
KA11 5AE
Advance Bookings **T**: 01294 311649
Holes: 18
Yardage: 6639 yds
SSS: 73

Annanhill Golf Club

Irvine Road, Kilmarnock
Ayrshire KA1 2RT
Advance Bookings **T**: 01563 521644
Secretary: T Denham
Concessions Available: Yes

FACILITIES AVAILABLE:

PG CP B D

COURSE 1: ANNANHILL

Holes: 18
Yardage: 6269 yds
SSS: 70
Party advance bookings **T**: 01563
554061, e-mail: rebeccaroxburgh
@eastayrshire.gov.uk. No party
bookings on Saturdays.

Kilbirnie Place Golf Club

Largs Road, Kilbirnie, Ayrshire
KA25 7AT
Advance Bookings **T**: 01505 683398
Holes: 18
Yardage: 5500 yds
SSS: 67

Caprington Golf Club

Ayr Road, Kilmarnock, Ayrshire
KA1 4UW
Advance Bookings **T**: 01563 521915
Concessions Available: Yes

FACILITIES AVAILABLE:

CC DR PG PS CP B D

COURSE 1: CAPRINGTON GOLF CLUB

Holes: 18
Yardage: 5718 yds
SSS: 68

Fees:	Round	Daily
Weekdays:	£10.60	£14.00
Weekends:	£20.00	£25.50

Party advance bookings
T: 01563 554061, e mail
rebeccaroxburgh@eastayrshire.gov.uk.
No party bookings on Saturdays.

Largs Golf Club

Irvine Road, Largs, Ayrshire
KA30 8EU
Advance Bookings **T**: 01475 673594
Holes: 18
Yardage: 6155 yds
SSS: 71

Routenburn Golf Club

Routenburn Road, Largs
Ayrshire KA30 8QA
Advance Bookings **T**: 01475 673230
Holes: 18
Yardage: 5604 yds
SSS: 68

Ballochmyle Golf Club

Mauchline, Ayrshire KA5 6LE
Advance Bookings **T**: 01290 550469
Holes: 18
Yardage: 5990 yds
SSS: 69

Strathclyde

Maybole Golf Course

Memorial Park, Maybole
Ayrshire KA19 7DX
Advance Bookings **T**: 01292 612000
Holes: 9
Yardage: 2652 yds
SSS: 33

Muirkirk Golf Club

Furnace Road, Muirkirk, Ayrshire
KA18 3RE
Advance Bookings **T**: 01290 661257
Holes: 9
Yardage: 2690 yds
SSS: 66

New Cumnock Golf Club

Lochill, Cumnock Road
New Cumnock, Ayrshire
KA18 4BQ
Advance Bookings **T**: 01290 338848
Holes: 9
Yardage: 2675 yds
SSS: 66

Doon Valley Golf Club

1 Hillside, Patna, Ayrshire
KA6 7JT
Advance Bookings **T**: 01292 531607
Clubhouse **T**: 01292 550411
Visitor Restrictions: Yes

FACILITIES AVAILABLE:

PG CP B

COURSE 1: DOON VALLEY

Holes: 9
Yardage: 5858 yds
SSS: 70

Fees:	Round	Daily
Weekdays:	£6.50	£9
Weekends:	£6.50	£9

Prestwick Golf Club

2 Links Road, Prestwick, Ayrshire
KA9 1QG
Advance Bookings **T**: 01292 477404
Holes: 18
Yardage: 6544 yds
SSS: 73

Prestwick St. Cuthbert Golf Club

East Road, Prestwick, Ayrshire
KA9 2SX
Advance Bookings **T**: 01292 477101
Club Established: 1899
Email: secretary@stcuthbert.co.uk
Website: www.stcuthbert.co.uk
Clubhouse **T**: 01292 477101
Secretary: J Rutherford
T: 01292 477101
Visitor Restrictions: Yes
Concessions Available: Yes

FACILITIES AVAILABLE:

CC PG CP B D

COURSE 1: PRESTWICK ST CUTHBERT

Holes: 18
Yardage: 6470 yds
SSS: 71

Fees:	Round
Weekdays:	£24
Weekends:	£32

Flat Parkland Course

Prestwick St. Nicholas Golf Club

Grangemuir Road, Prestwick
Ayrshire KA9 1SN
Advance Bookings **T**: 01292 477608
Holes: 18
Yardage: 5952 yds
SSS: 69

Skelmorlie Golf Course

Belthglass Road, Skelmorlie
Ayrshire PA17 5ES
Advance Bookings **T**: 01475 520152
Holes: 18
Yardage: 5030 yds
SSS: 65

Fullarton Golf Course

Harling Drive, Troon
Ayrshire KA10 6NF
Advance Bookings **T**: 01292 312464
Holes: 18
Yardage: 4870 yds
SSS: 63

Kilmarnock (Barassie) Golf Club

29 Hillhouse Road, Barassie
Troon, Ayrshire KA10 6SY
Advance Bookings **T**: 01292 313920
Holes: 18
Yardage: 6817 yds
SSS: 74 SEE PAGE 53

Lochgreen Golf Course

Harling Drive, Troon
Ayrshire KA10 6NF
Advance Bookings **T**: 01292 312464
Holes: 18
Yardage: 6822 yds
SSS: 73

Royal Troon Golf Club

Craigend Road, Troon
Ayrshire KA10 6EP
Advance Bookings **T**: 01292 311555
Holes: 18
Yardage: 6641 yds
Par: 72
SSS: 73

Turnberry Hotel & Golf Courses

Turnberry, Ayrshire KA26 9LT
Advance Bookings **T**: 01655 331000
Holes: 18
Yardage: 6976 yds
Par: 69
SSS: 72

Auchenharvie Golf Complex

Moorpark Road, West Stevenston
Ayrshire KA20 3HU
Advance Bookings **T**: 01294 603103
Holes: 9
Yardage: 5203 yds
SSS: 66

West Kilbride Golf Club

Fullerton Drive, West Kilbride
Ayrshire KA23 9HT
Advance Bookings **T**: 01294 823911
Holes: 18
Yardage: 6247 yds
SSS: 71

Ardeer Golf Club

Greenhead Avenue, Stevenston
Ayrshire KA20 4JX
Advance Bookings **T**: 01294 464542
Holes: 18
Yardage: 6409 yds
SSS: 71

Darley Golf Course

Harling Drive, Troon
Ayrshire KA10 6NF
Advance Bookings **T**: 01292 312464
Holes: 18
Yardage: 6501 yds
SSS: 72

Dunbartonshire

Windyhill Golf Club

Baljaffray Road, Bearsden
Dunbartonshire G61 4QQ
Advance Bookings **T**: 0141 942 2349
Holes: 18
Yardage: 6254 yds
SSS: 70

Clydebank & District Golf Club

Glasgow Road, Hardgate
Clydebank, Dunbartonshire
G81 5QY
Advance Bookings **T**: 01389 383407
Holes: 18
Yardage: 5825 yds
SSS: 68

Clydebank Municipal Golf Course

Overton Road, Dalmuir
Clydebank, Dunbartonshire
G81 3RE
Advance Bookings **T**: 0141 952 8698
Holes: 18
Yardage: 5349 yds
Par: 67
SSS: 66

Vale of Leven Golf Club

Northfield Road
Bonhill, Alexandria
Dunbartonshire G83 9ET
Advance Bookings **T**: 01389 752351
Club Established: 1907
Email:
clubadministrator@valeoflevengolfclu
b.www.valeoflevengolfclub.org.uk
Website: www.valeof
levengolfclub.org.uk
Clubhouse **T**: 01389 752351
Secretary: Richard Barclay
(administrator)
T: 08707 498950
Fax: 08707 498950
Pro: Barry Campbell
T: 01389 752351
Fax: 08707 498950
Visitor Restrictions: No Saturdays
Mar/Oct
Concessions Available: on application

FACILITIES AVAILABLE:

CC PG PS CP B D

COURSE 1: NORTHFIELD

Holes: 18
Yardage: 5167 yds
Par: 67
SSS: 66

Fees:	Round	Daily
Weekdays:	£16	£20
Weekends:	£24	£30

Excellent parkland course with
magnificent views over Loch
Lomond.

Dullatur Golf Club

Glen Douglas Drive
Craigmarloch, Cumbernauld
Dunbartonshire G68 0DW
Advance Bookings **T**: 01236 723230
Holes: 18
Yardage: 6253 yds
Par: 70
SSS: 70

Palacerigg Golf Club

Palacerigg Country Park
Cumbernauld, Dunbartonshire
G67 3HU
Advance Bookings **T**: 01236 721461
Holes: 18
Yardage: 6444 yds
SSS: 71

Westerwood Hotel Golf & Country Club

Westerwood, 1 St Andrews Drive
Cumbernauld, Dunbartonshire
G68 0EW
Advance Bookings **T**: 01236 457171
Holes: 18
Yardage: 6616 yds
SSS: 72

Cardross Golf Club

Main Road, Cardross
Dumbarton, Dunbartonshire
G82 5LB
Advance Bookings **T**: 01389 841350
Club Established: 1895
Email: golf@cardross.com
Website: www.cardross.com
Clubhouse **T**: 01389 841213
Secretary: I.T. Waugh
T: 01389 841754
Fax: 01389 842162
Pro: Robert Farrell
T: 01389 841213
Visitor Restrictions: Yes

FACILITIES AVAILABLE:

CC PG PS CP CH B D

Holes: 18
Yardage: 6469 yds
Par: 71
SSS: 72

Fees:	Round
Weekdays:	£28
Weekends:	£40

Dumbarton Golf Club

Broadmeadow, Overburn Avenue
Dumbarton, Dunbartonshire
G82 2BQ
Advance Bookings **T**: 01389 732830
Holes: 18
Yardage: 6027 yds
Par: 71
SSS: 69

Loch Lomond Golf Club

Rossdhu House, Luss
Dunbartonshire G83 8NT
Advance Bookings **T**: 01436 655555
Holes: 18
Yardage: 7060 yds
Par: 71
SSS: 72

Strathclyde

Bearsden Golf Club

Thorn Road, Bearsden, Glasgow
Dunbartonshire G61 4BP
Advance Bookings **T**: 0141 942 2351
Holes: 9
Yardage: 6014 yds
SSS: 69

Douglas Park Golf Club

Hillfoot, Bearsden, Glasgow
Dunbartonshire G61 2TJ
Advance Bookings **T**: 0141 942 0985
Club Established: 1897
Website:
www.douglasparkgolfclub.net
Clubhouse **T**: 0141 942 2220
Secretary: J G Ferguson
T: 0141 942 0985
Fax: 0141 942 0985
Pro: David B Scott
T: 0141 942 1482
Fax: 0141 942 1482
Visitor Restrictions: Visitors welcome
Wed/Thur only
Concessions Available: No
Regular Closures: None

FACILITIES AVAILABLE:

CC BH PG PS CP B D

COURSE 1: DOUGLAS PARK

Holes: 18
Yardage: 5962 yds
Par: 69
SSS: 69
Designed by: Willie Fernie
Fees: Round
Weekdays: £23
Weekends: £31

Milngavie & Bearsden support
eight clubs between them; this
has to be one of the most
attractive with the spectacular
view down the 18th among the
finest in the west of Scotland. It's
not long – just under 6000 yards
– but there's a fine mix of holes
with five par threes.

Hayston Golf Club

Campsie Road, Kirkintilloch
Dunbartonshire G66 1RN
Advance Bookings **T**: 0141 775 0882
Holes: 18
Yardage: 6052 yds
SSS: 70

Helensburgh Golf Club

25 East Abercromby Street
Helensburgh, Dunbartonshire
G84 7SQ
Advance Bookings **T**: 01436 674173
Club Established: 1893
Email: thesecretary@
helensburghgolfclub.org.uk
Clubhouse **T**: 01436 674173
Secretary: Mrs Kim Print
T: 01436 674173
Fax: 01436 671170
Pro: Mr David Fortheringham
T: 01436 675505
Visitor Restrictions: visitors welcome
weekdays only

FACILITIES AVAILABLE:

CC PG PS CP B D

COURSE 1: HELENSBURGH

Holes: 18
Yardage: 6104 yds
Par: 69
SSS: 70
Designed by: Old Tom Morris / James
Braid
Fees: Round
Weekdays: £25
Weekends: £35

A lovely moorland course with
panoramic views across Loch
Lomond and the Clyde estuary.
Excellent bar and dining facilities
are available.

Kirkintilloch Golf Club

Todhill, Campsie Road
Kirkintilloch, Dunbartonshire
G66 1RN
Advance Bookings **T**: 0141 776 1256
Holes: 18
Yardage: 5269 yds
Par: 70
SSS: 66

Balmore Golf Club

Balmore, Torrance
Dunbartonshire G64 4AW
Advance Bookings **T**: 01360 620240
Holes: 18
Yardage: 5542 yds
SSS: 66

Lanarkshire

World Heritage Golf Links

Arbory Brae Golf Course
Coldchapel Road, Abington
Lanarkshire ML12 6RW
Advance Bookings **T**: 01555 664634
Holes: 9
Yardage: 1885 yds
Par: 34

Airdrie Golf Club

Glenmavis Road, Airdrie
Lanarkshire ML6 0PQ
Advance Bookings **T**: 01236 762195
Holes: 18
Yardage: 6004
Par: 70
SSS: 69

Bellshill Golf Club

Orbiston, Bellshill
Lanarkshire ML4 2RZ
Advance Bookings **T**: 01698 745124
Holes: 18
Yardage: 6264 yds
SSS: 71

Biggar Golf Club

The Park, Broughton Road
Biggar, Lanarkshire
ML12 6HA
Advance Bookings **T**: 01899 220618
Holes: 18
Yardage: 5416 yds
SSS: 66

Cambuslang Golf Club

Westburn, Cambuslang
Lanarkshire G72 7NA
Advance Bookings **T**: 0141 641 3130
Holes: 9
Yardage: 6146 yds
SSS: 69

Carnwath Golf Course

1 Main Street, Carnwath
Lanarkshire ML11 8JX
Advance Bookings **T**: 01555 840251
Holes: 18
Yardage: 5953 yds
SSS: 69

Carluke Golf Club
Mauldslie Road, Hallcraig
Carluke, Lanarkshire
ML8 5HG
Advance Bookings **T**: 01555 770574
Club Established: 1894
Email: admin-
carlukegolf@supanet.com
Clubhouse **T**: 01555 771070
Secretary: Tom Pheely
T: 01555 770574
Pro: Ricky Forrest
T: 01555 751053
Visitor Restrictions: No visitors at
weekends

FACILITIES AVAILABLE:

PG PS CP B D

COURSE 1: CARLUKE

Holes: 18
Yardage: 5899 yds
SSS: 69
Fees: Round
Weekdays: £23
Weekends: £28

Picturesque parkland course
overlooking the Clyde valley.
Noteable features – the 11th a
short par 3 with a considerable
drop from tee to green and the
12th a short par 4.

Crow Wood Golf Club
Garnkirk Estate, Muirhead
Chryston, Lanarkshire G69 9JF
Advance Bookings **T**: 0141 779 2011
Holes: 18
Yardage: 6261 yds
SSS: 71

Coatbridge Golf Centre
Townhead Road, Coatbridge
Lanarkshire, ML5 2HX
Advance Bookings **T**: 01236 421492
Holes: 18
Yardage: 5877 yds
SSS: 68

Drumpellier Golf Club
Drumpellier Avenue, Coatbridge
Lanarkshire ML5 1RX
Advance Bookings **T**: 01236 424139
Holes: 18
Yardage: 6227
SSS: 70

East Kilbride Golf Club
Nerston, East Kilbride
Lanarkshire G74 4PF
Advance Bookings **T**: 01355 247728
Holes: 18
Yardage: 6419 yds
SSS: SSS71

Torrance House Golf Club
Strathaven Road, East Kilbride
Lanarkshire G75 0QZ
Advance Bookings **T**: 01355 249720
Holes: 18
Yardage: 6415 yds
SSS: 71   **SEE PAGE 49**

Mount Ellen Golf Club
Johnstone House, Johnstone
Road Gartcosh, Lanarkshire G69
8EY
Advance Bookings **T**: 01236 872277
Holes: 18
Yardage: 5525 yds
SSS: 67

Alexandra Golf Course
Alexandra Parade, Sannox
Gardens, Glasgow, Lanarkshire
G31 3BS
Advance Bookings **T**: 0141 5561294
Holes: 9
Yardage: 2008 yds
Par: 60
SSS: 61

Bishopbriggs Golf Club
Brackenbrae Road, Bishopbriggs,
Glasgow, Lanarkshire G64 2DX
Advance Bookings **T**: 0141 772 1810
Holes: 18
Yardage: 6041 yds
SSS: 69

Blairbeth Golf Club
Fernbra Avenue, Rutherglen
Glasgow, Lanarkshire G73 4SF
Advance Bookings **T**: 0141 6343355
Holes: 18
Yardage: 5518 yds
Par: 70
SSS: 68

Bothwell Castle Golf Club
Blantyre Road, Bothwell
Glasgow, Lanarkshire G71 8PJ
Advance Bookings **T**: 01698 853177
Holes: 18
Yardage: 6240 yds
SSS: 70

Calderbraes Golf Club
57 Roundknowe Road, Uddingston
Glasgow, Lanarkshire G71 6NG
Advance Bookings **T**: 01698 813425
Holes: 9
Yardage: 5046 yds
Par: 66
SSS: 67

Cathcart Castle Golf Club
Mearns Road, Glasgow
Lanarkshire G76 7YL
Advance Bookings **T**: 0141 638 9449
Holes: 18
Yardage: 5832 yds
Par: 68
SSS: 68

Cathkin Braes Golf Club
Cathkin Road, Rutherglen
Glasgow, Lanarkshire G73 4SE
Advance Bookings **T**: 0141 634 6605
Holes: 18
Yardage: 6208 yds
SSS: 71

Cawder Golf Club
Cadder Road, Bishopbriggs
Glasgow, Lanarkshire G64 3QD
Advance Bookings **T**: 0141 772 5167
Holes: 18
Yardage: 6244 yds
SSS: 71

Cowglen Golf Club
301 Barrhead Road, Glasgow
Lanarkshire G43 1AU
Advance Bookings **T**: 0141 632 0556
Holes: 18
Yardage: 6079 yds
SSS: 70   **SEE PAGE 50**

Strathclyde

East Renfrewshire Golf Club
Pilmuir, Newton Mearns Glasgow,
Lanarkshire G76 6RT
Advance Bookings **T**: 01355 500256
Holes: 18
Yardage: 6097 yds
SSS: 70

Eastwood Golf Club
Loganswell, Newton Mearns
Glasgow, Lanarkshire G77 6RX
Advance Bookings **T**: 01355 500261
Holes: 18
Yardage: 5864 yds
SSS: 69

Esporta Dougalston Golf Club
Strathblane Road, Milngavie
Glasgow, Lanarkshire G62 8H
Advance Bookings **T**: 0141 955 2400
Holes: 18
Yardage: 6354 yds
SSS: 72

Glasgow Golf Club
Killermont, Bearsden, Glasgow
Lanarkshire G61 2TW
Advance Bookings **T**: 0141 942 2011
Holes: 18
Yardage: 5968 yds
SSS: 69

Haggs Castle Golf Club
70 Dumbreck Road, Glasgow
Lanarkshire G41 4SN
Advance Bookings **T**: 0141 427 1157
Holes: 18
Yardage: 6426 yds
SSS: 71

Kirkhill Golf Club
Greenlees Road, Camsbuslang
Glasgow, Lanarkshire G72 8YN
Advance Bookings **T**: 0141 641 8499
Holes: 18
Yardage: 6030 yds
SSS: 68

Knightswood Golf Course
Lincoln Avenue, Glasgow
Lanarkshire G13 3DN
Advance Bookings **T**: 0141 959 6358
Holes: 9
Yardage: 2703 yds
SSS: 68

Lenzie Golf Club
19 Crosshill Road, Kirkintilloch
Glasgow, Lanarkshire G66 5DA
Advance Bookings **T**: 0141 776 6020
Holes: 18
Yardage: 5984 yds
SSS: 69

Lethamhill Golf Course
Hogganfield Loch
Cumbernauld Road, Glasgow
Lanarkshire G33 1AH
Advance Bookings **T**: 0141 770 6220
Holes: 18
Yardage: 5836 yds
Par: 70
SSS: 69

Linn Park Golf Course
Simshill Road, Glasgow
Lanarkshire G44 5TA
Advance Bookings **T**: 0141 637 5871
Holes: 18
Yardage: 4952
Par: 65
SSS: 65

Littlehill Golf Course
Auchinairn Road, Glasgow
Lanarkshire G64 1UT
Advance Bookings **T**: 0141 772 1916
Holes: 18
Yardage: 6228
Par: 70
SSS: 70

Pollok Golf Club
90 Barrhead Road, Glasgow
Lanarkshire G43 1BG
Advance Bookings **T**: 0141 6321080
Holes: 18
Yardage: 6257 yds
SSS: 70

Whitecraigs Golf Course
72 Ayr Road, Giffnock
Glasgow, Lanarkshire G46 6SW
Advance Bookings **T**: 0141 639 4530
Holes: 18
Yardage: 6013 yds
Par: 70
SSS: 70 **SEE PAGE 51**

Williamwood Golf Club
690 Clarkston Road, Glasgow
Lanarkshire G44 3YR
Advance Bookings **T**: 0141 637 1783
Holes: 18
Yardage: 5878 yds
SSS: 69

Hamilton Golf Club
Riccarton, Ferniegairn, Hamilton
Lanarkshire ML3 7UE
Advance Bookings **T**: 01698 282872
Holes: 18
Yardage: 6243 yds
Par: 70
SSS: 71

Strathclyde Park Golf Club
Motehill, Hamilton
Lanarkshire ML3 6BY
Advance Bookings **T**: 01698 429350
Holes: 9
Yardage: 3147 yds
SSS: 70

Lanark Golf Club
The Moor, Whitelees Road
Lanark, Lanarkshire ML11 7RX
Advance Bookings **T**: 01555 663219
Holes: 18
Yardage: 6423 yds
SSS: 71

Larkhall Golf Course
Burnhead Road, Larkhall
Lanarkshire ML9 3AB
Advance Bookings **T**: 01698 889597
Holes: 9
Yardage: 6754 yds
Par: 72
SSS: 72

Hollandbush Golf Club
Acretophead, Lesmahagow
Lanarkshire ML11 0JS
Advance Bookings **T**: 01555 893484
Holes: 18
Yardage: 6218 yds
SSS: 70

Clober Golf Club
Craigton Road, Milngavie
Lanarkshire G62 7HP
Advance Bookings **T**: 0141 956 1685
Holes: 18
Yardage: 4963 yds
SSS: 65

Hilton Park Golf Club
Stockmuir Road, Milngavie
Lanarkshire, G62 7HB
Advance Bookings **T**: 0141 956 4657
Holes: 18
Yardage: 6054 yds
Par: 70
SSS: 70

Milngavie Golf Club
Laighpark, Milngavie
Lanarkshire G62 8EP
Advance Bookings **T**: 0141 956 1619
Holes: 18
Yardage: 5818 yds
SSS: 68

Easter Moffat Golf Club
Mansion House, Plains, Moffat
Lanarkshire ML6 8NP
Advance Bookings **T**: 01236 842878
Holes: 18
Yardage: 6222 yds
SSS: 70

Dalziel Park Golf & Country Club
100 Hagan Drive, Motherwell
Lanarkshire ML1 5RZ
Advance Bookings **T**: 01698 862862
Holes: 18
Yardage: 6200 yds
SSS: 70

Douglas Water Golf Club
Ayr Road, Rigside
Lanarkshire ML11 9NP
Advance Bookings **T**: 01555 880361
Holes: 9
Yardage: 2495 metres
SSS: 69

Colville Park Golf Club
Jerviston Estate, Merry Street
Motherwell, Lanarkshire
ML1 4UG
Advance Bookings **T**: 01698 263017
Club Established: 1924
Clubhouse **T**: 01698 263017
Secretary: Mr Leslie Innes
T: 01698 262808
Pro: John Curry
T: 01698 265779
Visitor Restrictions: No visitors at weekends

FACILITIES AVAILABLE:

PG PS CP B D

COURSE 1: COLVILLE PARK

Holes: 18
Yardage: 6265 yds
Par: 71
SSS: 70
Designed by: James Braid
Fees: Round
Weekdays: £15
Weekends: £20

Parkland course with a wooded first six holes. The course is a good test of golf and well worth a visit.

Wishaw Golf Club
55 Cleland Road, Wishaw
Lanarkshire ML2 7PH
Advance Bookings **T**: 01698 372869
Holes: 18
Yardage: 6073 yds
SSS: 69

Strathaven Golf Club
Overton Avenue, Glasgow Road
Srathavon, Lanarkshire
ML10 6NL
Advance Bookings **T**: 01357 520421
Holes: 18
Yardage: 6250 yds
SSS: 70

Shotts Golf Club
Blairhead Golf Course
Blairhead, Shotts
Lanarkshire ML7 5BJ
Advance Bookings **T**: 01501 820431
Holes: 18
Yardage: 6205 yds
Par: 70
SSS: 70

Deaconsbank Golf Course
Rouken Glen Golf Centre
Stewarton Road (Junction A726)
Thornliebank, Lanarkshire
G46 7UZ
Advance Bookings **T**: 0141 6387044
Holes: 18
Yardage: 4800 yds
SSS: 63

Renfrewshire

Erskine Golf Club
Golf Road, Bishopton
Renfrewshire, PA7 5PH
Advance Bookings **T**: 01505 862302
Holes: 18
Yardage: 6086
SSS: 69

Ranfurly Castle Golf Club Ltd
Golf Road, Bridge of Weir
Renfrewshire PA11 3HN
Advance Bookings **T**: 01505 612609
Holes: 18
Yardage: 6284 yds
SSS: 71

Caldwell Golf Club Ltd
Uplawmoor, Caldwell
Renfrewshire G78 4AU
Advance Bookings **T**: 01505 850616
Holes: 18
Yardage: 6207 yds
SSS: 70

Bonnyton Golf Club
Eaglesham, Renfrewshire
G76 0QA
Advance Bookings **T**: 01355 302781
Holes: 18
Yardage: 6252 yds
SSS: 71

Strathclyde

Elderslie Golf Club

63 Main Road, Elderslie
Renfrewshire PA5 9AZ
Advance Bookings **T**: 01505 322835
Holes: 18
Yardage: 6175 yds
SSS: 70

Fereneze Golf Club

Fereneze Avenue, Barrhead
Glasgow, Renfrewshire G78 1HJ
Advance Bookings **T**: 0141 881 1519
Holes: 18
Yardage: 5908 yds
SSS: 70

Gourock Golf Club

Cowal View, Gourock
Renfrewshire PA19 1HD
Advance Bookings **T**: 01475 631001
Club Established: 1896
Email:
ADT@gourockgolfclub.freeserve.co.uk
Clubhouse **T**: 01475 631001
Secretary: Alan D Taylor
T: 01475 638307
Fax: 01475 638307
T: 01475 636834
Fax: 01475 638307
Visitor Restrictions: Not after 4.30
weekdays, before 4.00 Sat
Concessions Available: 2-Fore-1,
Bunkered
Regular Closures: Winter Mats
Nov/Apr inclusive

FACILITIES AVAILABLE:

CC PG PS CP B D

COURSE 1: GOUROCK

Holes: 18
Yardage: 6408 yds
Par: 73
SSS: 72

Fees:	Round	Daily
Weekdays:	£20	£27
Weekends:	£27	
On application		

A testing moorland course with
spectacular views across the firth
of Clyde to the hills of Argyle.

SEE PAGE 54

Greenock Golf Club

Forsyth Street, Greenock
Renfrewshire PA16 8RE
Advance Bookings **T**: 01475 720793
Holes: 27
Yardage: 5838 yds
SSS: 68

Greenock Whinhill Golf Club

Beith Road, Greenock
Renfrewshire PA16 9LN
Advance Bookings **T**: 01475 724694
Holes: 18
Yardage: 5504 yds
SSS: 68

Cochrane Castle Golf Club

Craigston, Johnstone
Renfrewshire PA5 0HF
Advance Bookings **T**: 01505 320146
Holes: 18
Yardage: 6226 yds
SSS: 71

Kilmacolm Golf Club

Porterfield Road, Kilmacolm
Renfrewshire PA13 4PD
Advance Bookings **T**: 01505 872139
Holes: 18
Yardage: 5890 yds
SSS: 69

Lochwinnoch Golf Club

Burnfoot Road, Lochwinnoch
Renfrewshire PA12 4AN
Advance Bookings **T**: 01505 842153
Holes: 18
Yardage: 6025 yds
SSS: 71

Barshaw Golf Club

Glasgow Road, Paisley
Renfrewshire PA1 3HJ
Advance Bookings **T**: 0141 889 2908
Holes: 18
Yardage: 5703 yds
SSS: 67

Paisley Golf Club

Braehead, Paisley
Renfrewshire PA2 8TZ
Advance Bookings **T**: 0141 884 3903
Holes: 18
Yardage: 6466 yds
SSS: 72

Ralston Golf Club

Strathmore Avenue, Ralston
Paisley, Renfrewshire PA1 3DT
Advance Bookings **T**: 0141 882 1349
Holes: 18
Yardage: 6091 yds
SSS: 69

Gleddoch Golf Club

Langbank, Port Glasgow
Renfrewshire PA14 6YE
Advance Bookings **T**: 01475 540711
Holes: 18
Yardage: 6332 yds
SSS: 71   SEE PAGE 55

Renfrew Golf Club

Blythswood Estate
Inchinnan Road, Renfrew
Renfrewshire PA4 9EG
Advance Bookings **T**: 0141 886 6692
Club Established: 1894
Email:
secretary@renfrew.scottishgolf.com
Website:
www.renfrew@scottishgolf.com
Clubhouse **T**: 0141 886 2124
Secretary: Ian Murchison
T: 0141 886 6692
Fax: 0141 886 1808
Pro: D Grant
T: 0141 885 1754
Fax: 0141 886 1808
Visitor Restrictions: Mon to Thur only

FACILITIES AVAILABLE:

CC PG PS CP B D

COURSE 1: RENFREW

Holes: 18
Yardage: 6818 yds
Par: 72
SSS: 73
Designed by: Commander D Harris

Fees:	Round
Weekdays:	£30
Weekends:	£40

Port Glasgow Golf Club

Devol Road, Port Glasgow
Renfrewshire PA14 5XE
Advance Bookings **T**: 01475 704181
Holes: 18
Yardage: 5712 yds
SSS: 68

Angus

Arbroath Golf Course
Arbroath Artisan
Golf Club

Elliot, Arbroath
Angus DD11 2PE
Advance Bookings **T**: 01241 875837
Club Established: 1903
Clubhouse **T**: 01241 872069
Secretary: J. Knox
Pro: L. Ewart
T: 01241 875837
Visitor Restrictions: Not before 10am
at W/Ends

FACILITIES AVAILABLE:

CC PG PS CP CH B D

Holes: 18
Yardage: 6185 yds
SSS: 70

Fees:	Round	Daily
Weekdays:	£18	£24
Weekends:	£24	£32

SEE PAGE 75

Letham Grange Golf Club

Colliston, Arbroath
Angus DD11 4RL
Advance Bookings **T**: 01241 890373
Holes: 18
Yardage: 6968 yds
Par: 73
SSS: 73

Piperdam Golf Course

Fowlis, By Dundee
Angus DD2 5LP
Advance Bookings **T**: 01382 581374
Holes: 18
Yardage: 6025 yds
Par: 72
SSS: 72

Brechin Golf and
Squash Club

Trinity, Brechin, Angus DD9 7PD
Advance Bookings **T**: 01356 625270
Club Established: 1893
Clubhouse **T**: 01356 622383
Secretary: Mr Ian A Jardine
T: 01356 622383
Fax: 01356 626925
Pro: Stephen Rennie
T: 01356 625270
Fax: 01356 625270
Visitor Restrictions: Occasional
Concessions Available: No

FACILITIES AVAILABLE:

CC BH PG PS CP B D

COURSE 1: BRECHIN

Holes: 18
Yardage: 6096 yds
SSS: 70

Fees:	Round
Weekdays:	£20

Relatively flat parkland course
with scenic views. A good test of
golf. Visitors welcome. £20 a
round (weekdays) Excellent value
midweek package £35.

Panmure Golf Club

Burnside Road, Barry
Carnoustie, Angus DD7 7RT
Advance Bookings **T**: 01241 853120
Holes: 18
Yardage: 6317 yds
SSS: 71

Ballumbie Castle

3 Old Quarry Road, Dundee
Angus DD4 0SY
Advance Bookings **T**: 01382 770028
Holes: 18
Yardage: 6127 yds
Par: 71

Caird Park Golf Course

Caird Park, Mains Loan
Dundee, Angus DD4 9BX
Advance Bookings **T**: 01382 438871
Holes: 18
Yardage: 5772 yds
Par: 69
SSS: 68

Carnoustie Golf Links

Links Parade, Carnoustie
Angus DD7 7SE
Advance Bookings **T**: 01241 853789
Email: administrator@
carnoustiegolflinks.co.uk
Website:
www.carnoustiegolflinks.co.uk
Secretary: Willie Gardner (Acting
Secretary)
Fax: 01241 852720
Pro: L Vannet
Visitor Restrictions: Yes

FACILITIES AVAILABLE:

CC PS PG CP C CH B D

COURSE 1: CHAMPIONSHIP COURSE

Holes: 18
Yardage: 6936 yds
Par: 72
SSS: 75
Designed by: James Braid

Fees:	Round	Daily
Weekdays:	£80	£80

COURSE2: BURNSIDE COURSE

Holes: 18
Yardage: 6020 yds
Par: 69
SSS: 69   SEE PAGE 74

Fees:	Round	Daily
Weekdays:	£25	£25
Weekends:	£40	£40

COURSE 3: BUDDON LINKS

Holes: 18
Yardage: 5420 yds
Par: 66
SSS: 67
Designed by: Alliss and Thomas

Fees:	Round	Daily
Weekdays:	£20	£20
Weekends:	£40	£40

A three course complex including
the world famous Championship,
venue of the 1999 Open. One of
the most difficult tests of golf in
the world. The other two courses
provide a perfect balance to the
Championship being shorter
although tighter.

Camperdown Golf Course

Camperdown Park, Dundee
Angus DD2 4TF
Advance Bookings **T**: 01382 623398
Holes: 18
Yardage: 6344 yds
SSS: 72

Forfar Golf Club

Cunninghill, Arbroath Road
Forfar, Angus DD8 2RL
Advance Bookings **T**: 01307 463773
Holes: 18
Yardage: 6052 yds
SSS: 70

Kirriemuir Golf Club

Northmuir, Kirriemuir
Angus DD8 4LN
Advance Bookings **T**: 01575 572144
Holes: 18
Yardage: 5553 yds
SSS: 67

Downfield Golf Club

Turnberry Avenue, Dundee
Angus DD2 3QP
Advance Bookings **T**: 01382 825595
Email: downfieldgc@aol.com
Website: www.downfieldgolf.com
Clubhouse **T**: 01382 825595
Secretary: Mrs Margaret Stewart
T: 01382 825595
Fax: 01382 813111
T: 01382 889246
Visitor Restrictions: Yes

FACILITIES AVAILABLE:

CC BH PG PS CP B D

Holes: 18
Yardage: 6800 yds
Par: 73
SSS: 73

Fees:	Round
Weekdays:	£31
Weekends:	£44

Monifieth Golf Links

Princes Street, Monifieth
Angus DD5 4AW
Advance Bookings **T**: 01382 535553
Holes: 18
Yardage: 6655 yds
SSS: 72   SEE PAGE 78

The Edzell Golf Club

High Street, Edzell
Angus DD9 7TF
Advance Bookings **T**: 01356 648462
Club Established: 1895
Email:
secretary@edzellgolfclub.demon.co.uk
Clubhouse **T**: 01356 648235
Secretary: Ian Farquhar
T: 01356 647283
Fax: 01356 648094
Pro: Alistair Webster
T: 01356 648462
Fax: 01356 64884
Visitor Restrictions: Yes

FACILITIES AVAILABLE:

CC BH DR PG PS CP CH B D

COURSE 1: EDZELL

Holes: 18
Yardage: 6348 yds
SSS: 71
Designed by: Bob Simpson

Fees:	Round
Weekdays:	£23
Weekends:	£33

COURSE 2: WEST WATER

Holes: 9
Yardage: 2057 yds
Par: 32
SSS: 60
Designed by: Graeme Webster

"Golfers who are visiting the
Angus area cannot afford to miss
what is one of Scotland's true
hidden gems." *Golf Monthly*, June
1999. "Quality it most certainly
exudes; the glorious setting at the
foot of the Southern Grampians
is perfection" *Scotland Home of
Golf 2001/2002*

Montrose Links Trust

Traill Drive, Montrose
Angus DD10 8SW
Advance Bookings **T**: 01674 672932
Holes: 18
Yardage: 6533 yds
SSS: 72   SEE PAGE 77

Isle of Arran

Shiskine Golf and Tennis Club

Blackwaterfoot, Isle of Arran
KA27 8HA
Advance Bookings Phone: 01770
860226
Club Established: 1896
Email: info@shiskinegolf.com
Website: www.shiskinegolf.com
Clubhouse Phone: 01770 860226
Secretary: Mrs Fiona Crawford
Phone: 01770 860548
Fax: 01770 860205
Visitor Restrictions: None

FACILITIES AVAILABLE:

CC BH PG PS CP CH D

Course 1: Shiskine
Holes: 12
Yardage: 2823 yds
Par: 42
SSS: 41
Designed by: Willie Fernie

Fees:	Round	Daily
Weekdays:	£13	£20
Weekends:	£17	£20

A good test of golf in a wonderful
setting. Advance booking advised.
SEE PAGE 99

Brodick Golf Club

Brodick, Isle of Arran KA27 8DL
Advance Bookings **T**: 01770 302349
Holes: 18
Yardage: 4736 yds
SSS: 64

Lamlash Golf Club

Lamlash, Brodick, Isle of Arran
KA27 8JU
Advance Bookings **T**: 01770 600196
(Starter)
Holes: 18
Yardage: 4640 yds
SSS: 64

Machrie Bay Golf Club

Machrie Bay, Brodick
Isle of Arran KA27 8DZ
Advance Bookings **T**: 01770 850232
Holes: 9
Yardage: 2143 yds
SSS: 62

Corrie Golf Club

Sannox, Isle of Arran KA27 8JD
Advance Bookings **T**: 01770
810223/600403
Holes: 9
Yardage: 1948 yds
SSS: 61

Lochranza Golf Course

Lochranza, Isle of Arran
KA27 8HL
Advance Bookings **T**: 01770 830273
Holes: 18
Yardage: 5487 yds
SSS: 69

Whiting Bay Golf Course

Golf Course Road, Whiting Bay
Isle of Arran KA27 8QT
Advance Bookings **T**: 01770 700487
Holes: 18
Yardage: 4405 yds
Par: 63
SSS: 63

Isle of Bute

Port Bannatyne Golf Club

Bannatyne Mains Road
Port Bannatyne, Rothesay
Isle of Bute PA20 0PH
Advance Bookings **T**: 01700 504544
Holes: 18
Yardage: 5085 yds
SSS: 67

Rothesay Golf Club

Glebelands Road, Canada Hill
Rothesay, Isle of Bute
PA20 9HN
Advance Bookings **T**: 01700 502244
Holes: 18
Yardage: 5395 yds
SSS: 66

Isle of Cumbrae

Millport Golf Club

Golf Road, Millport, Ayrshire
KA28 0HB
Advance Bookings **T**: 01475 530311
Holes: 18
Yardage: 5828 yds
SSS: 69   SEE PAGE 98

Isle of Colonsay

Isle of Colonsay Golf Club

Machrens Farm, Isle of Colonsay
PA61 7YP
Advance Bookings **T**: 01951 200364
Holes: 18
Yardage: 4475
SSS: 72

Isle of Gigha

Isle of Gigha Golf Club

Isle of Gigha, PA41 7AA
Advance Bookings **T**: 01583 505242
Club Established: 1986
Secretary: John Bannatyne
T: 01583 505242
Visitor Restrictions: None

FACILITIES AVAILABLE:

BH   CP   CH

COURSE 1: ISLE OF GIGHA

Holes: 9
Yardage: 5042 yds
SSS: 65
Designed by: Course Commitee
(1986)

Fees:	Round	Daily
Weekdays:	£10	£10
Weekends:	£10	£10

Picturesque parkland course with
spectacular views of the Mull of
Kintyre and Knapdale.

Isle of Islay

Islay Golf Club: The Machrie Hotel & Golf Club

Port Ellen, Isle of Islay PA42 7AN
Advance Bookings **T**: 01496 302310
Holes: 18
Yardage: 6225 yds
SSS: 70   SEE PAGE 100

Isle of Lewis

Stornoway Golf Course

Lady Lever Park, Stornoway
Isle of Lewis HS2 0XP
Advance Bookings **T**: 01851 702240
Holes: 18
Yardage: 5252 yds
SSS: 67

Isle of Orkney

Orkney Golf Club

Grainbank, St. Ola, Kirkwall,
Isle of Orkney KW15 1RD
Advance Bookings **T**: 01856 872457
Holes: 18
Yardage: 5406 yds
SSS: 67

Isle of Skye

Isle of Skye Golf Club

Sconser, Isle of Skye
Isle of Skye IV48 8TD
Advance Bookings **T**: 01478 650235
Holes: 9
Yardage: 4677 yds
SSS: 64

Skeabost Golf Club

Skeabost House Hotel
Skeabost Bridge, Isle of Skye
IV51 9NP
Advance Bookings **T**: 01470 532215
Holes: 9
Yardage: 3114 yds
SSS: 30

Isle of Tiree

Vaul Golf Club

Scarinish, Isle of Tiree PA77 6XH
Advance Bookings **T**: 01879 220319
Holes: 9
Yardage: 2911 yds
SSS: 35

Shetland

The Shetland Golf Club

Dale, Gott, Shetland
Shetland Islands ZE2 9SB
Advance Bookings **T**: 01595 840369
Holes: 18
Yardage: 5776 yds
SSS: 68

Accommodation Guide

BORDERS

Abbotsford Arms Hotel
63 Stirling Street,
Galashiels TD1 1BY
Tel: 01896 752517
Fax: 01896 750744
*Mintole Classic Gold

Type of Accomodation Hotel, STB 4 stars
Number of Rooms 123
Room Facilities Sat. TV, Pay TV, 24hr Room
Service, Tea/Coffee, Trouser Press, all en-suite
Season Dates All year
Prices £90-120

Special Features
Small, friendly hotel.
Central situation for 20
golf courses in area, near
town centre. Good food
at reasonable prices

Ashlyn Guest House
7 Abbotsford Road,
Galashiels TD1 3DP
Tel: 01896 752416
Fax: 01896 752416
E-mail: ashlyn7@hotmail.com

Type of Accomodation B&B
Number of Rooms 3
Room Facilities All en-suite, TV, Tea/Coffee, CH
Season Dates All year
Prices £45 per double room B&B

Special Features
Old Mill House
Totally non-smoking
Special rates for
Torwoodlee Golf Course

Kings Arms Hotel
M & H Dalgety
High Street, Melrose TD6 9PB
Tel: 01896 822143
Fax: 01896 823812

Type of Accomodation Hotel, STB 3 stars
Number of Rooms 24
Room Facilities All en-suite, Phone, TV, Tea/Coffee
Season Dates All year
Prices B&B from £32.50pppn, BBEM from £42pppn

Special Features
Log fires, Real ales,
extensive menus

King's Hotel
56 Market Street,
Galashiels TD1 3AN
Tel: 01896 755497
Fax: 01896 755497
E-mail: kingshotel@talk21.com

Type of Accomodation Hotel
Number of Rooms 7
Room Facilities All en-suite, TV, Tea/Coffee
Season Dates All year
Prices Single £46pn, Twin/Double £36pppn

Special Features
Car park, Restaurant and
Bar all on site

CENTRAL

Radisson SAS
Airth Castle & Hotel
Airth by Falkirk
Stirlingshire FK2 8JF
Tel: +44 1324 831411
Fax: +44 1324 831329
www.radissonsas.com

Type of Accomodation Hotel, STB 3 stars
Number of Rooms 13
Room Facilities All en-suite
Season Dates March to October
Prices £BBEM £60pp

Special Features
2 restaurants, 2 bars, Health
centre (gymnasium, sauna,
steam room, solarium,
whirlpool) 9 conference and
banqueting rooms

DUMFRIES AND GALLOWAY

Ash Lodge & Mint Cottage
Sandyhills & Kirkcudbright
Tel: 01557 332337
Mobile: 07850 138596
E-mail: fiona@thomsonholidaysdirect.com
www.thomsonholidaysdirect.com

Type of Accomodation Self Catering,
STB 3 stars
Number of Rooms 3 bed (sleeps 8/9) &
2 bed (3/4)
Room Facilities N/A
Season Dates All year
Prices from £199-£520 & £199-£299

Special Features
There are 31 golf clubs within
Dumfries & Galloway 16 of
which are within 20 miles of
Ash Lodge. On site swimming
pool, bar, restaurant & beach.
Mint Cottage is situated in
the heart of historic High St.
in Kirkcudbright.

Birkhill Hotel
16 St Mary's Street, Dumfries
DG1 1LZ
Tel: 01387 253418
Fax: 01387 253418
E-mail: birkhill@aol.com

Type of Accomodation Hotel
Number of Rooms 1 Single, 3 Double/Family
Room Facilities En-suite, TV, Tea/Coffee
Hotel Facilities Dining room, bar, car parking
Season Dates All year
Prices Single: £38, Double: £49, based on 2 sharing

Special Features
Small friendly family-run hotel where a warm welcome is assured. Located near town centre, two minutes from railway station. Home cooked food available and entertainment 4 nights per week.

Baron's Craig Hotel
Rockcliffe by Dalbeattie,
Kirkudbrightshire DG5 4QF
Tel: 01556 630225
Fax: 01556 630328
E-mail: info@baronscraighotel.co.uk
www.baronscraighotel.co.uk

Type of Accomodation Hotel
Number of Rooms 25
Room Facilities En-suite, most with sea-views
Season Dates All year
Prices upon application

Special Features
Luxurious accomodation with tempting menus and fine wines. Ideally situated for access to several courses including the superb Southerness course.

Beechwood Country House Hotel
Mr S Michaelides
Harthope Place, Moffat,
Dumfriesshire DG10 9HX
Tel: 01683 220210
Fax: 01683 220889

Type of Accomodation Hotel STB 4 Star,
AA 2 Star, 1 Rosette
Number of Rooms 7
Room Facilities En-suite and fully equipped
Hotel facilities Restaurant, car parking
Season Dates February to December
Prices BBEM £64pp

Special Features
Small friendly family-run hotel with the highest of standards, welcoming atmosphere, with access to numerous surrounding golf courses

Friars Carse Country House Hotel
Auldgirth
Tel: 01387 740388
E-mail: fc@pofr.co.uk
www.patch.uk.com

Type of Accomodation Hotel
Prices Short break packages available on B&B on half or full board

Special Features
A former baronial Hall set in 45 acres of woodland stretching to the River Nith.Within 30 minutes of 8 fine golf courses.

Gables Hotel
1 Annan Road, Gretna,
Dumfrieshire DG16 5DQ
Tel: 01461 338300
Fax: 01461 338626
E-mail: info@gables-hotel-gretna.co.uk
www.gables-hotel-gretna.co.uk

Type of Accomodation Hotel
Number of Rooms 31, all en-suite, including 4 luxury rooms with 4-poster beds
Room Facilities Telephone, TV, Hairdryer, Tea/Coffee
Hotel Facilities Bar and restaurant Conference and function facilities.
Season Dates All year
Prices From £50 to £130 per room (inc. full Scottish breakfast)

Special Features
Courses nearby: Gretna, Powfoot, Lochmaben, Dumfries (2), Lockerbie, Haddom Castle, Carlisle (2) – all within easy driving distance. Fishing and shooting also available.

Royal Four Towns Hotel
Mr Fawcett
High Road, Hightae, DG11 1JS
Tel: 01387 811711
Fax: 01387 811988
www.royalfourtowns.co.uk

Type of Accomodation Hotel
Number of Rooms 5 Double en-suite bedrooms
Room Facilities TV, Tea/Coffee facilities
Hotel Facilities Restaurant, car parking
Season Dates All year
Prices BB from £30pppn

Special Features
Hotel with a village atmosphere, serving traditional home cooked food, situated within easy driving distance of numerous courses including Lockerbie, Dumfries and Lochmaben.

Accomodation Guide

LOTHIAN

Craigesk
Miss A R Mitchell
10 Albert Terrace, Musselburgh,
East Lothian EH21 7LR
Tel: 0131 665 3344/3170
Fax: 0131 665 3344
E-mail: craigesk-b-b@faxvia.net

Type of Accomodation STB 5 star
Number of Rooms 20
Room Facilities All en-suite, DD phones,
Tea/Coffee, Trouser Press, CTV
Season Dates 30th Dec - 18th Dec
Prices DB&B from £50pppn

Special Features
Near all East Lothian golf
courses. 20 minutes from
Edinburgh. Private parking.

Fisherman's Hall
Jan & Bill Boggan
The Banks, South Queensferry
EH30 9SL
Tel: 0131 3313878
Fax: 0131 3315867

Type of Accomodation Beach house (4 stars)
Number of Rooms 4 bedrooms + 2
Room Facilities Fully equipped
Season Dates All year
Prices £350 - £750 per week

Special Features
Spectacular views of the
Bass Rock, Forth Islands
and sunsets – only 30
minutes from Edinburgh.
Beside quiet harbour.

Golf Hotel
34 Dirleton Avenue, North Berwick
Tel: 01620 892202
Fax: 01620 892290
E-mail: simon@thegolfhotel.net
www.thegolfhotel.net

Type of Accomodation Family-run hotel
Number of Rooms 13
Room Facilities 10 with en-suite
Season Dates All year
Prices Rates on application, Special winter rates

Special Features
Ideally situated for all 18
of East Lothian's golf
courses. Only 30 minutes
from Edinburgh.

Harbour House Hotel
North Berwick
Tel: 01620 892529
E-mail:
sheila@harbourhousehotel.com
www.harbourhousehotel.com

Type of Accomodation Hotel
Number of Rooms 11
Room Facilities All en-suite, TV, phone,
internet connection
Season Dates All year
Prices £35pppn B&B

Special Features
Good old-fashioned
Scottish hospitality.

The Monks' Muir
Haddington, East Lothian
EH41 3SB
Tel: 01620 860340
Fax: 01620 861770
E-mail: d@monksmuir.com
www.monksmuir.co.uk

Type of Accomodation Caravan park
Number of Rooms 35 static plus touring
Room Facilities TV, toilets, 1-3 bed
Season Dates all year
Prices £130 - £440 per week

Special Features
On-site shop and cafe.
Childrens' play area.
2 shower blocks.

Tell them you saw them in Scotland Home of Golf

FIFE

The Royal Hotel
Townhead, Dysart, Fife KY1 2XQ
Tel: 01592 654112/652109
Fax: 01592 598555

Type of Accomodation Hotel
Room Facilities TV, Radio-alarm, hospitality tray
Prices On application

Special Features
Friendly, family-run hotel situated in National Trust village of Dysart. Over 20 courses within 30 minutes drive. Comfortable lounge to relax in after golf.

The Craw's Nest Hotel
Mrs Eleanor Bowman
Bankwell Road, Anstruther
Fife KY10 3DA
Tel: 01333 310691
Fax: 01333 312216
enquiries@crawsnesthotel.co.uk
www.crawsnesthotel.co.uk

Type of Accomodation Hotel
Number of Rooms 50
Room Facilities En-suite, Tea/Coffee, Trouser press, Hairdryer, Direct Dial
Season Dates All year
Prices B&B from £30pppn

Special Features
The Craw's Nest Hotel is a family run hotel offering the best in Scottish hospitality. Only ten minutes drive from St Andrews and one hour from Edinburgh.

STRATHCLYDE

Boars Head Hotel
4 Main Street, Colmonell, Girvan, Ayrshire KA26 0RY
Tel/Fax: 01465 881371
E-mail: alasdair@boarshead-colmonell.freeserve.co.uk
www.boarshead-colmonell.freeserve.co.uk

Type of Accomodation Hotel
Number of Rooms 6
Room Facilities All En-suite
Hotel Facilities Bar, Evening meals available
Season Dates All year
Prices B&B from £19.50

Special Features
Peaceful village location with 15 courses within an hour's drive including Turnberry and Troon. Discount golfing rates available.

Calton Hotel
187 Ayr Road, Prestwick KA9 1TP
Tel: 01292 476811
Fax: 01292 673712
E-mail: hotelreservation@talk21.com

Type of Accomodation Hotel
Number of Rooms 37
Room Facilities En-suite, TV, Telephone, Tea/Coffee, Trouser press, Hairdryer
Season Dates All year
Prices upon application

Special Features
Carvery, lounge bar, 100-seat restaurant. Convenient for Troon and Prestwick St Nicholas Golf Courses.

Savoy Park Hotel
16 Racecourse Road,
Ayr KA7 2UT
Tel: 01292 266112
Fax: 01292 611488
E-mail: mail@savoypark.com
www.savoypark.com

Type of Accomodation Hotel
Number of Rooms 15
Room Facilities En-suite, TV, Sky TV, Tea/Coffee, hairdryer
Season Dates All year
Prices single £55–£65pn, double £37–£47.50 pppn

Special Features
Traditional red sandstone building, Lounge bar and restaurant. Central to many golf courses.

South Beach Hotel
Troon
Tel: 01292 312033
E-mail: info@southbeach.co.uk
www.southbeach.co.uk

Type of Accomodation Hotel, STB 3 stars
Number of Rooms 34
Room Facilities All en-suite
Season Dates All year
Prices single £35–£65 B&B, twin/double £60–£87, superior twin/double £75–£95

Special Features
Restaurant, 2 bars, drying rooms, secure club storage.

Accommodation Guide

Aberdeen Patio Hotel
Beach Boulevard,
Aberdeen AB24 SEF
Tel: 01224 633339
Fax: 01224 638833
E-mail: patiosales@globalnet.co.uk
www.patiohotels.com

Type of Accomodation Hotel, STB 4 stars,
highly commended, AA 4 stars
Number of Rooms 124
Room Facilities All en-suite, leisure club
Season Dates All year
Prices Single (Mon-Thurs) £88 B&B
(Fri, Sat, Sun £42), Double (Mon-Thurs) £98 B&B
(Fri, Sat, Sun £55),

Special Features
5 minutes from Royal
Aberdeen Course,
20 others within 30
minutes drive. Driving
range and golf superstore
2 minutes drive away.

The Banff Links Hotel
Swordanes, Banff AB45 2JJ
Tel: 01261 812414
Fax: 01261 812463
E-mail: swordanes@btinternet.com

Type of Accomodation Hotel
Number of Rooms 8
Room Facilities All en-suite
Season Dates All year
Prices Special golfing breaks and group discounts

Special Features
Great choice of courses

Banff Springs Hotel
Golden Knowes Road,
Banff AB45 2JE
Tel: 01261 812881
Fax: 01261 815546
E-mail: info@banffspringshotel.co.uk

Type of Accomodation Hotel, STB 3 star
Number of Rooms 31
Room Facilities All en-suite. Gymnasium
Season Dates All year
Prices B&B from £36 pp

Special Features
Plenty of golf courses
within a short drive.
'Taste of Scotland'
Restaurant.

The Burnett Arms Hotel
25 High Street, Banchory
AB31 5TD
Tel: 01330 824944
Fax: 01330 825553
E-mail: theburnett@totalise.co.uk
www.burnettarms.co.uk

Type of Accomodation Hotel, AA 2 stars,
RAC 2 stars, STB 2 stars
Number of Rooms 16 (6 twin, 6 dbl, 4 sgl)
Room Facilities All en-suite, Remote TV
+ Sky, Phone, Tea/Coffee. H/dryer
Season Dates All year
Prices Single £40-£55, Twin/Dbl £56-76,
Discounts for parties of 10 golfers or more

Special Features
Situated only 3 minutes
from 2 18-hole courses
with 20 others within 30
minutes.

The County Hotel Banff
Banff, Aberdeenshire AB45 1AE
Tel: 01261 815353
Fax: 01261 818335
E-mail:
enquiries@thecountyhotel.com
www.thecountyhotel.com

Type of Accomodation Hotel
Number of Rooms 5, 1 Family room,
1 4-poster double, 1 twin, 1 single, 1 double
Room Facilities 4 en-suite, 1 private b/room
Season Dates All year
Prices £38-£75 per room

Special Features
Walking distance to Duff
House and the Royal Golf
Course. Beautiful views
over coast. French cuisine.

Kilmarnock Arms Hotel
Cruden Bay,
Aberdeenshire AB42 OHD
Tel: 01779 812213
Fax: 01779 812153
www.kilmarnock-arms-hotel.co.uk

Type of Accomodation Hotel
Number of Rooms 14
Room Facilities All en-suite
Season Dates All year
Prices On application

Special Features
New Falcon Restauarant,
public & lounge bar.
5 mins walk from Cruden
Bay golf course.
30 minutes from
Aberdeen and central for
local courses.

Tell them you saw them in Scotland Home of Golf

The Marcliffe at Pitfodels
North Deeside Road, Pitfodels,
Aberdeen AB15 9YA
Tel: 01244 861000
Fax: 01244 868860
E-mail: enquiries@marcliffe.com
www.marcliffe.com

Type of Accomodation Hotel STB 5 star
Number of Rooms 42
Room Facilities En-suite
Season Dates All year
Prices On application

Special Features
Close to Royal Aberdeen
and many other golf
courses in area. Excellent
restaurant.

The Seafield Hotel
19 Seafield Street,
Cullen, Moray AB56 4SG
Tel: 01542 840791
Fax: 01542 840736
E-mail: info@theseafieldarms.co.uk
www.theseafieldarms.co.uk

Type of Accomodation 3 star Hotel
Number of Rooms 21
Room Facilities All en-suite (most with bath &
shower), hospitality tray, TV and CH
Season Dates All year
Prices Single from £42, Twin/double from £37.50pp

Special Features
Close to beach and Cullen
Golf Course. 15 courses
within 30 minutes drive.
Outdoor activities can be
arranged.

The Spires Executive Apartments
531 Great Western Road, Aberdeen
Tel: 01224 209991
www.thespires.co.uk

Type of Accomodation Apartments
Number of Rooms 2 bedroomed apartments
Room Facilities Well-serviced
Season Dates All year
Prices On application

Special Features
Ideal for your golf break.
One night stay upwards.

TAYSIDE

Dalhousie Lodge
Edzell, by Brechin,
Angus DD9 6SG
Tel: 01356 624566
Fax: 01356 623725
E-mail:
dalhousieestate@btinternet.com

Type of Accomodation Lodge, full-board,
short-stay and self-catering
Number of Rooms 7, sleeping up to 12
Room Facilities Well equipped
Season Dates All year
Prices On application

Special Features
Comfortable, secluded
country house. Many
championship golf courses
within easy reach.

Grey Harlings House
Mrs Janet Scrimgeour
East Links, Montrose,
Angus DD10 8SW
Tel: 01674 673980

Type of Accomodation Guest House
Number of Rooms 5
Room Facilities En-suite, Colour TV,
Tea/Coffee facilities
Season Dates All year
Prices B&B £20pp

Special Features
Situated on 2 golf courses.
25 minutes to Carnoustie.
Numerous other links and
inland courses nearby.

The George Hotel
22 George Street, Montrose,
Angus, Scotland DD10 8EW
Tel: 016746 75050
Fax: 016746 671153
E-mail:
reception@thegeorge-montrose.c.uk

Type of Accomodation Hotel
Room Facilities All en-suite, Sat TV (free
movie/sports channel), Telephone, Tea/Coffee
facilities
Hotel Facilities function suite, restaurant, bar
Prices On application

Special Features
Family-owned hotel in
the heart of Montrose.
Excellent centre for
walking, angling, sight-
seeing and golf.

Taymouth Castle Estate
2 The Square, Kenmore,
Perthshire PH15 2HH
Tel: 01887 830 765
Fax: 01887 830 830
www.fishingnet.com/taymouth

Type of Accomodation Self-catering cottages
situated throught the estate. all are fully equipped
and within walking distance of the Kenmore
Country Club

Special Features
Free unlimited golf at
Taymouth Castle Golf
Course and free access
to the local country club
swimming facility

Accommodation Guide

Ascot House
7 Cawdor Street, Nairn IV12 4QD
Tel: 01667 455855
Fax: 01667 451900
E-mail: ascot7nairn@aol.com

Type of Accomodation Guest House, STB 3 star
Number of Rooms 11
Room Facilities 1 single, 2 double, 1 twin,
5 executive suites
Season Dates All year
Prices B&B £20-£35ppn

Special Features
2 minutes walk to town
centre and ideally located
for Nairn's 2 Championship
golf courses.

Feith Mhor Lodge
Station Road, Carrbridge
Inverness-shire PH23 3AP
Tel: 01479 841621
E-mail: feith.mhor@btinternet.com
www.feith.mhor@btinternet.co.uk

Type of Accomodation Guest House
or self-catering house
Number of Rooms 6
Room Facilities All en-suite
Season Dates Alll year
Prices B&B from £20 to £28 pppn

Special Features
Beautiful country setting
– 1 mile from village.
6 golf clubs in easy reach
– Abernethy, Boat of
Garten, Carrbridge,
Granton-on-Spey,
Kingussie & Newtonmore

Gigha Hotel
Isle of Gigha
Argyll PA41 7AA
Tel: 01583 505254
Fax: 01583 505244
www.isle-of-gigha.co.uk

Type of Accomodation Hotel, STB 3 stars
Number of Rooms 13
Room Facilities All en-suite
Season Dates March to October
Prices BBEM £60pp

Special Features
Nearby Achmore Gardens
and our 9 hole golf course
with beautiful views.

Glenaveron
Golf Road, Brora,
Sutherland KW9 6QS
Tel: 01408 621601
E-mail: glenaveron@hotmail.com
www.glenaveron.co.uk

Type of Accomodation Guest House, STB 4 stars
Number of Rooms 3 (1D, 1T, 1F)
Room Facilities All en-suite, non-smoking
Season Dates All year
Prices BB single from £28-£33,
D/T from £25-£28

Special Features
3 minutes walk to Brora
Golf Course and only 25
minutes drive to Royal
Dornoch Golf Course.

Glen Mhor Hotel
9-12 Ness Bank,
Inverness, IV2 4SG
Tel: 01463 234308
Fax: 01463 713170
www.glen-mhor.com

Type of Accomodation Hotel
Number of Rooms 45, Singles, Doubles,
Twins, Executive Rooms and Junior suites
Room Facilities All en-suite, TV, Tel/Modem,
Season Dates All year
Prices B&B from £41 pppn, sharing to £60ppn

Special Features
2 restaurants, riverside
location, parking available.
28 courses within 1 hour
drive, including Royal
Dornoch and Nairn. 3 local
courses (Tee times can be
reserved).

Kinloch House Hotel
By Blairgowrie, PH10 6SG
Tel: 01250 884237
Fax: 01250 884333

Type of Accomodation Hotel
Number of Rooms 20
Room Facilities En-suite, phone, TV,
trouser press
Season Dates All year
Prices DB&B single £90, double/twin from £195,
suite from £230

Special Features
3 rosette restaurant, health
and fitness centre. Teetime
booking facility.

Tell them you saw them in Scotland Home of Golf

Accommodation Guide

The Mansion House Hotel
The Haugh, Elgin,
Moray IV30 1AW
Tel: 01343 548811
Fax: 01343 547916
E-mail: reception@mhelgin.co.uk

Type of Accomodation Hotel, STB 4 star,
highly commended, AA 3 star
Number of Rooms 23
Room Facilities All en-suite. Leisure facilities
Season Dates All year
Prices Single £80 B&B, Double £120 B&B

Special Features
Elegent, welcoming hotel
set within private
woodland. 10 golf courses
within 10 miles.

Navidale House Hotel
Helmsdale, Sutherland KW8 6JS
Tel: 01431 821258
Fax: 01431 821531
www.contact-my-idea.com/
navidale/navidalehouse.htm.

Type of Accomodation Hotel and 2 Lodges
Number of Rooms 10
Room Facilities All en-suite
Season Dates All year
Prices DB&B £60pp

Special Features
Recently refurbished to a
high standard and ideally
located for golfing.

Pitgrudy Caravan Park
Poles Road, Dornoch,
Sutherland IV25 3HY
Tel: 01862 821253
Fax: 01862 821382
www.host.co.uk

Type of Accomodation Caravan Park, STB 5 star
Season Dates May to September
Prices 40 touring pitches, 10 holiday caravans
Number sleeping 2 to 5
Shops near Yes
Season dates May to September
Prices £7.50 per pitch per night,
Caravans £95 - £295 per week

Special Features
Golfers' paradise with
several golf courses within
a short drive

Silver Sands Leisure Park
Mr G Kerr
Covesea, West Beach, Lossiemouth
Morayshire IV31 6SP
Tel: 01343 813262
Fax: 01343 815205
E-mail:
holidays@silversands.freeserve.co.uk
www.silversands.freeserve.co.uk

Type of Accomodation Caravan Park,
Thistle, STB 4 stars
Number of Units 45
Number sleeping 6/8
Shop near? Yes
Season Dates March to October
Prices From £175. Touring from £7.50

Special Features
Next to Moray Golf Club.
Ideal base for many
courses throughout
Morayshire

Some useful numbers

Rail	**National Rail Enquiries**	0845 7484 950
Flights	**British Airways**	0845 773 3377
	British Midland	0870 607 0555
	Easyjet	0870 600 0000
	Go	0870 607 6543
Car hire	**Avis**	0870 606 0100
	Europcar	0845 722 2525
	Hertz	0870 599 6699
Travel news	**AA**	0870 550 0600
	RAC	0906 470 1740
Weather	**Glasgow Met. Office**	0845 300 0300

Golfing Notes

1

2

3

4

5

6

7

8

9

10

11

12

13

14

15

16

17

18

		Quantity:
Billy Casper's Scottish Golf Collection	£50.00	☐

Framed Photos:

Billy Casper Masters win – Original Signature	£300.00	☐
Gary Player USPGA win – Original Signature	£300.00	☐
Byron Nelson – Engraved Signature	£200.00	☐

OTHER PLAYERS AVAILABLE ON REQUEST

Framed **Masters flag** with one original Signature	£500.00	☐

SIGNATURE DESIRED: _____

ADDITIONAL SIGNATURES AVAILABLE ON REQUEST

Special Request Items:

Item desired: _____

Signature(s): _____

Name: _____

Address: _____

_____

_____ Postcode: _____

Toatal Amount Due: [:   ]

I enclose a cheque ☐

Please charge my VISA ☐   MASTERCARD ☐

Card Expiry Date ☐☐ ☐☐

Card Number ☐☐☐☐☐☐☐☐☐☐☐☐☐☐☐☐

Signed [   ]

For further information see pages 24 and 25

GOLF EVENT SERVICE

please complete and return this form to receive further
details of our golf event services:

Name: _____

Company: _____

Position: _____

Date and location of proposed event if known:

_____

_____

Address: _____

_____

_____ Postcode: _____

Telephone: _____

Fax: _____

E-mail: _____

Any other information: _____

_____

_____

_____

_____

For further information see page 25

Please return form to:

Pastime Publications 5 Dalgety Avenue, Edinburgh EH7 5UF Scotland U

Golfing Notes

1

2

3

4

5

6

7

8

9

10

11

12

13

14

15

16

17

18

Need help planning your holiday?

Amethyst Travel and Golf
Rowan House, Glasdale, Comrie, Perthshire PH6 2JX
Tel: 01764 670509
E-mail: info@amethyst-travel.com
Fax: 01764 670584

www.amethyst-travel.com

Alyth Golf Desk Ltd
Leroch, Alyth, Blairgowrie PH11 8NZ
Tel: 01828 633323
Fax: 01828 633888

E-mail: strathmoregolf@sol.co.uk
www.alythgolfdesk.co.uk

Golf packages to suit every taste and budget. Over 60 courses. One call takes the hassle out of your holiday.

Golf Connections
9 Hopeward Mews, Dalgety Bay, Fife KY11 9TB
Tel: 01383 820211
Fax: 01383 820211

E-mail: enquiry@golfconnections.co.uk
www.golfconnections.co.uk

Tailor made golf tours for Scotland. On and off course activities to meet individual requirements of male and female golfers.

Golf Roots Scotland
29 Haldane Avenue, Haddington, East Lothian EH41 3PG
Tel: 01620 829604
Fax: 01620 829604

E-mail: enquiries@golfroots.co.uk
www.golfroots.co.uk

Personalised tours for discerning golfers. We will organise all golf, accommodation and transport – you can relax and enjoy the golf.

Ian McIntosh Travel
22 Braehead Grove, Edinburgh, EH4 6BG
Tel: 0131 339 2995
Fax: 0131 339 3284

E-mail: ritamcintosh@ianmcintoshtravel.freeserve.co.uk

Tailor-made itineraries including accommodation, tee-times, transport for all of Scotland except the Old Course. Lead name, handicaps required.

Qualitee Golf Tours
18 Inchmurrin Cresent, Balloch, Dunbartonshire G83 8JJ
Tel: 01389 750830
Fax: 01389 755968

E-mail: dphipps@btconnect.com

Our sole aim is to provide you, our valued client, with the best value for money golf package you'll find.

Travel Scot World

5 South Charlotte Street, Edinburgh EH2 4AN
Tel: 0131 226 3246
Fax: 0131 220 1271

E-mail: sales@travelscotworld.uk.com
www.scotworldtravel.co.uk

We provide expert advice on the golf courses and accommodation around Scotland. Whatever your client's golfing requirements, Travel Scot World can provide a solution.

Tayleur Mayde Golf Tours

21 Castle Street, Edinburgh, EH2 3DN
Tel: 1 800 847 8064 (USA)
Fax: 0131 225 9113

E-mail: info@tayleurmayde.com
www.tayleurmayde.com

The Scotland Tours
Company Ltd

30 Canmore Street, Dunfermline, Fife KY12 7NT
Tel: 01383 727999
Fax: 01383 727927

E-mail: enquiries@scotland-tours.com
www.scotlandgolftours.com

Prompt service, quality locations, great golf, ideal vehicles, detailed itineraries – for high quality well-organised golf tours, contact Scotland Tours.

Thistle Golf (Scotland) Ltd

Suite 423, The Pentagon Centre, 36 Washington Street, Glasgow G3 8AZ
Tel: 0141 248 4554
Fax: 0141 248 4554

E-mail: info@thistlegolf.co.uk
www.thistlegolf.co.uk

High quality tailor made golf tours throughout Scotland including tee-times, accommodation, vehicle hire and sightseeing. Corporate days also arranged.

Wilkinson Golf

The Boathouse, Hawkcraig Road, Aberdour, Fife KY3 OTZ
Tel: 01383 861000
Fax: 01383 861010

E-mail: gary@wilkinsongolf.com
www.wilkinsongolf.com

Tailor made golf vacations around Scotland and Ireland. Itineraries to suit all budgets and size of group.

If calling from outwith the UK, replace the initial '0' with '+44'

Tell them you saw them in Scotland Home of Golf

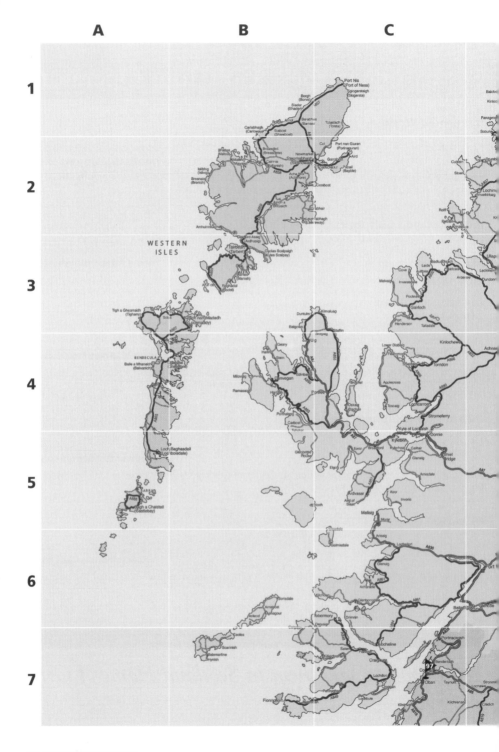

WESTERN ISLES

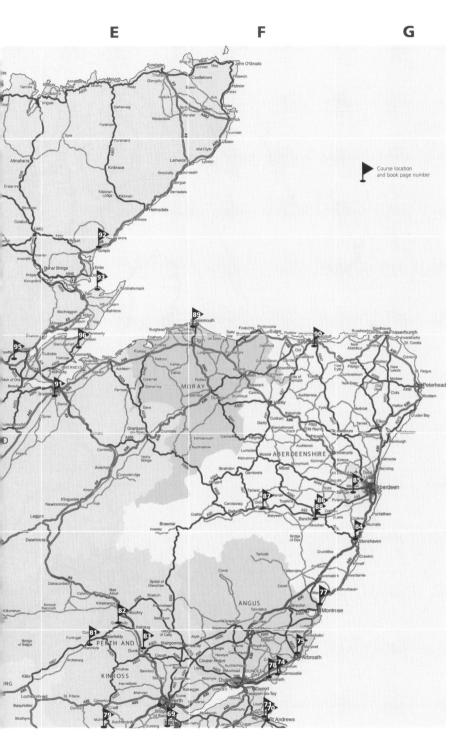

Course location
and book page number

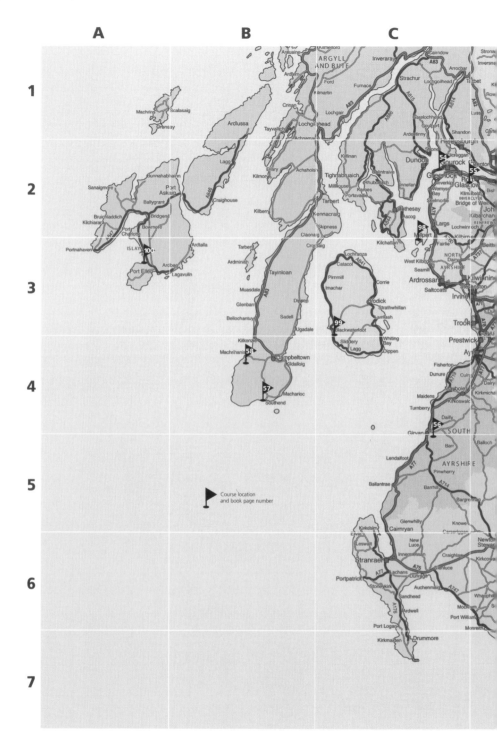

Course location
and book page number

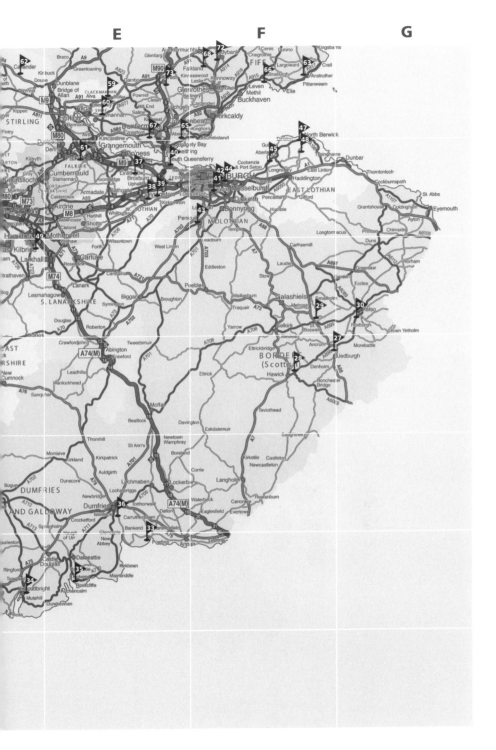

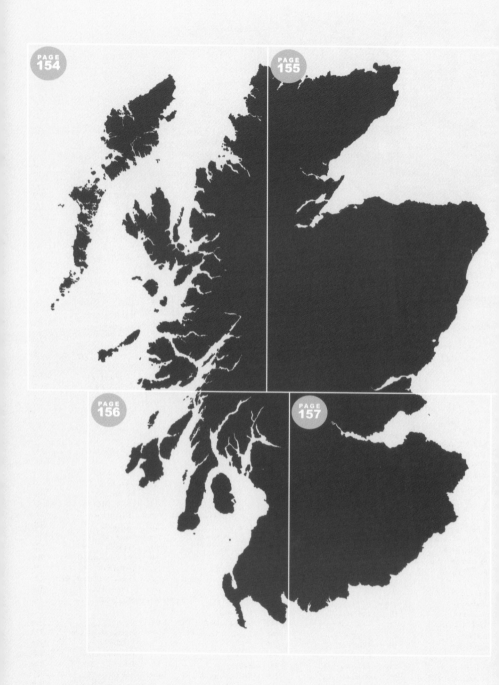

PAGE
154

PAGE
155

PAGE
156

PAGE
157

INDEX

INDEX